the
take the easy way
simplistic answers — who/what
when where
Public vs complex one (item, why, who?)
harder
in
long run
↓
symphony

→ Don't confuse "personal curiosity" w/ "hard
bargaining"
— not smart
cut off interruptions) soft on people
flexibility hard on problem

→ Pacing

Everyone of you will get something different out of this trainy — differ —
— enhance + increase your flexibility, tools, strategies
— place
new ways to move when u need too — more options
tied onto bears, INTENT, INQUIRY — BALANCED VOICES —

invisible/
— intangible
— shadow negotiation"
— shaping conversation"

Everyday
Negotiation

Everyday Negotiation

Navigating the Hidden Agendas in Bargaining

Deborah M. Kolb, Ph.D.

and

Judith Williams, Ph.D.

FOREWORD BY WILLIAM URY

JOSSEY-BASS
A Wiley Imprint
www.josseybass.com

Published by Jossey-Bass
A Wiley Imprint
989 Market Street, San Francisco, CA 94103-1741   www.josseybass.com

Jossey-Bass books and products are available through most bookstores. To contact Jossey-Bass directly call our Customer Care Department within the U.S. at 800-956-7739, outside the U.S. at 317-572-3986 or fax 317-572-4002.

Jossey-Bass also publishes its books in a variety of electronic formats. Some content that appears in print may not be available in electronic books.

Library of Congress Cataloging-in-Publication Data
Kolb, Deborah M.
     [Shadow Negotiation.]
     Everyday negotiation: navigating the hidden agendas in bargaining/
By Deborah M. Kolb and Judith Williams.
        p. cm.— (The Jossey-Bass business & management series)
Previously published: New York: Simon & Schuster, 2000, under title:
Shadow negotiation: how women can master the hidden agendas that determine bargaining success.
Includes bibliographical references and index.
     ISBN 0-7879-6501-4 (alk. paper)
     1. Negotiation.   I. Williams, Judith.   II. Title.   III. Series.
BF637.N4 K655 2003
658.4'052'082—dc21   2002012703

Printed in the United States of America
REVISED EDITION
PB Printing   10 9 8 7 6 5 4 3 2 1

The Jossey-Bass
Business & Management Series

Contents

Foreword

It was with particular pleasure that I accepted this invitation from my long-time colleague Deborah Kolb and her coauthor, Judith Williams, to write a foreword to this second edition of their illuminating book on the hidden dimensions of negotiation. When I read the first edition, titled *The Shadow Negotiation: How Women Can Master the Hidden Agendas That Determine Bargaining Success*, my first and repeated thought was how useful this book would be not only for women but for men as well. While the book draws on the insights of women in their negotiations, these insights are valuable for everyone every day. With this in mind, the authors have reframed this second edition, fittingly titling it *Everyday Negotiation*.

Among the many contributions this book makes to the growing literature on negotiation, three in particular stand out. Each represents a hidden strand of the process of negotiation. The first contribution is the book's focus on the *hidden context* of negotiation. Negotiation is not just about *what* is on the table but about *who* is at the table. What is their relationship, and what is their relative power? As the authors point out, context matters—a lot. And we all too often neglect the context in focusing on the substance alone. It makes sense that this valuable emphasis on context should arise from research into the experiences of women in negotiation in part because women—more than men—have tended to pay close attention to the relationship and in part because women have historically and unjustly often been placed in lower or weaker power positions. The book's second contribution has to do with the *hidden barriers* to negotiation. Perhaps the biggest barrier to negotiating effectively, as the book points out, lies within ourselves. It is our tendencies to underplay our strengths and read weakness into our situation (or, conversely, to read erroneous superiority into our position). We cannot hope to influence the other side if we cannot first learn to influence ourselves. The authors provide practical advice for how to position ourselves from within so as to be able to negotiate successfully for our interests.

The third contribution is to highlight the *hidden opportunities* to negotiate that exist in our everyday lives. Traditionally, most decisions at work or at home or in the community have been made hierarchically. Those at the top of the hierarchy—the king, the boss, the paterfamilias—gave the orders and the people on the bottom followed them. Thankfully, that situation is beginning to change in many places. Nowadays, whether it is in politics, business, or family life, negotiation—horizontal decision making—is becoming the pre-eminent process for making decisions. We no longer have to just say yes to the other party if they are in a superior power position or a traditionally superior relationship. As this book shows, we can position ourselves to negotiate effectively. We can enhance our power, and we can use the power of connection. Again, it is no coincidence that we can learn so much about these hidden opportunities from the experience of women—for they have often had to learn the hard way to challenge the traditions and power realities that have kept them from meeting their needs and pursuing their dreams.

Finally, Deborah Kolb and Judith Williams have succeeded in presenting these new understandings about the hidden dimensions of everyday negotiations in an engaging and accessible style, telling a host of insightful stories and offering an abundance of wise and practical advice. I hope that you, the reader, enjoy this book as much as I have.

Boulder, Colorado   William Ury
November 2002

Preface

For many years we have been talking to women about how they experience negotiation. What we learned from them was first published in *The Shadow Negotiation: How Women Can Master the Hidden Agendas That Determine Bargaining Success* (Simon & Schuster, 2000). The women told us some startling stories. These made us question common notions of what it means to be an effective negotiator and they carry important lessons about how successful results happen. When *Harvard Business Review* put *The Shadow Negotiation* on its list of the top ten business books of 2000, the editors noted: "The book is a negotiation guide for women, but it offers universal insights into the psychological tactics all individuals employ."

After publication of *The Shadow Negotiation*, talk show hosts would typically ask: "So how do women negotiate differently from men." The question gave us pause. We weren't after styles or approaches peculiar to women; we were after their insights into the negotiation process itself. Because of differences in perspective and power, the women we interviewed often had a different slant on the process from the one common in most commentary. The women's collective view revealed a dynamic that had previously been ignored or hidden in popular handbooks: in any negotiation there is a *shadow negotiation* taking place. The shadow negotiation parallels the negotiation over issues and can have as much, if not more, impact on the eventual outcome as the participants' specific interests. Whereas popular advice focuses on the *what* of a negotiation—the issues at stake—our discussion of the shadow negotiation illuminates the *how:* how bargainers treat each other, whether they will be adversarial or cooperative, whose voice counts, and the level of candor or openness.

The shadow negotiation

All bargainers—male and female—must manage the shadow negotiation if they want to have their issues heard and to understand the other person's concerns. The shadow negotiation, although first surfacing in stories from women, is not sex specific. Negotiation happens between people—regardless of gender, ethnicity, or status. Bargainers do not deal just with issues; they deal with each other. Success in everyday bargaining can hinge on how they handle the relational dimensions of the negotiation process. So, in this paperback edition, we have broadened our scope to include stories from men and we have changed the title. *Everyday Negotiation* reflects the integral part negotiation plays in our daily work lives—whether we are after a first job, a coveted promotion, a plum assignment, essential resources, or better communication. It also gives weight to our conviction that everyone—whether male or female—must contend with the dynamics of the shadow negotiation to be effective at the bargaining table.

relational dimensions

All the change that is taking place around us has upped the ante on negotiating skills. We think women have a lot to teach us all about this. As Anita Roddick, the founder of the Body

Shop, once said, "Any woman who has dealt with two children and one piece of toffee can negotiate any contract in the world."

o   o   o

We have accumulated many debts in the course of working on this book. First and foremost we are deeply grateful to the many students, friends and colleagues, casual acquaintances and complete strangers who were willing to share their experiences and perspectives with us. This book would not have been possible without their generosity. Several people were especially important in influencing our ideas. Lotte Bailyn, Sara Cobb, Joyce Fletcher, Debra Meyerson, Linda Putnam, the late Jeffrey Z. Rubin and our other colleagues at the Program on Negotiation at Harvard Law School and the Center for Gender in Organizations at the Simmons Graduate School of Management provided continual support. Kitty Pell and Christine Power helped us with their early enthusiasm and willingness to conduct some initial interviews. Without the patience of our agent Loretta Barrett or the deft eye and gentle guidance of Fred Hills, our editor at Simon & Schuster, the hardcover edition would never have seen the light of day.

Since publication of that edition, we have accumulated additional debts. Carrie Menkel-Meadow, Kathleen Valley, and Michael Wheeler helped us think through the translation from a book for women to one for everybody. The enthusiasm and creativity of Kathe Sweeney, Todd Berman, Jesica Church, Mary Garrett, and Hilary Powers at Jossey-Bass made working on this expanded version a pleasure. Carol Frohlinger, our partner at theshadownegotiation.com, has been unflagging in her support and we are grateful to her as a colleague and friend.

Jonathan Kolb pored over the many drafts with good humor, sharpening our ideas and our prose as he went along. But it is from our children—Samuel, Elizabeth, Megan, and Tamsen—that we probably learned most about how to thread our ways through the multiple shadow negotiations in our lives.

Boston, Massachusetts   Deborah M. Kolb
November 2002   Judith Williams

Everyday Negotiation

Introduction

RECOGNIZING THE HIDDEN AGENDAS IN EVERYDAY NEGOTIATION

The alarm goes off at six. By six-thirty coffee is brewing—along with an argument. The contractor has finally agreed to look at the storm damage. You cannot get away this afternoon. Besides, it's your spouse's turn. You covered the last crisis. Do you risk delay and reschedule, come up with a workable alternative, or hold firm?

First on the agenda at the office is a meeting with your boss. As you suspected, she rejects the team's proposed media campaign. You think she's wrong. How can you convince her? Should you try? What happens to the team's morale if you don't?

Office space is being reorganized. Last year you compromised. Not this time. Your department has run out of room for new hires.

Over a working lunch, you meet with two junior members of your team who have come up with a terrific idea. How do you encourage them and at the same time point out that the proposal needs a lot of work?

You get a late telephone call from your most important customer. He's having second thoughts about those price revisions that the two of you talked about. Can you find a solution—perhaps a slower schedule for the increases—so that he's comfortable and you don't blow your budget projections?

You finally head home. You will tackle that one tomorrow.

Sound familiar? A day on the job seldom goes by without the need to negotiate cropping up. We routinely deal with conflicting priorities and juggle multiple demands on our energies. Suggestions for change—in policy, practice, product, or service—often meet resistance and require rounds of negotiation. Our responsibilities may exceed the official authority we have to get things moving. We cannot tell people what to do. They feel no special obligation to listen, let alone follow orders. Even with the clout to impose our will, we sometimes hesitate to use it, fearing a chill in working relationships that stifles creativity and constructive criticism. Whether we are building support or overcoming resistance, we are negotiating. In fact, whenever we need something from someone else—a job, better cooperation, more time, or more money—we negotiate.

Most of this bargaining plays out in the informal exchanges that are part of the warp and woof of daily life. We drop by a colleague's office for a chat or enlist a mentor's help over coffee. Circumstances are more likely to find us vying for a raise or trying to restore a fractious team to equilibrium than taking part in the public drama of a mega-merger or celebrity deal. Yet we often let these visible, high-stakes negotiations shape our notions about negotiation itself and, in turn, the abilities and skills needed for success. When we associate negotiation with big-time deal making, emphasis falls on tangible results: the record-setting salary Katie Couric exacts from NBC or Steve Case's coup in putting together a huge entertainment conglomerate at AOL/Time Warner.

Deal making like this is rooted in the transaction—in getting the best deal. It works from an economic model. *Maximizing* is the name of the game, and we often carry the approach over to our everyday negotiations. We want the best car for the least money. We take advantage of a depressed real estate market to buy that condo we've had our eye on. But within the transaction, we are ready to do some horse-trading. We hanker for a red sports car, but settle on the metallic gray if the price is right. We swap a higher down payment on the condo to get a lower interest rate on the mortgage.

Transactions seem to call out for negotiation. They are moments of exhilaration for some and of dread for others. We rejoice when we get a plum assignment and sense failure when we don't come home with the starting salary we were after. But most of our daily bargaining does not have such a concrete scorecard. Even when it does, other factors intrude on the negotiation process.

Restricting negotiation to formal deal making skews our sense of what is possible through negotiation. Suspecting that we are neither sufficiently artful nor naturally persuasive, we let opportunities to negotiate slip by us, unclaimed or unnoticed. Cramped by circumstance, we don't consider negotiation a possibility. We just make do and move on, not realizing that we might have bargained. Often, from lack of training or experience, we fail to recognize that we are in the midst of a negotiation until it is too late to change the outcome. Even when we are well aware that we are negotiating and of the stakes involved, we may have trouble getting the person we're negotiating with to listen, much less cooperate with us.

For the last several years we have been talking to women about what happens in their everyday negotiations. As they experienced negotiation, the tried-and-true methods of deal making came up short. It's not always so easy to get to yes as it seems on the pages of popular negotiation books or in seminars.[1] The women's accounts of actual negotiations alerted us to broader challenges than the deal-making approach suggests. They often faced an unwilling seller or buyer. Then the greatest obstacle was getting the other person to the table. Once there, they encountered barriers in communication. They had to do more than resist efforts to put them at a disadvantage; they also had to deepen the conversation if they hoped to achieve any dialogue on the problem. Collectively, their comments keyed on two major concerns:

- How to position themselves in the negotiation conversation so that the other person was willing to take them seriously

- How to position the other person so that he or she was willing to cooperate in reaching a mutual solution

As the women we interviewed talked about what happened in their everyday negotiations, the emphasis shifted from deal making to problem solving. Their commentary centered not so much on particular results, but on the process used in getting them.[2] Occasionally they did have transactions to negotiate, but even these had relational issues where the common notions of deal making offered only partial help. Their insights have important messages for everyone who negotiates, which turns out to be all of us—male and female. Any negotiation can involve subtle or not-so-subtle differentials in status or skill, and men as well as women can find themselves in situations where the tide seems to be running against them for reasons that have little to do with the topic formally under consideration.

THE DEAL IS ONLY PART OF THE STORY

deal-making

Most popular advice on negotiation recommends that you focus on the elements of the deal and provides a strategic blueprint. Rather than wage a battle over a single issue, the advice suggests, think of the deal as a series of trade-offs among many issues. With a single issue at stake, any negotiation lurches toward a win-lose proposition. Someone is going to come out on top. If, however, you can break down a monolithic problem, discover it is actually made up of many different issues and interests, those differences give you room to find a compromise. No one wins everything, but no one loses everything either.

The fable of the orange bears out what these mutual-gains solutions can offer.[3] At the same time, it brings into sharp focus the shortcomings of a deal-making orientation. The fable takes place at Christmastime. Two sisters each plan to bake a cake for the festivities. Each recipe calls for an orange. But when the sisters check the larder, they find just one. An argument immediately erupts over who gets the orange. One sister complains that chiffon cake is wrong for the season. The other retorts that fruitcake may be traditional, but nobody likes it. Obvious solutions are out of the question. It being a holiday, they cannot borrow from the very neighbors who will later be their guests, and the stores are closed. The sisters, unwilling to compromise and bake only half a recipe, become more and more entrenched in defending their rights. It is an all-or-nothing contest. They cannot both get what they want. Or can they?

Preoccupied with winning, each overlooks the actual ingredients specified in the recipes. Amid the heat in the kitchen some pertinent facts emerge. The traditional fruitcake requires only the rind, while the delicate chiffon cake uses just the juice. Were one or the other sister to prevail, either the rind or the juice would go to waste. By focusing on what each needs and the possible trades, both sisters can get what they want. One sister carefully grates the rind off the orange, then hands the fruit over to her sibling for squeezing.

What a great deal, you think. If you just adopt this approach, you can become an accomplished negotiator. You have only to look for differences in needs and interests and propose solutions that play on those differences. The techniques are seductive in their promise of success.

The sisters have the luxury—not often found in actual negotiations—of getting right to problem solving. To solve the orange problem in the real world, each sister would have to work to bring the other to the point where she saw the value of negotiation and of compromise. Then, too, the solution is almost mythic in its symmetry. There is no overlap in the sisters' needs. Neither one's interest in the orange impinges on the other's. What happens if the problem is not quite so tidy? The easy win-win solution vanishes if one recipe calls for both rind and juice. One of the sisters would be forced to give up something she wants.

Nor does everyone come to the table prepared to play by the same rules or with the same ends in mind. The sisters' dispute, for example, could mask resentments that have nothing to do with oranges. The older sister might be fed up with always having to accommodate a younger sibling. She might not want to make *any* deal that works for her sister. The younger sister, on the other hand, might not be willing to give an inch just because she really hates fruitcake. How do these feelings play out and how can they be handled?

Comments from our informants prompted us to dig deeper. The orange story did not ring true to their experiences. There was too much slighted or missing. Some of their most critical negotiations produced something much more elusive than a deal. Only by a semantic stretch could the results have been considered trades. They might have improved the perception of their performance, opened freer communication lines, inched a team closer to a cohesive whole, or lightened the apprehension over an impending change. Seldom did they reach good solutions when they focused all their attention on putting creative ideas on the table. They discovered that they needed to devote equal energy to shaping the conversation in which those ideas were heard—claiming their voice and listening to the other person.

A Broader, Deeper Look

Almost without exception our interviewees could analyze the issues driving a negotiation with great skill. They exhibited equal ingenuity in coming up with creative solutions—or trades. Just what the mutual-gains model suggests. But their efforts did not always meet with success. And the reasons the negotiation faltered give us a window on the bargaining process. They also throw into question some basic assumptions behind the mutual-gains approach. Let's look at some of these assumptions.

Focus on the problem. Seldom do negotiators have the luxury of paying attention only to the problem. In real-life negotiations unspoken wants and expectations come into play that interfere with "getting to yes." Negotiators have histories—established ways of doing things and resolving conflict. They have accepted, if sometimes unarticulated, standards of conduct. They have complicated systems of relating as well as complex relationships with each other. These all bear on a negotiation. They frame its context.

Differences in influence can distort the balance at the table, affecting flexibility and candor on both sides. How can you convince the other person to accept a creative trade when he or she sees no need to trade at all? Conversely, those with power can have trouble persuading subordinates to be honest and forthright with them. How do people who lack bargaining power because of their position in an organization, their professions, their age, their gender, their race, their class, or their ethnicity make negotiations happen? How do those with influence create an atmosphere where those with less authority aren't afraid to communicate openly?

Without doubt, focusing on possible trades can take you further than you're likely to get with adversarial win-lose confrontations. The people involved in any negotiation *do* have different interests. By capitalizing on those differences, you *can* come up with trade-offs, rind for juice. You can swap something you don't care about for something that does matter to you. You may have a different appetite for risk or be operating under different time constraints, and you can take advantage of those disparities. You can pay or be paid in different currencies, exchanging part of the raise you wanted for an extra week's vacation. But no matter how creative you are in searching out mutual benefits, you cannot take the people out of the problem. Sometimes people *are* the problem.

Know what you want. You may know what you want, but being in a good position to get it can be an entirely different matter. Even when bargainers recognize that negotiation is a possibility, they can have trouble getting themselves into a good position to negotiate. Afraid of causing dissension or doubting their persuasive powers, they set their sights low and prepare to settle for less than they want or deserve. To counteract these tendencies, they need to do some careful stock taking, not just brainstorming.

Going into a negotiation, bargainers are not always clear about what they want. Nor do objectives always remain the same over the course of a negotiation. Attitudes and goals can shift on both sides of the table. Moreover, the main issue being negotiated may not be the whole story. Even bargainers adept at defining their objective do not always grasp its full scope or the implications of taking a certain path. Delighted at capturing a promotion or a high-visibility assignment, for example, they overlook the conditions—reduced workload or increased resources—necessary to make a success of that new job or assignment.

Willingness to negotiate. Mutual-gains approaches pretty much assume that self-interest is a sufficient motivator. Sometimes an attractive set of trade-offs does provide the necessary incentive. But not everyone is always ready to negotiate through a problem.

Something more, it seems, is required than an elegant solution. Before you can propose or weigh possible trades, you may have to do some serious strategizing to get the other party to the table, particularly someone who is perfectly content for things to remain as they are. Sure you can schedule a meeting with your boss; that does not mean that you can convince your boss to talk about your increased responsibilities or the compensation and recognition that should go along with them. A whole array of strategic moves, not creative ideas alone, are needed to make an unwilling bargainer see any personal advantage in negotiating with you.

Once at the table, challenges become a natural part of a negotiation's give-and-take. Frequently bargainers meet expecting to work on a deal or resolve a problem only to find their credibility questioned and their ideas shrugged off. Challenges like these put them on the defensive. Before those previously identified objectives can be pursued, these challenges must be met.

Bargainers operate out of enlightened self-interest. In the mutual-gains world, bargainers are essentially independent actors bent on realizing personal goals. Assertive, objective, and cool under pressure, they probe each other for information. They care about the other person's concerns more or less as a means to an end—to the extent that those concerns help or hinder their case.[4]

This individualistic approach—which has been called the pursuit of "enlightened self-interest"[5]—takes into account only half of the negotiation equation. Any negotiation is a form of social interaction; it involves a *you* and a *them*. Complex relationships can exist between bargainers, and those relationships have weight. They often determine whether good solutions will even be entertained.

Of course, personal agendas matter. You're negotiating because you want something, after all. If you're not going to be a forceful advocate for yourself, who is? But too narrow a focus on individual goals can get in the way of the communication needed to reach a good solution. Real skills and an attitude about the other person often essential to success can drop by the wayside or be co-opted when only self-interest is sought, however enlightened.

Creative ideas carry the day. The deal-making or mutual-gains orientation skews the negotiation process toward rational and objective analysis. It assumes you can pretty much figure out what motivates other people and trade on that. It's great if you can gain their trust, but you don't really need to work at getting their cooperation. They will jump at creative ideas that meet their needs. As rational decision makers, you assume, they are bound to make the right choices.

Rationality and objectivity, however, do not always rule at the bargaining table. Dispositions toward conflict, biases, remembered slights or successes, and the feelings that the participants have about each other intrude on the process. Personal preoccupations encroach. Dirty dishes in the sink or an impending deadline can have more impact than frequent flyer miles on where a family decides to spend its vacation. A bargainer sure of losing ground at the office might feel obliged to take a strong stand. Worries about a valued colleague whose job is in jeopardy or about the extra time needed to care for a frail parent can shape a case. To get to yes, these hidden agendas must be brought out into the open.

○   ○   ○

Intrigued by these stories, we realized that common assumptions about negotiation failed to capture the relational dynamics. We needed to take a broader look to find out what negotiators had to do to get another person to the table and be heard. We also needed to go deeper to understand how negotiators, once into the process, create spaces for mutual engagement and connection.

THE SHADOW NEGOTIATION: ADVOCACY AND CONNECTION

Our interviews produced several compelling insights into the negotiation process. A good idea alone rarely carries the day. Going after mutual gains is a worthy goal, but it is not enough. You have to know how to get there and have the tools at hand.

Negotiations, it turns out, are not purely rational exercises in the pursuit of self-interest or the development of creative trades. They are more akin to conversations that are carried out simultaneously on two levels. First there is the discussion of substance—what the bargainers have to say about the issues. But then there is the interpersonal communication that takes place—what the talk encodes about their relationship.[6] Yes, people bargain over issues; but they also negotiate how they are

going to negotiate. All the time they are bargaining over issues, they are conducting a parallel negotiation in which they work out the terms of their relationship and their expectations. Even though they seldom address the subject directly, they decide between them whose interests and needs command attention, whose opinions matter, and how cooperative they are going to be in reaching an agreement. This interchange, often nonverbal and masked in the stands taken on issues, has a momentum all its own quite apart from the substance of what is being discussed.

We call this parallel negotiation the *shadow negotiation*. The shadow negotiation takes place below the surface of any debate over the issues. As bargainers try to turn the discussion to their advantage or persuade the other side to cooperate in resolving the issues, they make assumptions about themselves—how much leverage they have and what they can legitimately demand. They make assumptions about the other person—about that person's wants, weaknesses, and probable behavior. They size each other up, poking here and there to find out where the give is. They test for flexibility, trying to gauge how strongly an individual feels about a certain point.

The shadow negotiation is no place to be a passive observer. You can maneuver to put yourself in a good position or let others create a position for you.[7] Your action—or inaction—here determines what takes place in the negotiation over issues. If you don't move to direct the shadow negotiation to your advantage, you can find the agreement tipping against you.

Slight changes in positioning can cause a major shift in the dynamics within the shadow negotiation. To have a credible voice on the issues, you must create the conditions for that voice to be heard. At the same time, you must make room for the other person's voice.

Advocacy. To hold your own in the shadow negotiation, you don't need to be tough or aggressive.[8] You do need, however, to get in a good position to advocate for your interests. This premise is basic. Not everyone starts out well positioned. At times bargainers get in their own way. Unsure of themselves or their ideas, they undermine their advocacy. To be effective, you must recognize any self-imposed limitations and deal with them.

At other times, the situation creates an uneven playing field.[9] Strategic moves can establish greater parity in the conversation. They can be used to underscore the benefits of dealing with you fairly and the costs of stonewalling or avoidance. Once into the negotiation, the other side may try to gain the upper hand and put you on the defensive. You resist these challenges by turning them—interrupting to break the momentum, diverting a personal attack back to the issues, naming the tactic, or correcting the faulty impression the other person is trying to foist off on you. These turns are critical if you want to get your ideas heard and credited.

The impressions you create in the shadow negotiation determine how much give-and-take there will be over the issues and influence any agreement you make. You must be ready to move in the shadow negotiation, not just to promote your interests but to block any attempt to undermine your credibility. Through a series of strategic moves and turns you tell the other person that you will not and do not need to settle for less than you deserve.

Connection. The messages you send in the shadow negotiation establish your advocacy. But you cannot pay attention only to how *you* are positioned in the negotiation. Any good solution requires compromise, concessions, and creativity on both sides. Concentrate only on your agenda, promote it at the other party's expense, and he or she has little incentive to cooperate. Regard the other person as the enemy and pretty soon he or she starts acting like one—blind to the interests you share.

To find common ground, you have to work together, not against each other. This is where the *skills of connection* come into play. Connection should not be confused with active listening or manipulation. It stems from a genuine recognition that understanding must exist on both sides of the table before an agreement can be reached. It takes sensitivity and responsive action to draw out what other people have on their minds in a negotiation. Often these hidden agendas are their real agendas. Unless bargainers are explicitly encouraged to talk about them, they will hesitate, fearing that any candor will be used against them. They don't want to tip their hands.

There is a pragmatic reason behind this attentiveness to relationship building in the shadow negotiation. Show the others involved that you value them and their ideas, and there is a good chance they will reciprocate. You'd be surprised how quickly they become open in voicing the reasons for their demands *and* receptive to listening to yours. But establishing connection with the other party does a good deal more than facilitate equal airtime. When you each feel free to engage in an open exchange that flows both ways, you can confront the real issues rather than their proxies. As different perspectives emerge, the dialogue can lead to truly transformative solutions that no one at the table had considered before. Because all the issues have been aired, mutual understanding grows and solutions are more apt to be long lasting. The conflict no longer simmers below the surface, only partially resolved. Most real-life negotiations involve multiple issues that bear on each other in interacting layers. Without candid discussion, that complexity never appears. *complexity*

Advocacy and connection go hand in hand in successful negotiation, and you establish the terms of both in the shadow negotiation. Using strategic moves and turns, you create your space in the conversation. You cannot let a need for responsive and open exchange hold your interests hostage. You lay the groundwork for dialogue with a forceful advocacy, not with tough or competitive posturing. The other person has to have something and someone to connect with for the skills of connection to work. A strong sense of what you need out of a negotiation insulates you from having collaborative moves read as signs of weakness and a prelude to concession. Similarly, attempts at getting connected cannot be transparent ploys to further self-interest. They must be based in genuine interest and curiosity—a conviction that the other person has something to contribute to any solution.

Together, advocacy and connection enable you to build a relationship across differences; together, they cement a commitment to working collaboratively on a mutual solution. When bargainers talk freely about what really matters, the impact ripples into the future. Not only do they communicate better on the current problem, their communications improve going forward. Negotiation ceases to be simply a platform for making good trades. It becomes a place where learning actually takes place, and the participants carry that greater understanding forward.

INSIDE A SHADOW NEGOTIATION

Let's take a look inside a shadow negotiation and chart its impact on the way the issues are framed and resolved. Elizabeth and Will are physicians in a small HMO located in a suburb outside Atlanta. The two, both in their early thirties, get along well. One or the other must be on duty when the center is open, and they routinely split weekend and evening shifts. But friction erupts over the summer vacation schedules.

WILL: I'm going on a fishing trip with three other guys the last week in June. Pencil me in for that time slot.

ELIZABETH: Well, um, actually, that's not okay. That week is a problem for me. My mother's moving into a new apartment. Remember? She has to be out of our old house by the end of the month, and I've promised to help pack up and get her settled in her new place.

WILL: I can't change my plans. If I don't go, the trip gets canceled and our deposit's down the drain. Shift your mother's move back a week.

ELIZABETH: I feel terrible about this, but that would really upset my mother. We'd have to put everything in storage. She can't move into the new place until the first.

WILL: So? She's going to have to put some stuff in storage anyway, and she could stay with you for the week.

ELIZABETH: Now *that* I really don't want to do. How about splitting the week? I could move her in over the weekend. . . . It would be a hassle, but then you could leave on Monday.

WILL: You gotta be kidding. My buddies would be halfway down the river.

Will slips his claim into a casual conversation with no warning, catching Elizabeth off-guard. He also introduces the issue not as a request to be negotiated, but as a statement of fact. He tries to gain the advantage by taking a hard line, and Elizabeth starts a one-way negotiation with herself when she suggests a compromise.

The two go round and round, Will holding out for the week and Elizabeth putting out suggestions for compromise. Will loses his temper. Upset, Elizabeth starts to waver. To buy some peace, she says she'll put on her thinking cap.

Both Elizabeth and Will are at fault here. Each made plans without checking the other's schedule. Despite mutual responsibility and some need to make a deal on the vacation, they are not equally prepared to negotiate. They focus on the outcome while their real conflict proceeds in the shadow negotiation. Will feels he can keep control by staking a claim and stonewalling. He uses emotion strategically, a move he knows will put Elizabeth on the defensive. Elizabeth fails to respond to his challenges and stays in a defensive position. The shadow negotiation tips against her as Will sees the positive results of his tactics, and she assumes responsibility for working out a solution.

Elizabeth spends an evening puzzling through what they should do. She focuses only on the possible deal that can be made. Her mother, although difficult, can stay for a week. The experience just won't be pleasant for either of them. If Elizabeth is going to shuffle things around, suffer the inconvenience, she wants something in return. Summer is coming. She'll trade first choice on the duty roster for July and August. That seems fair to her.

ELIZABETH: You can have the vacation week. (Will smiles.) But I want first dibs on the summer schedule. (Will stops smiling.)

WILL: No way. What does the call schedule have to do with vacation? You don't really need that week. You just said so. Done. Finished. Thanks.

ELIZABETH: Not hardly. You get the week. I get first choice this summer. That's a fair trade. If you don't give me the summer, you can't have the week.

WILL: This is going nowhere. I'm not going to tie up my summer.

Will and Elizabeth have reached a pivotal moment—that point when a negotiation can move forward along various paths or become deadlocked. How did they get here? The situation has all the ingredients needed for some creative deal making. Surely they can come up with a solution.

Perhaps, but only perhaps. They may have a mutual problem, but they have not worked out in the shadow negotiation any recognition that compromise will be necessary on both sides. Without this acknowledgment, any resolution remains precarious. Will continues to stonewall, believing he can wear Elizabeth down. Elizabeth continues to hunt for a solution, not realizing that Will is after full capitulation. Elizabeth's efforts to accommodate Will's needs signal to him that she probably won't put up more than a token fight for the week. In a way, her flexibility feeds his intransigence.

Neither displays much concern about the other's difficulties. Will assumes it's easy to shift around an elderly parent. Elizabeth silently disparages the greater importance Will attaches to going fishing with his buddies than he accords her family obligations. Mentally she trivializes what Will would consider a loss of face with his friends if he backs out and with her if he backs down. Little understanding exists on either side.

Will and Elizabeth have come to an impasse. Impatient with going round in circles, Will decides to bluff. "We'll flip a coin," he says. "Heads and the week's mine."

His stratagem trips him up. Elizabeth, rather than giving in as he expects, goes along. The toss turns up tails. A few days later, a business conference comes up for one of Will's friends, and the fishing trip gets rescheduled anyway. But Will never tells Elizabeth.

Advocacy, Connection, and the Shadow Negotiation

Even though the toss goes Elizabeth's way, she remains dissatisfied. They didn't do such a good job negotiating, she thinks, if the two of them let chance solve such a trivial problem. Elizabeth replays the negotiation in her mind, looking for where she went wrong, wondering whether she might have discovered the right solution if she just kept at the problem.

Elizabeth does not go astray in how she approaches the problem of the vacation schedule. That is pretty simple. She stumbles in the shadow negotiation. While she concentrates on the problem, searching for a workable compromise, Will puts all his efforts into getting his own way. By taking sole responsibility for the problem, she leads Will to believe that she will be the one making all the concessions. Once Will solidifies this position in the shadow negotiation, no amount of creative problem solving on Elizabeth's part can change the perceptions at work. Will simply interprets those efforts as signals that she will give him what he wants.

The failure here, however, does not all rest with Elizabeth. Will would rather trust Lady Luck than back down or compromise. He views the whole process as a game to be won rather than a problem to be worked out together, and nothing that Elizabeth does in the shadow negotiation changes that opinion.

In the following chapters we lay out a different path to becoming an effective negotiator that can help you avoid these needless impasses. Our blueprint for success draws equally on advocacy and connection. A thoughtful advocacy gets you into a position where you can be comfortable and effective pressing your demands. An equally important part of this advocacy comes in <u>convincing your counterpart that negotiation will ben-</u> efit both of you.

In the <u>best negotiations, strong advocates connect with each other.</u> The person with whom you are negotiating must be able to see your efforts to get connected as something more than a prelude to concession. <u>Collaborative dialogue</u> requires some reciprocity, some give-and-take and openness to other perspectives. As a forceful advocate <u>you establish your voice in that dialogue.</u> As a connected negotiator you engage <u>the other side</u> in a conversation in which <u>differences can surface without personal discord.</u> The relationship building implicit in connection should not, however, be confused with creating a superficial harmony. It does not demand that you satisfy the interests of others at the cost of your own. You do not foster a climate in which innovative proposals can be generated by making concessions unilaterally nor by being the only one cooperating. Both advocacy and connection require disciplined and deliberate efforts. They build on each other.

To give you a preview of how advocacy and connection support each other, let's rewind Elizabeth and Will's negotiation back to where Elizabeth proposes to trade the vacation week for first choice on the summer call schedule. In this replay, Elizabeth moves to check Will's efforts to tip the shadow negotiation in his favor.

WILL: You gotta be kidding! This is going nowhere. I'm not going to tie up my summer.

ELIZABETH: Okay. Time out. *We* have a problem. I'm fresh out of ideas. And you don't have any. Maybe we should just let Joe (*the medical director*) decide.

Instead of ignoring Will's tactics, Elizabeth names them and refuses to accept full responsibility for coming up with a solution. This turn shifts the dynamics. Elizabeth puts Will on notice. She is not going to do all the compromising and produce all the ideas. Will has to pull his weight if he doesn't want to involve the medical director. Elizabeth figures Will won't want to appear to his boss as someone who cannot work out a simple conflict in vacation schedules. Of course, she doesn't either. She banks on the threat being enough to get Will to be more flexible. Simultaneously, she takes away Will's veto power and restores balance to the shadow negotiation.

A repertory of strategic moves is always necessary when you are negotiating and never more so than when you are dealing with someone who considers any negotiation a zero-sum game and plays to win. The people with whom you negotiate need to know that they cannot hold out for a solution that works only for them before you can convince them to take you and your interests seriously. Elizabeth achieves this objective. Will immediately begins to backpedal.

> WILL: Let's not be so hasty. We don't need to drag Joe in.

Elizabeth can take her victory and run. But Elizabeth's charge in the shadow negotiation is to do more than get the upper hand. She needs Will's cooperation to reach a decision that they both can accept. After all, they are still going to be working together long after Elizabeth's mother is settled into her new apartment and summer is over. Elizabeth cannot rest with issuing a threat. An outcome forced by her is just as unproductive as one imposed by Will. Under either scenario, resentments would fester. She is after Will's participation, not his capitulation. She couples the strong strategic move with a connected overture to draw Will back into the discussion.

> ELIZABETH: If we don't ask Joe to intervene, I'm not sure what we can do. We're both in a tight spot. I know I wouldn't want to disappoint my friends. But I wasn't kidding when I said I was tapped out in the idea department. What do you think we should do?
>
> WILL: I guess I didn't expect this to be such a big deal. It's gotten all out of proportion. Why don't we just. . . .

Elizabeth comes right out and asks for Will's cooperation. She forces him to admit that they have a mutual problem and share responsibility for it, but she is careful to express her concern for his predicament. She never tries to apportion the blame for letting the situation deteriorate. Rather, by acknowledging Will's concerns, she creates an opening for him to respond in a more constructive, participatory way. He may not. But she has given him the chance, and she still reserves the option of forcing the issue.

o   o   o

Negotiating skills are critical for everyone today. Not only do we call on them in special situations when we take on a new job or buy a car. We need them every day to get done what needs doing at work and home. The more skillful we become as advocates in a collaborative process, the more we can expand our opportunities. When we use advocacy purposefully, not to overpower the opposition but to establish credibility, we lay the groundwork for building mutual respect. Negotiators who trust each other can probe deeper, more candidly, and the prospects for innovative solutions increase geometrically. In a complex and rapidly changing world, no one can have all the answers. The possibility of dialogue, the opportunity to create one, to benefit from other viewpoints, other people's skills—this is part of the promise of everyday negotiation.

Part One

The Power of Advocacy

Promoting Your
Interests Effectively

Chapter 1

Staying Out of
Your Own Way

Areporter once asked Yogi Berra what advice he would give aspiring ballplayers. After puzzling for a minute, the veteran catcher produced one of his signature comebacks. "Ya gotta dress for every game." Berra, seldom out of the Yankee lineup, was talking about more than putting on his pads and mask. To play well, you had to be ready, pumped up, and prepared to face what was thrown your way. That's what the tools of effective advocacy do for you in a negotiation. They don't just put you in the game. They help ensure that you will be ready to hit whatever is tossed your way, be it a sneaky curve or an unexpected fast ball.

Part of that readiness is confidence in yourself and your ability to hold your own. Before you can convince the other person of anything, you first have to believe that you are in a good position to push for your demands. It's tough to get up for a negotiation when you look at your chances of success with a jaundiced eye. Why bother to negotiate at all? Who wants to get into a struggle one is just going to lose? Pushed by a colleague, pressured by a boss, or limited by circumstances, it often seems easiest to acquiesce quietly or keep quiet altogether. Why risk the unpleasantness? It's tough to be persuasive when you think your case is shaky. Unconvinced of its merits, you are bound to have a hard time convincing anyone else. Better, you think, to cave before the other side pokes holes in your argument or laughs. Then again maybe if you come on strong, assume an assurance you don't really feel, they won't notice the weaknesses.[1] It's tough to force yourself to negotiate when you have been burned in the past or feel uncomfortable pressing for something you want. Ironically, it's equally tough to get good results when you're over-confident. Be too sure of yourself, and you can overshoot without first testing whether your goals are reasonable. Unrealistic demands make you look uninformed or, worse, foolish.

Before you can negotiate effectively with others, you may have some negotiating to do with yourself. Successful advocacy begins with preparation—both psychological and factual. You must be convinced that your demands are legitimate and defensible. You need to see a negotiation as an opportunity that opens up choices, not as an occasion that requires you to over-sell and overpromise or one that forces you to take what is offered. Many successful negotiations begin with a resounding no. But to get past that no, you must first see the possibility of a yes. Once you step back and take a realistic look at what is possible, you would be surprised how often you can turn around even a seemingly no-win situation.

Sometimes you can be your own worst enemy. By not taking the simple steps needed to empower yourself in a negotiation, you can get in your own way even before the actual bargaining starts. Underestimating one's own strengths is as deadly as overestimating those of a bargaining counterpart, but it is common. On tenuous ground, people tend to pull back on demands and narrow their options from the beginning. When outflanked or outgunned, they go silent because they don't see much point in speaking up any more. And now and then they just walk away without making any attempt to even the odds. At the other extreme, convinced they hold all the right cards, they dig in their heels, substituting rigidity for persuasiveness.

PITFALLS IN NEGOTIATION

The negotiation process is difficult enough without carrying a self-imposed handicap. Negotiations can be filled with all sorts of pitfalls. The other side tries to gain the upper hand at your expense. People prod here and poke there in the shadow negotiation, looking for an advantage or a vulnerability to exploit. But you don't have to help them. The first step on the way to becoming an effective negotiator is to recognize how you get in your own way. Here's a sampling of common pitfalls:

- Missing opportunities for negotiation
- Disliking the process
- Seeing only weakness
- Bargaining yourself down
- Feeling overconfident
- Making sure everyone is happy
- Confusing toughness and effectiveness

Missing Opportunities for Negotiation

To negotiate, you have to realize that it is possible. Otherwise the moment slips by. Opportunities are missed for lots of reasons. Sometimes, confronted with what seems to be a final decision, it's easy to forget that no decision is final until it is accepted. Faced with what seems to be an immovable barrier or just plain stubbornness, a negotiator can jump to a hasty conclusion and take *no* as the last word. The office manager flatly refuses to discuss health-care benefits. Part-time workers are never included on the company policy. Your new coworker has an annoying habit of vocally second-guessing your decisions on major accounts. You mention the need for some ground rules, but she cuts you off. When you accept a no as the end of the conversation, you foreclose on the possibility of negotiating through the problem.

Other times, the situation does not seem to lend itself to negotiation. Both these reasons converged for Karen when she was given a new and exciting account at her advertising agency. Karen's optimism swelled. She saw the assignment as a vote of confidence and hesitated to mention the heavy load she was already carrying. She put in longer and longer hours. Challenged by the new account and aware of its visibility in the agency, she kept on top of it, but gradually her other accounts began to slip. Copy was a day late getting to the designers. She had to reschedule several important meetings with other clients. Over the course of several weeks, the slippage raised eyebrows. Even though no one in the agency contested her performance on the new account, it was not the unalloyed success she expected.

Karen missed a negotiating moment. She considered the new assignment a flattering fait accompli. She did not see the

possibilities for negotiating what she needed to make the
assignment a success. She could have bargained to lighten up
her current responsibilities or to restrict them to oversight. She
could have negotiated for more resources and actively sought
the managing partner's guidance or support on the account.
Having negotiated none of these preconditions, she could not
do her best and so her great assignment turned out to be not so
great, overall.

Karen did not want to make waves. Haggling over terms of
the assignment, she thought, would create the wrong impression and make the agency directors think their confidence mis-
placed. But, more than that, she associated negotiation with
hard bargaining—with buying a car or holding back rent from
a landlord because the heat was off. Negotiation, to her mind,
was not part of the equation when she was presented with what
seemed to be an order from the top. Karen needed to delegate
responsibility for work on accounts she could not serve well,
and that responsibility was negotiable had she realized it.

Even within peremptory decisions there is generally room
for some give-and-take, but you have to be aware of the possibility and act on it. Before going along with imposed solutions
and shutting down your options, try to discover the reasons
behind the rationale. There may be less onerous answers. But
to uncover them, you have to get the discussion going. Negotiation is always, or almost always, a possibility.

Disliking the Process

Some opportunities to negotiate are not so much missed as dismissed. Negotiation, in fact, is considered a dirty word. The
gamesmanship is off-putting. If what it takes to be an effective

negotiator is self-absorption and fluency in boasting, the price is too high. It is not so hard to go after support for a project or defend a team member. But when it comes to asking for something of personal benefit, that's a different matter. "Anti-pushers" might want a raise or a high starting salary or more time to work up a proposal, but they don't want to press too hard for it. The self-promotion involved borders on selfishness. Besides, it's a waste of time—much more pleasant and efficient to spend that hour getting the job done or being with family and friends than jockeying for an edge.

Distaste leads to avoidance. Better not to play the game than feel like a fraud. A museum curator in her mid-twenties, for example, carries around an image of herself that makes negotiation painful. "All my life," she says, "I have been taught to put others ahead of myself. I still have trouble seeing myself as a negotiator. It feels foreign and uncomfortable to sit down and decide what I want and how to get it. Whenever I do this, I feel as though I am being selfish." Clearly the curator's attitudes straitjacket her ability to make demands. She will pay a price—always waiting for someone to come to her with a fair solution. But the price she pays may not be so high as the one exacted from a man who doesn't want to appear pushy.

Richard, a shy but creative product manager, is uncomfortable pushing for himself. Just prior to his recent performance review, he reflected on his quandary: "My wife's no longer working. She has been after me to ask for more money at my review to cover our lost income. But I have a good relationship with my boss. He always goes out of his way to help me." Richard worries that any pressure will offend his boss and jeopardize their relationship. That is a risk he does not want to take.

Both the curator and the product manager confuse being sensitive to others with giving in to their demands. People make demands in negotiations. That is the reason to negotiate in the first place. But they can choose how they phrase those demands. Avoidance is not the answer. It prevents you from finding your voice and deprives others of the opportunity to hear what you really think. The issue is not whether to negotiate but how to negotiate in a way that feels authentic and still gets you what you want.

Seeing Only Weakness

Many people go into negotiations suspecting they will lose. This expectation then drives their thinking. Why should my customer meet my terms, they reason, when so many other vendors are waiting in line? I have spent too many years in a low-paying job in a nonprofit agency; I will never get the salary I want in the corporate sector. My boss is going to do what he wants anyway. Why should I raise a cautionary voice? Better for him to see me as a team player than someone who complains all the time. Negativity like this is an almost sure-fire guarantee that the negotiation will start with you being psychologically one-down. A fixation on weakness can cause you to exaggerate everything that works against you. It can also blind you to real strengths. In either case, it becomes progressively more difficult to recognize, much less use, what you actually have going for you. Nick's approach to a job search is a good example of the damage negative thinking can do.

Nick had been riding the dot-com wave, but suddenly crashed. Within months of his first child's birth, he was laid off.

All his friends were out of work. Being around them only added to his depression. It was just luck that Nick heard about a promising opening. Nick was grateful for making the final round. Any of his friends would jump at an offer. He was convinced the other candidates would be in the same boat.

When the offer came, Nick was disappointed, but grabbed it. Pleased, the principals in the firm heaved a sigh of relief. They needed someone who was technologically savvy and capable of writing in comprehensible English. Nick was the first person they had interviewed who fit that bill. Nick knew he brought a unique combination of skills to the table, but his negative focus prevented him from parlaying those advantages into a higher salary.

With weakness looming large, you can overlook the strengths you actually have. When pushed hard, you may lack the necessary resilience to stay in the negotiation. When intimidated or challenged, you may rigidly defend your claims or take the path of least resistance and retreat. A focus only on weakness shortchanges you and limits your ability to use the assets you do have. Most people harbor doubts about being able to reach their goals. What makes the difference is whether you allow these very natural doubts to control your actions.

Bargaining Yourself Down

Self-doubt creates another problem. Others don't have to whittle down opening demands; you do the work for them. Before you even start to negotiate—for a new job, a shift in career path, or more open communication with a client or a coworker—chances are good that you carry on a private debate in your head. What do I want? What are the odds of my getting it? Am I up to fighting that battle once again? Do I have a choice?

All too often more than goals are set in these internal dialogues. They are the place where the first concessions in the negotiation are made. Before opening the discussions, you start to bargain yourself down. Sure you contributed to the group's effectiveness and to bottom-line profits. A 10 percent raise seems justified and realistic. But then the second-guessing starts. "My boss will never agree to that," you argue mentally. "I'm good, but maybe not that good. I'd probably be making more than the rest of the group. Business hasn't been so good. I'll start a bit lower—8 percent sounds more like it."

This private rationalizing may be faultless. The boss may consider a 10 percent raise totally out of line. But the point is that she doesn't have an opportunity to react to your request. You've decided ahead of time what her response will be and don't test whether that anticipated scenario is in fact what would happen.

Once you make that first concession in your head, you lower your aspirations and lose ground before the negotiation even opens. These diminished goals become self-fulfilling prophecies as the shadow negotiation plays out.[2] You ask for less than you want in the hopes of getting something or of avoiding a messy confrontation. Once you settle for an 8 percent raise in your head, that figure usually turns out to be the most you can get, regardless of what you might deserve or the other person might give.

When you worry that your demands will be hard to swallow and reduce them rather than trying to make them more palatable, you handicap yourself from the start in the shadow negotiation. You let self-doubt dominate your thinking. The central issue is not whether you can get something, but how to get what you want.

Feeling Overconfident

Overconfidence can present as many problems as self-doubt. Confidence plays a critical role in successful negotiation. It allows you to stay in a negotiation when it gets tough. But you can have too much of a good thing. Cockiness can lead to peremptory or outrageous demands that are out of touch with the reality of the situation. Rather than coming across as positive and assured, overly confident bargainers can appear arrogant and, all too often, poorly informed. Overestimating the strength of their position, they incorrectly assume the other side is not in good shape.

Jeff and Mike, two partners in a high-tech start-up, had developed search-engine software for online daily news. Jeff and Mike were convinced of its technical superiority; the software was faster and more efficient than anything on the market. An approach from a large news organization convinced them that they could make a great deal—if not with this organization, then with another.

At the first meeting, the two addressed the newspaper's questions and concerns in a cursory fashion. Eager to cut to the chase, they put a number on the table for the use of the program. The figure astounded the team from the newspaper. "That's out of the question. XYZ Corp.'s engine may be slower, but it costs a quarter of that."

The pair's overconfidence led them to throw out a completely unrealistic figure that exposed their inexperience. The deal fell through. It was months before Jeff and Mike had another nibble.

As Jeff and Mike discovered, being too sure of your case can block out the information you need to make that case and to engage in the give-and-take of a negotiation. The other person writes off the exaggeration as overselling and overpromising and can be insulted by the disregard these acts signal.

Making Sure Everyone Is Happy

Sometimes you can get trapped by a desire to satisfy everyone. To make the others happy (or happier), you try to be nice or to smooth things over. Maybe you don't want to appear overly aggressive or unsympathetic. Maybe you have trouble with winning when victory comes at her expense or his public loss of face. Whatever the reason, you stumble—most often, by giving back what you deserve. That's what Beth did in a negotiation with another editor.

> *We were fighting over a new title. The book fit nicely in my list and I argued my case pretty strenuously. The other editor finally threw up his hands and said, "Okay, Beth. It's yours." Did I accept that? Oh, no. I tossed the ball back at him. I told him he could keep the book. I could tell just from the look on his face how much the decision meant to him. He'd had a rough couple of months. But I warned him that we needed to set up some guidelines. Otherwise, next time around, I wouldn't give an inch.*

Did they ever set up any guidelines? No. Beth smoothed things over with her fellow editor, but at cost only to her.

Efforts to please sometimes stem not from an urge to paper over difficulties but from an understandable urge to look good to everyone. Ken was hired by a major accounting firm to help with its growing business in China. Ken had passed his CPA exams on the first try. Impatient with the audit work that the partners considered critical to his long-term effectiveness on the China accounts, Ken jockeyed to make a move from audit to tax. Ken realized assignments had to be negotiated, but didn't think it was a good career move to turn down a request from a partner. After committing to take over a key audit, he promised the same block of time to a tax partner. A week before the audit was scheduled to start, the scheduling conflict surfaced. Ken's efforts to please produced the opposite effect. Unable to say no to either partner, he made both furious. His mixed messages threw off conflicting signals and prompted the decision makers to wonder whether he was devious or simply indecisive.

Negotiations abound with nonverbal cues. At the first sign of displeasure, you can retreat rather than use these messages as a wedge to open a dialogue. Looking to be fair to everyone, you can sometimes forget about being fair to yourself. If you adjust what you want in response to what the other person wants, you fail to reckon the end cost of these concessions. Intent on peacemaking, you may not think about the price of that peace until it is too late. Caring about the other person in a negotiation is good, but not when it is totally one-sided.

Confusing Toughness and Effectiveness

Negotiators who want to make everybody happy are always looking for ways to please. Tough negotiators, on the other hand, are looking for ways to win. For them, any negotiation produces winners and losers. Tough negotiators begin bargaining prepared to fight. A cartoon from a couple of years ago captures this attitude: It pictures a group of people standing around a table, papers are flying, and one man is leaving the room. The caption reads: "He's a great negotiator in a Mike Tyson kind of way." Prepared for a fight, the tough negotiator typically finds one as the process almost immediately lurches toward an adversarial contest. The risks of this approach are substantial.

Brenda, a successful sales executive in an outplacement firm, took a tough stance with her boss over the signing of a stiff noncompete agreement. She worried that he would misinterpret any conciliatory overture on her part as prelude to capitulation. Supported by an attorney's advice, she took a hard line. Her boss reacted to her tough approach and responded in kind. He kicked her off the management committee. Now worried about being fired or losing face in the organization, Brenda signed the noncompete—without being able to negotiate any qualifications to soften its impact for her. There were any number of ways a mutually satisfactory agreement could have been reached, but Brenda's tough stance precluded any discussion of them. The negotiation became a war of wills. That is the risk of equating toughness and winning with effectiveness. The resistance it generates often produces the opposite results from those intended.

o   o   o

These acts of self-sabotage take place in the shadow negotiation. A lack of information or understanding prompts some people to overplay their hands. What they see as a full house is really only a pair of threes; they just don't know it or don't bother to find out. Others take one look at the cards and immediately question whether they have a winner. Doubt creeps in and they fold, whether that is warranted or not.

Four Steps to Stay Out of Your Own Way

Before you can put the qualities and skills you bring to any negotiation to work, you need a solid grounding. Confidence in a negotiation comes not so much from knowing you are in complete control as from recognizing what control you *do* have. The more realistic you can be in assessing the situation, the more effective you will be as a negotiator. A superficial pep talk is not adequate preparation. Successful advocacy depends on a hard-edged appraisal of where you stand and what you can do to improve your situation. There are four steps you can take to prepare yourself. Each step is simple, yet together they provide you with the self-awareness and situational insights that you need to negotiate effectively. As your understanding expands, so does your confidence in your ability to deal with the situation.

- ○ **Take stock.**
  Deliberately inventory the skills and experience you bring to the table. Often you will find hidden resources that you are not using. Look at what makes you feel vulnerable. Then you can plan ahead to compensate.

- ○ **Learn as much as you can.**
  An informational vacuum creates anxiety. Gather the facts that support your case, but also find out as much as you can about the other person and his or her situation. Pertinent information helps you set your agenda and stick to it.

○ **Develop alternatives.**
When you have all your negotiating eggs in one basket, you feel (and are) dependent on how the negotiation turns out. Having other options available increases your flexibility. You can objectively decide whether it is better for you to make a deal or walk away. You are not captive to any particular solution.

○ **Get fresh perspectives.**
It is easy to get trapped in your own thinking. Talking to others whose judgment you trust can help you see the situation in a new light. Often you come away with suggestions that orient you more positively or more realistically.

Acts of self-sabotage often do more to harm a bargainer's position than the other side's tactics even contemplate. Protect yourself from self-inflicted strikes. Take stock of where you are and where you want to go. Probing like this tells you what information you need and where your resources could use a little shoring up. In a nutshell, think long and hard not just about what works to the other party's advantage but about what works to yours. This process not only helps you stay out of your own way; it strengthens your hand.

A Case of Self-Sabotage
Historian Thelma Aronberg faced a situation that made her ripe for self-sabotage. Thelma, at thirty-six, was a tenured professor in the American studies program at a liberal arts college in Ohio. An outspoken perfectionist, she pushed herself on all fronts. Students flocked to her lively and somewhat eccentric classes in pop culture and film. Colleagues had come to expect an original and iconoclastic approach in her publications, but could not

quibble with her meticulous research. All in all, Thelma was not a woman you would expect to sabotage herself. But that's what happened when her department head dropped by for what Thelma thought was a friendly chat. Thelma, away for the past week giving a long-scheduled seminar, had missed the monthly department meeting and was anxious to catch up.

BRAD: How did your seminar go?

THELMA: Fine. Great group, lots of interchange, lively discussion.

BRAD: Well, you missed an interesting faculty meeting. Congratulations are in order. We selected you department chair.

Brad's announcement sent Thelma reeling. After three years waiting to adopt a baby, her new daughter was about to arrive at the same time that her first book was due at the publisher. She could not imagine how she could manage the extra load.

THELMA: This is a joke, right?

BRAD: Uh-uh. The vote was unanimous.

THELMA: That's crazy, insane. I couldn't possibly take on the chairmanship now.

BRAD: Look, it's your turn. The chair is supposed to rotate every two years. That's department policy. But this is my second stint. I'm not putting in a third.

THELMA: Can't you get somebody else?

BRAD: You're the only one who isn't pulling her weight. Everybody's got work to get out. Everybody's stretched. And everybody else has done a stint.

The insinuation that she was not a team player cut. Thelma was not a freeloader who let others carry the departmental burdens. She shouldered more than her share of committee work and student advising. Apparently those efforts did not count. If the department did not consider her a team player, and her colleagues were prepared to force the issue when she was so inundated, Thelma thought, maybe it was time to look for an appointment somewhere else.

Feeling undervalued, overburdened, and angry, Thelma saw resignation as the only way out of the predicament. The timing was impossible. She couldn't just go along. The consequences would be disastrous. From where she was sitting, Brad's request sounded like an order, not the opening of a discussion. But was it? Had Thelma felt more in control, she could have turned her negative perspective around. Her position was stronger than she realized. We will return to Thelma and how she resolves her quandary after we explore the resources she eventually taps.

Take Stock

Once self-doubt takes over or the choices you have seem equally unattractive, as they did for Thelma, you risk distorting the situation beyond recognition. Preoccupied with your vulnerability, you may read only weakness in your position and see no way out. At this point, step back and take stock. What personal resources are you forgetting? What assets do you have at hand that you are not using? You want this inventory to be as complete and precise as possible. Ask yourself four questions to firm up this self-evaluation:

QUESTION #1. *First ask yourself why the other person is negotiating with you at all. What do you have that she wants or he needs?*

People don't negotiate without reasons. Negotiation happens because everyone involved wants something and stands to benefit from the negotiation. The other party sees immediate advantages or potential gains in the future. What are those? What do you offer? This line of questioning shifts your focus from why you need them to why they need you. That change in emphasis, by forcing you to look at your strengths, prevents you from getting bogged down in the weaknesses of your position. It gave Pat, a twenty-seven-year-old reporter, a needed edge in a difficult negotiation. Pat was angling to be appointed press agent for a political campaign and had a lot working against her.

> *I wanted to break away from pure news reporting. This job opening was my first real shot at doing that. But I had no name recognition in political circles. I wasn't just green. I was young. Except for the volunteers, everyone on the campaign was at least fifteen years my senior and seasoned.*

Right off, the candidate started testing Pat in the shadow negotiation. He stressed her inexperience. Hiring her, he said, posed some real risks. The press agent in any campaign was highly visible. If she came on board, she would be learning the tricks of the trade at his expense. In exchange, she should be willing to be paid at a bargain-basement hourly rate. Pat wanted the job at any price. The figure he quoted was not much different from what she was earning as a reporter. But few reporters pull down big salaries. In a political campaign low pay meant your opinions did not carry much weight. If Pat accepted the candidate's offer, she risked being silenced before she even started.

But Pat, having taken stock, had a good handle on what she brought to the campaign. Every time the candidate pointed to a weakness, Pat countered. Yes, she was green, but none of the seasoned professionals on the campaign had her journalism skills. No, she was not paid much as a reporter, but she had earned another currency he badly needed: wide contacts among the press.[3] By keeping the candidate focused on her talents and how they met his needs, she was able to negotiate a salary in keeping with the demands of the job and the prevailing pay scale.

Knowing your own value, what you bring to the table, gives you a psychological edge. You have the means at hand to divert attention away from areas where you might be weak. But don't do your inventory in the abstract. Make a list of five good reasons why the other party needs you. This exercise will help you reframe the situation. The realization that the needs don't run in just one direction puts you on a more even footing. You may want something from the other party, but you also have something he or she wants from you.

QUESTION #2. *Ask yourself what happens when you have been successful in a negotiation.*

Experience can be a great teacher in negotiations. The more you negotiate, the more adept you can become. But that only happens if you learn to bank your experiences. You have to see how success in one situation can carry over and fortify you in another. You may be better at negotiation than you realize. Look at situations that have gone well and ask yourself why. By exploring the reasons behind your successes, you often gain insights that point to possible ways of getting unsatisfactory encounters back on track.

Emily used this technique to save her business. She'd started her own public relations firm after apprenticing at a large agency in Atlanta. Despite a growing client list, she was barely keeping afloat financially. The mounting pressure on her bottom line forced her to confront why. She did fine negotiating the initial contracts. The problem came later. She did too much unpaid work for her clients. Every time her clients asked for additional services, she undercut her profits. It was a vicious cycle. She couldn't bring herself to say no, and because she didn't, her clients kept making more and more requests. "In a way, I renege on my own contracts. I cannot say no to clients. I know it and they know it."

Emily was no novice at negotiation. Besides starting her own company, she had spearheaded a successful anti-smoking campaign in her community. "I cared about clean air. But the campaign was not personal. It was a cause." Emily felt sure of her ground when she stood up to angry restaurant owners. "When tempers got hot, I could always deflect the personal attacks and my stake in the outcome by going to the facts."

Emily realized she needed a comparable fail-safe mechanism when she negotiated with her clients on reimbursement for additional work. She found it by revising her basic contract so that it included an itemization of services that were not covered. Whenever clients suggested expanding the original scope of work, she had everything in black and white. The issue became not whether they would pay for these extra services, but how much.

Everyone has a success story to tell. These can be converted to learning experiences. The experience does not have to be drawn from your work environment to be translated to it. Perhaps you convinced the condo association to put in some landscaping or managed to get a great deal on uniforms for your softball team. Analyzing those successes gives you insights into what makes a negotiation work for you. Do you prefer to take your risks in small doses rather than all at once? Do you prevail by persistence? Are you so organized that when you begin bargaining your argument contains no loose ends? Or do you rely on your reading of people to come up with a creative solution? Times when you are successful are moments for learning. As your understanding of why they happen becomes clear, you can try to create those same conditions in situations where you might not feel so confident.

QUESTION #3. *Ask yourself what you know about the other party and the situation.*

Past negotiations can teach you a lot, but so does your wider experience. A curious thing often happens to people when they negotiate. They forget what they know once an encounter gets tagged as a "negotiation." They don't carry over to a negotiation the cues and observations that get them through the give-and-take of their daily routines. They may have been absorbing information about people or group dynamics, but they don't use it during a negotiation. Get in touch with what you do know. Over time, you gain insights into what motivates people and how they are likely to behave. Tap into those observations. They are incredible resources to bring into play. They helped Rob not just hold his own in a difficult negotiation, but to do well. Rob had spent years with a national sporting goods manufacturer. After a period of stunning success, the firm started to have problems. Charged with bringing down costs, Rob saw no alternative to shipping production offshore and several rounds of layoffs. Rob agreed to oversee the turnaround, but he exacted some concessions. "I didn't like what I was seeing from top management. I wanted an insurance policy." It turned out he needed one. After he managed a 30 percent cut in the payroll, Rob was fired. "It was a case of shoot the messenger, but there was a shocker." The company reneged on Rob's insurance policy. He sued.

Convinced that he was ill equipped to handle the negotiations, Rob was about to leave the settlement talks to the lawyers. Then the lawyers began asking for documentation. That's when Rob realized he had an unexpected asset. He knew the company and the players inside out.

> *I had worked there since the beginning. I know how they operate. The CEO is tough as nails and a consummate manipulator. But she cares how people see her. I knew she'd deal if she thought that this would get out.*

Capitalizing on a hidden strength, Rob began to take an active role in the suit. Eventually the company settled and the settlement hinged to a great extent on the information Rob was able to feed the attorneys.

Realizing how much you know about the other party empowers you in a negotiation. It can be key when dealing with someone difficult, as Rob discovered. Cues you absorb about negotiating styles contain valuable hints on how to deal with the other person. Understanding the tack he or she is likely to take helps you plan your own strategy—whether you are negotiating a difficult assignment or a severance package.

You have to be deliberate in your efforts at getting in touch with what you know. Familiarity often dulls perception, and you miss the obvious. At one of our workshops Annette asked us for advice on dealing with a slick salesman like her boss. "I give him reasons why we should make a change or go after a certain client, and he couldn't care less. He just wants to get things off his desk." Annette didn't need advice. She had only to act on what she already knew. All she had to do was to keep her boss informed. He would let her know if he had any objections.

QUESTION #4. *Ask yourself what about certain situations makes you feel vulnerable. Where are you vulnerable?*

Assets and resources have a flip side. You have to pay attention to your weaknesses too. Knowing you have a gap in your skills or background, you can figure out ways to bridge it. Look back over your past experiences. What situations have given you trouble? What has made you feel vulnerable? How do you test yourself? Do you always get what you want? Does that success mean that you are an effective advocate or that you are asking for too little? In certain circumstances do you tend to avoid conflict, blame yourself, or take on the burden of making everyone feel good?

Just thinking about troublesome experiences alerts you to occasions when you slip into self-sabotaging patterns or find your confidence threatened. Once you understand what trips you up, you can figure out what you need to do to compensate. Gina, an entrepreneur, considers her lack of academic credentials a potential liability when she bargains. A retailing whiz with an uncanny ability to coax money out of investors, she never got past high school. That her backers, her customers, and her staff have long since ceased to care about her educational background is not the issue. Because Gina thinks they do, because she believes it, that perception is a liability. It undermines her confidence in the shadow negotiation.

Recognizing this, Gina masters the ins and outs of any proposal and learns as much as she can about the people she will face. "Most people aren't so thorough," she admits. "But I never got an education. I don't have a college diploma, much less an MBA. Preparation helps me fight my lack of confidence. I know I know my stuff, degrees or not."

Being alert to what triggers your vulnerabilities allows you to plan ahead. When warning alarms trip, you can fall back on rehearsed responses. If you discover you have a tendency to bargain away your advantage at the last minute, a mantra—"Keep it yourself, stupid"—comes in handy. It is not an ironclad insurance policy, but it may keep you on your toes. Brian, a Peace Corps veteran turned investment banker, negotiates large municipal bond deals. Aware that he can get caught up in a municipality's needs, he resists the pressure to close. He always gives himself a night to go over the fine print once more. Knowing that he has this time in reserve prevents him from making hasty commitments.

Rather than leave to chance whether your vulnerabilities will be exploited in the shadow negotiation, anticipate occasions when that is likely to happen. Forewarned, you can control them, not vice versa. Armed against the worst, you can avoid falling into bad habits and approach any negotiation with confidence.

Learn as Much as You Can

Information is a valuable commodity in negotiations. We've seen what knowing about yourself and tapping into what you know about the other party can accomplish. But imagine what would happen if you had perfect information. You would understand exactly how to present your case and the responses you needed to have ready. You could predict what the other person would be willing to give. You could anticipate which arguments would sway her, which might get his attention. Perfect information would take away all the uncertainty and much of the anxiety. Unfortunately, bargainers rarely enjoy this luxury, but the more you can discover, the more realistic your assessment of the situation becomes.

Two distinct kinds of information come into play in negotiations. *Factual information* provides the hard data—the pertinent facts and the intelligence about policies, practices, and precedents—that you use to back up your arguments. *Scouting information* helps you predict the hearing that those arguments will get so you can fine-tune your approach.

Factual Information. To negotiate effectively, you must believe that your argument is defensible. A solid informational foundation helps support that conviction. With the pertinent facts on hand you won't be caught off stride when pointed questions come your way. You can supply concrete reasons why your proposal makes sense—why, for example, a gradual price increase in a contract is more likely to be accepted by a client than a smaller but immediate hike.

Facts extend well beyond quantitative data. They cover a whole host of organizational policies and precedents as well as comparisons that can be drawn from other sources. If, for example, you want to propose a flexible work schedule or matrixed relationship, you can make your argument more effectively if you can point to other examples in your organization or to arrangements at other companies that have worked well.

Facts in this broader sense, because they introduce objective or noncontroversial criteria into the discussion, can clear up misperceptions. They also come in handy when you need to block arguments rooted in personal bias. Alison, an oil executive in her late twenties, piggybacked a master's in international finance with an undergraduate degree in geology. Fluent in Arabic and Hebrew, she applied for a posting to the Middle East. Her boss turned her down. Given the status of women in that area of the world, he said, she could not be effective.

Alison knew, from a friend's experience in Cairo, that even in conservative countries women moved easily within the international business community. Instead of pushing against her boss's subjective mind-set, she pulled together information from government and nongovernmental sources. She was able to show, by industry, just how many American women worked in the Middle East. She also documented the difference in the way "foreign" women were treated in these countries. Her boss, who had been operating on a gut reaction and no concrete information, finally realized that he was on shaky (perhaps actionable) ground.

No place is the need for factual information keener than in salary negotiations.[4] You cannot pluck a salary request out of thin air. Without the appropriate information to back up that request, you run two substantial risks: demanding too little or demanding too much. Good information tells you when your request falls within industry, professional, and organizational standards and makes it that much easier to defend. Solid information also fortifies against that inevitable question: "What are you making now?" Prospective employers often use an applicant's current salary as a benchmark in deciding what to offer. This practice can create a problem for anyone who has been laid off or whose current salary isn't an adequate reflection of ability or responsibility.

Whatever your circumstances, the more you know about a job and the salary it should command, the more comfortable you will feel. First off, the information takes away some of the uncertainty. You can distinguish a fair offer from an insult. With a firm salary range in mind, you can focus the discussion on the qualifications needed for the job and what it should pay and steer clear of a subjective argument over what you are worth.

Concrete information affords solid protection—against both overselling and undervaluing. It also checks the temptation to bargain yourself down in that private debate that takes place in your head. Connie, a talented engineer in her late twenties, had spent six years at a start-up company. Frustrated at a salary that lagged industry standards and did not begin to compensate for long hours and heavy responsibilities, she decided to start job-hunting. Before she went out on any interviews, however, she knew she had to be prepared to justify the big jump in salary that she wanted.

> *Of course I did my homework, but the right information was not easy to find. I was comparing salaries at a small start-up with those at a big engineering firm. Instead of raises, we got stock options. These were worthless, but maybe not if the company took off. Still, I needed a logic for the number I put on the table.*

To build her case, Connie concentrated on what first-year engineers made at large firms when she graduated. She called the placement office at her university and discovered the salaries clustered in three groupings. (This example uses hypothetical numbers rather than real statistics for any particular field.)

Starting Salaries
$37,500–$35,000
$33,000–$30,000
$22,500–$19,000

Given her educational record and experience, Connie felt secure putting herself just under the top tier. She then projected what that number would be with annual raises—one at the inflation rate and another assuming a higher merit increase. She fixed on an appropriate merit raise, which she was convinced she would have earned, by talking to friends who graduated with her and worked at large firms.

Target Salary Range	Increase at Inflation (3 percent)		Merit Increase (6 percent)	
	Starting Level	Current Dollars	Starting Level	Current Dollars
$33,000–$30,000	$33,000	$38,500	$33,000	$44,500

The higher figure, $44,500, turned into Connie's opening demand. The lower one, $38,500, became her walk-away price. If an offer fell below that figure, she would turn it down. Unless you define this walk-away figure yourself, any prospective boss will mentally fix it at your current salary level. Connie's research gave her the ammunition she needed to deflect discussion away from her weakness—her current salary—to what the prospective job should command and the experience she brought to it.

Any equivocation on an acceptable range tempts a prospective employer to push an offer lower and lower. To resist, you need a logic for the number you put on the table. That logic translates facts and figures into a cohesive argument. When a demand seems legitimate given what you have discovered, it is much easier to defend to others.

Scouting Information. Not all crucial information comes in the form of facts and figures and clear-cut policies. You retrieve an altogether different species of information by sounding others out for their take on particular personalities or for their reading of an organization's politics and its culture. The more you know about the person you are going to be negotiating with, the more confidence you will have in your approach.

Often the outcome of a negotiation turns on the political environment in which it takes place. Decision-making routines, norms, the informal power structure—all these condition the response you are likely to get. Do your demands fall within normal practices or do you have to take special care? Are there precedents for what you are proposing? Who else will be affected? Is their reaction liable to be negative? If so, what can you do to turn that initial response around?

This kind of knowledge is generally not public. Nor is it uniform. Different people will have had different experiences with the same person, and these experiences color their opinions. No two people will have the same reading of office politics or the organization's culture. As a result, it is important to let your scouting range widely.

These scouting reports guide you as you figure out how best to approach the other party. Erika used them to get off on the right foot when she argued her case for a specific first assignment after completing the training program at a New York investment banking house. Erika wanted to be an options trader, but the decision was taken out of her hands. Instead, she was slated for the research department, a plum assignment. "I'd been a star in the training program, and in some ways the assignment was a reward. But not for me. I had my sights fixed on the trading floor."

Most of the trainees considered these assignment decisions final. Erika wanted to negotiate hers. At the same time, she had little interest in being branded a troublemaker. Before Erika started her scouting, she had no idea how receptive the management committee would be to an alternative suggestion from her. Having spent only a short rotation on the trading floor, she was even less certain how to approach the head trader. She also worried about the head of research. The woman had been something of a mentor, and Erika did not want a change in assignment to alienate her.

Erika, gregarious and not the least bit timid about approaching relative strangers, gathered information informally. To test the feasibility of even proposing a change in assignment, she talked to men and women in various departments who had completed the training program three or four years earlier. To get a better handle on the head trader's likely reaction, she went out for coffee with any options trader under thirty she could corral. Within a relatively short time, a clear picture began to emerge: This first assignment was critical to her career path. Requests for reassignment, while not common, had been successful in the past. With this feedback in hand, Erika shared her career plans with her mentor, being careful to make her appreciation of the woman's support explicit.

Scouting information not only lessened Erika's fears about the risks of putting in for the options desk. It pointed out how she should couch her proposal so that it would stir up the least resistance.

Scouting information allows you to anticipate problems. If your demands bump up against entrenched attitudes or established ways of doing things, you know where to fine-tune your request. If current practices come up short as far as you are concerned, you have clues on how you might work on revising those precedents. Bettina, pregnant with her first child, used this kind of information to develop a proposal for a flexible schedule.

Bettina, an operations manager in an automotive assembly plant in Detroit, knew any change in her schedule would automatically affect others. In the past, these arrangements had created problems in her company—both for management and for the women. To get management's side of the story, she quizzed her boss and other department heads about the headaches flexible schedules caused them. At the same time, she drew out women on the challenges they faced when they reduced their hours in the office.

"Face time," it turned out, was a big element in how employees were perceived. The increased emphasis on teams meant that if you weren't around, you gradually became invisible. "I talked to women on flexible schedules," Bettina recalls. "And I watched them. They missed important meetings and gradually got left out of the decision making. Then, feeling guilty about disappointing their bosses and not wanting to be excluded for career reasons, bit by bit they started putting in longer hours. Eventually they were working a full schedule for part-time pay."

With this scouting information in hand, Bettina could address many of management's concerns in her proposal. Her scouting reports also underscored the need to build in safeguards for herself and revealed where she would be most vulnerable. A high priority was ensuring that team meetings happened when she was there. Any proposal she made had to maintain her level of responsibility *and* prevent erosion of her time at home. To protect against slippage on either count, she incorporated a three-month review so that she and her boss could evaluate how the arrangement was working for both of them.[5]

Scouting information does more than cue you in to how to make a case. It can also provide ample clues about what cases you should not make. Art, an economist at a New England utility, saved himself from a bad career move by tapping his informal sources.

A call from a headhunter piqued Art's interest. "I had been with the utility for a while and was feeling stale. A company in Texas sounded great. But I knew that might be the fault of New England weather." Despite a Ph.D. in economics, Art could not decipher the company's annual report. "I started with the footnotes; that may have been a mistake." To find out, he called an accountant friend. There was prolonged pause before the reply came. "Art, I can't talk about that. We are running the numbers for one of their acquisitions. Umm . . . ah . . . take a look at the *Fortune* article." The picture of the company that emerged in *Fortune* diverged so dramatically from its go-go image that Art brought it up over lunch with a senior money manager in Boston, who warned, "I wouldn't go near that firm."

These cautionary signals put Art on alert. When nothing in the interviews convinced him that the aggressive management would change, Art rejected the company's offer. "I kicked myself the whole way back to Boston. They offered me an obscene amount of money." But it was a good decision, one that could not have been made without the early warning system Art tapped. The company was Enron.

Information increases your control over a negotiation. The more you know ahead of time, the more realistic you can be in setting your goals and the easier it is to figure out what steps you need to take to get what you want. This kind of control gives you confidence in what you are doing. And increased confidence makes it less likely you will sabotage yourself by caving in too soon or settling for less than you should.

Develop Alternatives

Information, in and of itself, bolsters confidence. Going into a negotiation prepared lessens the chances of being caught unawares. With the right information at your fingertips, it is easier for you to be firm and harder for others to brush off your arguments. But information does more than bolster your case. It forces you to clarify your options. Earlier we suggested you begin to prepare for a negotiation by taking stock and considering why the other party needs you. That is an important step, but you can take it further. You can analyze what will happen to each side if you cannot come to terms. What are your alternatives? What are the other person's? The answers to these questions reveal just how much flexibility you have in a negotiation. The better your alternatives are, the less your fate hangs on the negotiation's outcome and, paradoxically, the more influence you are likely to have over the terms of any agreement. In parallel, as your counterpart's alternatives worsen, yours improve.

Find Other Ways to Satisfy Your Needs. When the other party senses that you have no alternative but to take what is offered, he or she will be tempted to give as little as possible. With another job offer or another contract in your back pocket, you don't have to depend on the other party's generosity or go along with any ultimatums. You can decide what is best for you rather than have the other side do the defining. Alternatives, in effect, expand your bargaining power and enable you to *stay* in the negotiation.

The notion of alternatives is captured in an acronym— BATNA—which stands for the Best Alternative To a Negotiated Agreement.[6] Your BATNA answers the question: What will I do if we can't come to an agreement that meets my needs? Alice and Meg broadened their alternatives midstream in a negotiation when their firm's contract with its only client came up for renewal. The company that the two women ran provided part-time clerical services to a nearby university on a contractual basis. In turn, they filled their roster of workers with lower-income women from a job-training program initiated by the city.

As soon as the talks started, the university's vice president for financial affairs began pressing them on price. "He thought we were ripe for plucking," Meg commented. "Two naive, overeducated twenty-something women with lots of heart and no street smarts." Right off the bat, he cited the university-wide cost-cutting program and slashed Alice and Meg's fee until there was barely room in the numbers to cover their overhead. Panicked, they were on the verge of giving in just to secure the contract's renewal.

"Then we called a time out," Alice said. "We told him we needed a week to think over our decision." The two spent that time not in squeezing the last nickel out of their budget but in lining up other work. By the end of the week, they had secured verbal commitments that, altogether, represented more work than they could handle without staffing up.

The vice president attempted to start the next round of talks where the previous one had left off. "Sorry," Meg interjected. "If that is your budget allowance, we will have to scale back our services." No longer dependent on the university contract for survival, Alice and Meg could hold out for a fair price. Though they might have been able to remain firm without these other commitments, the temptation to go along with the vice president's ultimatum would have been much stronger. Having viable alternatives strengthened their resolve.

The vice president was surprised. Under the impression that the university remained their only client, he thought he would be able to dictate terms. Once Alice and Meg disabused him of that notion, they were able to work out a deal that each side could live with. The vice president actually became quite conciliatory. An efficient bottom line was only part of his mandate. The university had no interest in jeopardizing a contract that eased its tense relations with the city. He needed an agreement more than Alice or Meg guessed.

Alternatives strengthen your position, but they serve other important functions. First, they keep you focused on your goals. The discipline of sifting through alternatives forces you to identify the best option. Second, with other opportunities available, you don't run the risk of getting so caught up in the negotiation that reaching agreement—any agreement—becomes the goal. No deal is better than a bad deal—if you have an escape hatch. But don't make the mistake of overestimating the alternatives at your disposal. They must be real. Otherwise, they are just wishful thinking and can tempt you to overplay your hand.

What Is the Worst That Can Happen? It pays to think about worst-case scenarios. At times, your fallback position is to leave things the way they are. If you cannot strike a deal, you won't be any better off, but you also won't lose anything. If your other choices would leave you worse off, you are stuck with the present arrangement. When you find yourself in this situation, you don't have much room to bargain. You may have to resign yourself to taking less or paying more than you had hoped—and not just in terms of money. That's okay. There is no point in blaming yourself or faulting your negotiating skills. No one can negotiate effectively without some viable choices.

Charles, an IT manager, wanted to try out the powerful new sales management software just released. Testing the idea with the chief operations officer, he discovered he had no flexibility. The company was locked into its current vendor, whose CEO sat on the board and gave them a significant price break. Charles argued that the increased functionality outweighed the cost savings, but he was cut short by the COO. He wouldn't bring up the possibility of shifting to the CEO. He certainly wouldn't suggest a trial run. Charles was stuck. He had no other options to explore. Despite his reluctance and what he considered a potential conflict of interest, Charles had no choice but continue with the current software.

Don't Forget to Assess the Other Person's Alternatives. Having a good grasp on your alternatives gives you a realistic picture of your situation. But if you can learn more about the choices at the other party's disposal, the picture becomes even sharper. The reason is simple. What you think of your alternatives directly affects your assessment of the other side's position. If your alternatives don't look good, you almost automatically assume the other person has the upper hand. Marge, a freelance designer in her early forties, almost got caught in this trap. Until she actually investigated the other side's choices, she exaggerated the flexibility they enjoyed.

Marge had done some top-notch design work for ODI, one of the largest furniture dealers in North Carolina. Not long afterward, ODI's owners approached her. Instead of continuing to do contract work, why didn't she become a partner? The proposal they put to her was straightforward. They would supply office space and the needed capital. In exchange, she would provide in-house design expertise. On the plus side, the partnership would end her persistent cash-flow problems. On the downside, it might compromise her independence and her ability to work for other clients. The issues between them soon boiled down to one—office layout. The owners wanted Marge's space configured so that it appeared to be an extension of their design department. Marge insisted that her space be clearly defined so that her other clients would feel comfortable coming to the office.

This was a tough negotiation for Marge. ODI dwarfed her shoestring operation. What's more, the owners' enthusiasm for her work masked a veiled threat. Accept or they would find someone else. This hardball tactic made Marge suspicious. She knew only two other designers of her caliber in the Greenville area. She called both and discovered that neither would consider the arrangement that ODI had in mind. ODI would have to raid a competitor or persuade a designer to relocate—not exactly great alternatives for them. Marge's awareness of the owners' limited choices enabled her to push hard on her space demands. Had she taken the owners' reading of their options at face value, she would have found it much more difficult to resist their attempts to dominate her in the shadow negotiation.

Alternatives—yours and the other party's—go a long way in answering the question of who needs whom more in a negotiation. They provide a litmus test for the ability of either to walk away. When you have other options, you cannot be held captive to an imposed solution. When you know the constraints under which the other person is operating, you are much less inclined to grab any offer he or she puts on the table. And if your alternatives turn out to be poor, you don't waste time blaming yourself. You try for the best that you can hope to realize. An understanding of the alternatives on both sides of the table adds to your effectiveness as a negotiator precisely because it gives you a realistic picture of the cards you have to play.

Get Fresh Perspectives

So you have inventoried your assets, come to grips with your weaknesses, learned more about the situation and the players, and still things look bleak. The more you mull over your problem, the worse it looks. Sometimes, caught in your own myopia, you see no way out of a bad situation. But difficult negotiations need not be toughed out alone, nor should they be. Talking through a problem with family members, friends, and colleagues often gives you the support you need to face what you expect to be a troubling experience.

Seek Out Objective Advice. Informal consultants can do more than provide moral support and a safety valve. Removed from the immediate situation, they invariably have a different take on it. Nor are they subject to the same doubts you may have. Their outlook can help you filter out your biases and view your choices objectively.

Meredith, an attorney specializing in trust and financial planning, had built a committed practice among the new breed of entrepreneurs in Silicon Valley and the Bay Area's biotechnology firms. One of her first clients had recently died of AIDS. He left a large estate, a distraught and loving partner, and an appalled family. A week after his will was filed at probate, the family brought an injunction to remove Meredith as trustee. The grounds were incompetence. Meredith panicked. Even her wicked sense of humor disappeared.

> *I didn't know what to do. If I stepped down as trustee, it was an admission of incompetence and the worst kind of betrayal of James. His family is a powerhouse in this state. If I fought them, I was going to be slaughtered. Either way I would be ruined.*

Part of Meredith's strain was financial. She was spending all her time preparing her defense. Her billable hours shrank at the same time that her expenses escalated. She also worried about the quality of the work she had done for James. His condition had deteriorated rapidly, and they competed against the clock to finish the documents. Had she done a sloppy job in the rush?

Meredith knew she could not allow this state of paralysis to continue. She turned to colleagues at the Women's Bar Association for a detached look at the lawsuit. Unhampered by the emotions and strains Meredith was under, they walked her through the case. She was not in such bad shape legally. The work for her client was solid, defensible on its merits. She was, however, letting the opposing counsel's status overwhelm her. Her fears were understandable, they all agreed, but it was an emotional reaction, one that the lawyers on the other side were all too willing to exploit in the shadow negotiation.

Gradually Meredith's friends brought her to a new understanding. She was not so vulnerable as she assumed, but she was getting in her own way. Rather than increasing Meredith's gloom, this objective assessment sharpened her focus. She turned the case over to another lawyer and concentrated her attention on her clients, which relieved her financial stress. Several months later the suit was dismissed.

Tap the Experiences of Others. It is not unusual when you get into a bind in a negotiation to think, "Why me?" Preoccupied with your own difficulties, you assume no one else has ever had the same experience. By talking to colleagues you often discover you are in good company. Chris, a medical intern, looked forward to his upcoming rotation review with the chief resident. His first few months had been sleepless but productive, and he wanted to discuss a rotation in orthopedic surgery. Instead of a pat on the back, he got a laundry list of misdemeanors. Chris, taken aback, had no idea how to respond. It was not exactly the moment to talk about a future specialty.

In a smart move, Chris temporized and told the senior resident he needed to think about his feedback. He also mentioned the incident to a couple of second-year residents during a momentary lull on the floor. He was barely through his complaints when the two started to laugh. "You got off light. Carmichael chews up interns. He's famous for it." The comments set Chris's mind at rest. He needed the chief resident's recommendation and thought he had been singled out for unusual criticism. When he picked up the discussion with the resident, he mentioned a comment that he found useful and then moved quickly to solicit the resident's take on the pros and cons of various rotations.

Widen Your Focus. There is one last way fresh perspectives are helpful. Uncertainty about what to do can tempt you to narrow your choices. A troublesome decision seems more manageable when you can only choose yes or no. Simplification like this appeals because it reduces your decision points; at the same time it prevents you from considering other options. A wise counselor can often come up with an array of ideas that broadens your thinking. Suddenly you don't see yourself trapped in an either/or decision, whether to accept or to refuse. Esther, a junior partner in a consulting firm, reaped the benefits of an expanded perspective.

Esther's potential caught the eye of the managing partner, and he offered her a special assignment heading up a task force on diversity. This offer was a mixed blessing. Esther cared about diversity, but she also cared about keeping her career on track, and promotions at the firm went to the rainmakers who brought in new business. The task force would eat into hours she could spend on work that would be rewarded. To make matters worse, virtually no one turned down a special assignment from the managing partner.

Esther faced a dilemma. If she said yes, it would take her away from her primary work and hurt her career, but the managing partner would consider her a team player. If she said no, she could get on with what she saw as her "real" work, but the partner would be offended. Because the assignment appealed to her, she was tempted to agree and deal with the difficulties later. Before she made a final decision, she decided to run the pros and cons by her old business school professor. He quickly passed over the consequences of saying yes or no. Instead, he focused on Esther's real problem. She wanted to take on the assignment, but worried about the impact on her career. The dilemma came not from the assignment itself but from the importance the firm attached to it. Esther needed to convince the managing partner that this assignment had to carry as much value for the firm as rainmaking did before anyone would give its findings much weight, and that it would be a good move to make sure that it did so.

The managing partner had long been an advocate of increased diversity within the firm, and he immediately grasped the core issue when Esther laid out her reservations. As long as the diversity effort bore no relation to the firm's reward systems, no one would pay it much attention. Together Esther and the managing partner came up with an estimate of how much time the assignment would take to ensure first-rate results. They then reduced her other obligations by a corresponding amount. Finally, they began to analyze how those efforts translated to the firm's bottom line. They were after concrete ways of measurement so that organization building as well as rainmaking counted in decisions on who got promoted and who didn't.

It is not always easy to ask for help and not all advice is equal. Even close friends or colleagues can be tempted to tell you what they think you want to hear. Bent on making you feel better or avoiding an emotional discussion, they mask their real opinions. You may have to contract explicitly for candid advice and you must choose your consultants carefully. You don't want an overly rosy picture painted, but an unnecessarily bleak view is no help either. To understand where you stand, you need to corroborate both the good and the bad.

Objective feedback, whether positive *or* negative, invariably gives you a more realistic take on your situation. No matter how scrupulous your self-assessment or meticulous your information-gathering efforts, at times a correcting lens is needed. Informal consultants can confirm your suspicion that you are not in a particularly strong bargaining position. They can also encourage you to view the negotiation more positively by pointing out where you have become too narrowly focused or drawn questionable conclusions.

Thelma's Dilemma

We have laid out a series of steps that alert you to where you might get in your own way and what you can do to start your advocacy off on the right foot. These steps have a cumulative effect, reinforcing each other. To show how they can work together, we return to Thelma's story at the point where she is being pressured to take over as department head. Defensive and stretched to the limit, Thelma at first saw only an insoluble dilemma. She could not manage an infant, her teaching load, and the chair's additional duties. If she accepted, she saw two miserable years ahead. Angry with her colleagues and resentful of the time the chair's job would take away from her new baby, she decided the only way out was to resign.

Thelma called a friend at another school and poured out her tale of woe. Brad had accused her of being a freeloader when the department needed a team player. No one was sympathetic to her situation. She had pretty much made up her mind to resign. Thelma's friend surprised her. Instead of commiseration, she got a mini-lecture. Thelma did not realize she was engaged in a negotiation. And in a negotiation you have to think about what you want. Her friend then posed a question that puzzled Thelma at first. At what price, she asked, would Thelma take the chair's job? What sort of support would the department have to give her? Mulling over that question Thelma took the initial step in preparing an effective advocacy. She started thinking. Maybe she could bargain after all.

Thelma first looked at where she stood. Her position was actually pretty strong, when she stepped back a bit and considered it. Without doubt, she was the best person for the chair's job at that time. She had been a moving force on the college's curriculum committee. With her as chair, the department would gain a vocal spokesperson who could push the administration for reform. But, most important, the department needed her—whether or not she accepted the chair's job. As one of the college's most popular teachers, she wielded considerable influence with the administration—a big advantage in a budget-cutting atmosphere.

Thelma also realized she had some hidden assets she could bring into play. She was pretty good at reading people and situations—the kind of information all of us pick up but so often discount. She knew the department, and she knew Brad. She had watched him in action for almost a decade. He disliked complaints and looked for solutions, not more problems. He wanted to get rid of the chairmanship and would probably try to find the resources to make the job easier for her.

What's more, she had a lot of scouting information at her fingertips. As soon as the adoption agency notified her about the baby, she had sought out members of other departments to discover how they handled the dual burdens of work and family. But she still needed information on the arrangements that other departments made to lessen the extra load any chair took on. Did they supply additional staff support? Were teaching commitments reduced to free up time? A few quick telephone calls yielded the answers. Support staff was invariably provided, and teaching commitments reduced by at least one course.

With these arrangements in mind, Thelma began to craft a solution that met her needs and Brad's—his for somebody to take over as chair and hers to have the time and energy to enjoy her daughter. To give herself a fallback position, Thelma approached a colleague she had helped out in the past. Would he be willing to serve as co-chair the first year of Thelma's commitment if Thelma did all the organizational work from home? Yes, the colleague agreed, if Thelma returned the favor when his turn as chair came up.

Thelma was left with one thorny question. What demands could she make that were realistic and filled her needs?

I'll ask to teach one less course and for an assistant, just to be on the safe side.

The next morning Thelma put her conditions on the table. Brad did not even blink. He was perfectly willing to bargain.

As Thelma discovered, biased and distorted pictures of where you stand can wreak havoc on your capacity to negotiate. To argue your case effectively, you need to believe that you have something to bargain with and over. Otherwise opportunities slip by. Before you can engage the other party in a negotiation, you must make sure you are ready—psychologically and practically. A realistic fix on your bargaining position not only enables you to stay out of your own way, it focuses you on the positive steps you can take to support your demands. It's the bargainer's equivalent of being dressed for the game.

Chapter 2

Making Strategic Moves

Effective advocacy hinges on getting into a good position in the shadow negotiation and staying there. Usually that objective involves some deliberate maneuvering on your part. You want the other person to be receptive to your demands—or at least grant them a hearing. But just because you are primed to negotiate is no guarantee that your counterpart is anxious to meet you halfway.

Ready to sit down with a boss, a colleague, or a client, you may find that you have a reluctant bargainer on your hands. She stalls or ignores you, refusing to meet. Phone calls go unanswered. That important talk keeps being postponed. Even if you succeed in arranging a meeting, the negotiation never gets off the ground. He pays lip service to your ideas and immediately skips to his own agenda or changes the subject. Somehow you never manage to get a two-way conversation going. He has made up his mind before you open your mouth. She thinks that if she holds out long enough, you may relax your demands or stop bothering her.

It's perfectly normal to encounter resistance in negotiation. A good part of every bargainer's job is to persuade others to take his or her proposals seriously. It may seem obvious, but your first task is to get the other person to the table. Equally important, you must then convince him or her to engage in a process of give-and-take. Not all the giving or the taking can come from one side. Strategic moves are the means you use to coax reluctant bargainers to the table and ensure that the give-and-take goes both ways.

A willingness to negotiate is at some basic level a confession of mutual need. People negotiate when you have something they want and they cannot count on your falling in with their plans without getting something in return. These perceptions of mutual need play out in the shadow negotiation. When you seem to need the other person more than he or she needs you, the balance in the shadow negotiation can tilt dramatically against you. Differences in power or position, for example, can stymie fruitful exchange. Subordinates generally pay acute attention to a superior's demands, but they can encounter real difficulty in persuading a boss to listen to their demands. Managers who are in the minority due to their race or gender can find themselves excluded from important networks. They may have neither the personal clout and experience nor the organizational standing to convince others that talks should be started.

Even when bargainers are in a position to press their demands, they can find them being discounted. This happens for a lot of reasons. Some people acquire a reputation for going along so that others don't really expect them to voice strong objections. Their style of communicating may get in the way as they cloak their arguments in diffidence. Accustomed to working within a rigid chain of command, they may have hesitated to speak up in the past. Most bosses will keep piling on the work so long as an employee silently goes about completing the assignments on time without recognition or reward. Clients and colleagues, suspecting that someone is not likely to buck the system, will be tempted to press for concessions.[1] Bargainers can be left out of the informal discussions where the issues are really decided. By the time they offer their opinions, what they have to say is irrelevant. It's not just that they are not heard. Their ideas no longer count. Little by little, without conscious recognition on the bargainer's part, his or her bargaining power may have slipped away.

More than persuasive coaxing is needed when you bump up against attitudes like these in the shadow negotiation. You must bring the people you negotiate with to the point where they realize that they have to deal with you seriously and fairly. Just as there are steps you can take so that you come to the table with confidence, there are strategic moves you can make to convince other people to heed your demands. These moves convey exactly why they need to meet you halfway. Any reluctance they might have to negotiate with you fades once they are forced to admit that they will be better off if they deal with you *and* worse off if they don't.

GETTING INTO A GOOD POSITION

Strategic moves employ both the carrot and the stick to improve your negotiating position. Using incentives, the carrots, you make other people aware of the *benefits* of dealing with you. You point out the value they get in return, how negotiating with you works to their advantage. So long as the loan officer at the bank senses that you don't fit the profile of a good customer, and many single proprietorships in service industries do not, he or she is going to think twice about setting up a credit line for your new business. It is always safer to say no, after all. Denied loans don't appear on the bank's monthly watch list of troubled accounts. For the application to warrant more than a perfunctory review, the loan officer must be convinced that there are clear advantages (and precious little risk) in approving the loan.

Sticks operate in reverse. By exerting pressure on the other party, you underscore the *costs* to her if she continues to ignore you or to him if he persists in giving you a hard time. If they see few reasons to discuss your needs, you supply them by raising the stakes. Increased pressure may be in order when the prospect of negotiation holds some real disadvantages for the other party. He or she may be quite content to let things drift along as they are. A boss accountable to management for the department's cost cutting may be reluctant to give you a raise until you tell him you have another job offer. Business as usual is more comfortable than introducing an alien voice (yours) into the decision-making apparatus already in place—until, that is, the others realize you have a much-needed piece of information. A coworker who has been successful in persuading you to produce those late-night projections has a vested interest in not revisiting the issue, but may become far more amenable after you leave promptly several nights in a row.

Establishing your voice *as a negotiator* in the shadow negotiation is no small task. Your credibility will be questioned and your resolve tested. In situations where you are not the only one involved in making the decision, the other party must understand that you have the authority to commit your organization.

A supplier will always defer to the person in the firm he thinks has the final say and controls the checkbook. It doesn't matter that the account is your responsibility and you are the one making the sales calls. Your opinions won't carry any weight so long as he doubts your authority to make decisions or put his requisition through.

At times it can be awkward to use carrots and sticks on your own or they may not be enough to compel someone to negotiate with you. Strategic allies can pave your way by putting their credibility behind you. It also pays to plan ahead when you know an important negotiation is coming up. You can then move to influence its outcome by shaping the process. By anticipating resistance and lobbying behind the scenes, you can position your ideas and issues so that they are heard positively once the negotiation actually gets under way. Here's a quick summary of strategic moves you can use:

- **Hold out incentives.**
  In any negotiation, the other party controls something you need—more money, more time, more cooperation, better communication, an opportunity. That's why you want to negotiate in the first place. But your needs alone won't get anyone to the table. Your counterparts must recognize that you have something of value to them. Incentives make that value visible.

- **Step up the pressure.**
  The incentives you hold out may not convince someone to negotiate with you. He or she may be perfectly content to let things continue the way they are—in which case you have to raise the costs of not dealing with you. You can increase the stakes by letting him know you have other

alternatives and don't have to go along with his plans. You can bring people to the table by convincing them that taking no action on your demands is not an option. Things are going to change even if they continue to stall.

○ **Establish your authority.**
Unless the other party recognizes your authority, she will resist dealing with you. To have any control over the negotiating process, you must establish your credibility and, when others are involved in the decision-making process, your right to speak for them.

○ **Enlist support.**
In many circumstances, what you can accomplish on your own is limited. You can reinforce your efforts to influence the other party by enlisting allies. Strategically placed allies can ensure you get a favorable hearing. They can also bring pressure to bear on your behalf.

○ **Exert control over the process.**
You can move to structure the negotiation process by planting seeds for your ideas and gathering support for your agenda. Besides increasing your chances of encountering a positively disposed bargainer, behind-the-scenes efforts can prevent opposition from gaining momentum and make it less likely that your proposals will be rejected prematurely.

Laid down in black and white, these strategic moves seem very formal and premeditated, manipulative even. It is easy to slip into the mistake of thinking you can hold them in reserve, just for those big negotiations. You are not, after all, planning a major merger. You merely want to lower the decibel level at the weekly staff meeting. Just once it would be nice if you could make the arrangements with your client without discovering later that he has double-checked them with your boss. With all the cutbacks at work, you don't mind picking up some of the overload. But you would like to participate in the discussions over who is going to do what. None of these situations seems to call out for a strategic campaign. But unless you change the way the other party looks at them and at you, nothing about the situation will change for you in the shadow negotiation.

Strategic moves help you shape the game. They provide the means to increase your influence over a negotiation's course. They help you bring the other party to the table and even the odds once the real bargaining starts.

Fiona's Campaign

Fiona Sweeney faced a negotiation that turned out to be a pivotal point in her career. She had joined an international computer company when she graduated from college. Over the next eleven years, she steadily moved up the ranks. Calm, pragmatic, and thoughtful, she attributed her success to diligence. Her coworkers in the Albany plant singled out her intuitive feel for organizations. Her businessman father thought it was his doing.

Suddenly Fiona was promoted to controller of operations and transferred to Palo Alto. Never "one of the boys" in a predominantly male environment and a newcomer to the division, Fiona found California a jolting experience. Accustomed to thrashing out ideas with long-time colleagues, she felt isolated. And then her new boss gave her what seemed to be an impossible task. He charged her with negotiating a change in the company's decision-making processes. Despite a professed goal of customer satisfaction, the company was a series of fiefdoms, with little coordination even on major accounts. Even though the system almost guaranteed a constant level of customer dissatisfaction,

the sales managers had no inclination to change.
Instead, to protect commissions and their valued customers, they exerted pressure on production and quality control.

Fiona, new on the scene and ripe for testing,
needed all the strategic moves at her disposal to carry
out her assignment. First and foremost, she had to convince the various departments to take her seriously.
Only then could she begin to negotiate the significant
changes demanded by any real shift in an organization's
decision making. Once we explore the individual moves
that contribute to an effective advocacy, we will return
to Fiona's story to show how she integrated them into
a strategic campaign.

Hold Out Incentives

Incentives entice people to deal with you. These strategic
moves can take many forms, but they have one purpose. They
convince other parties that negotiating with you is in their best
interest. You cannot just tell them that you have something
valuable to offer; you have to *show* them. This demonstration
requires coming up with the right incentives and those, in turn,
depend on the specific circumstances.

You can have the best product or service in the world, a
long list of talents you have scrupulously inventoried, but you
won't get far in a negotiation if the other person is not in the
market for what you are selling. Value must be perceived as
valuable before you can turn it into an advantage. Your customer says she can get comparable services from other vendors,
and she won't pay a premium for yours. If you want that premium, you have to make clear what you provide that other sup-

pliers don't. The product launch comes off ahead of schedule. If no one knows that you made that happen, your contribution goes unnoticed. To be rewarded for it, you have to make it visible in the shadow negotiation. Even when your value is apparent to the other person, he or she may be tempted to discount it simply to maintain the upper hand in your relationship. When you let that happen, you shortchange your contribution and severely penalize yourself.

Make sure you have something the other person needs. Just because you are motivated and see clear benefits in what you offer, that doesn't mean you can be sure the other party will jump to the same conclusion. No matter how versatile the talents or services are that you bring, if the other party doesn't need them, then he won't have an incentive to deal with you. Your incentives must have some resonance with his needs. If you want his attention, you have to create that need.

At forty, Molly was a month away from finishing her MBA. Although she had begun her job search early, her prospects were not bright. Her age worked against her, but so did her résumé. Her entire work experience consisted of teaching English as a foreign language when her husband was stationed in Germany. "I was a blank page," she comments, "with a young daughter." Molly did, however, have considerable motivation: a need for financial security.

> *I never expected to work full time. But then my husband died suddenly. I went to business school to make sure that I could afford to send my daughter to college.*

Molly also had a game plan. She wanted to carve out a niche for herself in mergers and acquisitions. But after several chilly interviews it was apparent that no one was going to sign her up on a promise to work hard.

Molly decided she needed something concrete to bring to the negotiations. She went back to the drawing boards and developed a matrix of Internet software firms. She analyzed what niche each company filled in the emerging market. She then looked for synergies with established companies. With this work in hand, she wangled her way into three investment banking firms. None was interested in hiring her, but one found her project promising enough to give her a trial as a researcher—without pay or any staff support.

After getting her foot in the door, Molly faced the daunting task of creating a perception of value for what she was giving away and translating her trial period into a job. Only when her research began to yield real results did she approach the managing partner.

Joel didn't even realize how tentative our arrangement was. I told him I could not continue to work for free and had begun a job search. He had no idea they weren't paying me.

Her focus on a hot new market gave Molly leverage, an incentive for the managing partner to deal with her. Her research was just starting to produce results and he couldn't afford an interruption. Keeping her on was easier than training someone new. Once he came to this conclusion, Molly could negotiate terms. She had established her value.

Creating value is a key move in the shadow negotiation. Once you figure out what the other party actually needs, you can tailor your incentives so that they respond to those needs. You suddenly appear more useful than he or she realized. You don't always have to create this value out of whole cloth the way Molly did. But you do have to demonstrate it. You cannot leave it up to the other party to puzzle through how and where your talents or product might be useful. You have to make that connection yourself. The trick comes, as Molly discovered, in knowing what the organization values (or will value in the future) and then making it easy for the other person to see that you can do that valued work or provide the needed service. He or she then has a reason to negotiate with you.

Make your value visible. After assessing your situation, you may conclude, quite rightly, that you have a lot of value to offer. But somehow that value does not seem to be gaining you much ground in the shadow negotiation. Generally it is not working to your advantage because it is invisible. Value can be discounted on both sides of the table. Not only do you have to be aware of your value. You must make sure that it is firmly implanted in the other person's mind.

The value of the work you do disappears unless you claim it. The conference goes off without a hitch. If no one knows about the long hours you put in to make that happen, your contribution goes unnoticed. Unnoticed, it goes unrewarded. If you want to change that situation, you need to make your value visible.

Frequently the people we negotiate with must be reminded of our contributions. Rather than continue to be taken for granted, you can deliberately jostle their awareness. It does not take much to remind someone of what you do. You can interrupt your services for a bit. Toni was a partner in a growing architectural practice. Gradually, she had taken over the responsibility for making sure the office ran smoothly, clients paid promptly, and bills went out on time. She assumed these duties largely by default. Her partner had no interest in anything other than design. Before long he gave no credit to the effort and time Toni spent keeping the office on an even keel. Then Toni was invited by an old friend to give a talk in London.

About to prepare "instruction" sheets for her partner, Toni held off. She thought he might at least be curious about the procedures she had put in place. He wasn't. At the last minute, she asked if he wanted to go over them, but he just smiled. "No problem," he assured her. "I'll take care of everything." After a few days, in the course of which he had to make an emergency run to the bank to transfer funds, he had a good picture of what went on behind the scenes in his own office. The work Toni had been doing was no longer invisible. The experience left him with a new appreciation of the burden Toni had been carrying. He was now prepared to talk about sharing responsibilities so that they were both freer to get on with what they really enjoyed—designing.

For your value to influence a negotiation, you must take steps, however subtle, to ensure that it is right there on the table for both of you to see. We cannot stress this point enough. When your work disappears, so do your influence and your bargaining power.

Make certain the other party pays for your value. The person you are negotiating with may, in fact, have a good idea of your value. He or she may even appreciate the work you do. The sticky problem comes not in making your value visible but in making sure you get credit for it. The shadow negotiation turns into a tug of war in which you are pushed to retreat on your demands. You want a promotion; she pushes you to settle for praise and a pat on the back. You need incentives at hand to convince the other person that being valued means having your value rewarded.

Chris, a television executive, knew exactly what she contributed at the station. But she still faced two major obstacles when she decided to ask for a raise. She worked in an industry notorious for underpaying and overworking backroom people, and she reported to a boss, a lawyer by training, who prided himself on his reputation as an aggressive negotiator. "Al likes everyone to think he eats nails for breakfast. He would not hesitate to cram a take-or-leave-it proposition down my throat."

To get the raise she wanted (and deserved), Chris had to force Al to admit that she played a critical part in the station's operations and that she should be paid accordingly.

Chris drew on her flair for the dramatic and a rather puckish sense of humor to orchestrate the interview. She thought out each detail with a feeling for the dynamics in the shadow negotiation.

Al loved the exercise of power. He always conducted salary negotiations from behind a huge desk. The supplicants sat opposite him on a couch that sank to the ground, making them feel inconsequential. I brought one of the high stools we use in the studio with me to the meeting. From that perch, I wasn't swallowed up in a bottomless couch. I looked down on Al.

The negotiation began amicably. Al agreed to all but one of her requests. He gave her another week of vacation, a company car, and a first-class seat when she had to fly to the network's West Coast offices. But he would not budge on her demand for more money.

As they went back and forth, Chris's value to the station became abundantly clear.

> *I timed the meeting to occur during the busiest part of the day in the newsroom—at deadline when my presence was crucial. I purposely let producers interrupt us. They broke into the meeting several times to tell me about stories, tape editing, and satellite shots.*

Despite these timely interruptions, Al remained adamant: No raise. Chris got off her stool and looked at Al.

> *After a long silence, I said I hoped there would be no hard feelings. I thought he valued my work. Then I told him I had to get the newscast on the air and walked out of the office.*

When Chris left Al's office, she was not bluffing. She knew her value, Al knew her value. If he wanted to keep her, he was going to have to pay her a fair wage. Al sent his secretary after Chris. When she walked back into his office, he was sitting on the couch. "Let's talk money," he said.

Each of us brings different skills and expertise to bear in a negotiation. But, like Al, other people may discount what we offer in a negotiation, generally for a simple reason. They are going to have to pay for it—by giving us more money, or time, or cooperation. You can help them over this hurdle, but you have to do it in a way they understand and appreciate. Chris's high stool and the interruptions she prompted were symbolic actions that Al immediately read. Toni's trip to London jolted her partner, and they were able to come up with more equitable ways to share the office burdens. And Molly's project provided the managing partner with tangible evidence of the future contributions she could make to a firm engaged in mergers and acquisitions. The incentives you hold out, to be effective and increase your influence in a negotiation, must be recognizable and worth something to the other person.

Step Up the Pressure

Negotiation inevitably involves change. You open talks because you want something to be different. That something might be a salary, or a job, or a relationship. The right incentives can prompt your counterparts. The obvious advantages to them may make them amenable to negotiating that change with you. But holding out a carrot is not always enough. Caught in inertia and a dislike of change in any form, they may not mind passing up some possible advantage. Things are just fine the way they are. Why risk unsettling the situation? Abba Eban, Israel's former foreign minister, once observed that diplomats have "a passionate love affair with the status quo" that stills any forward movement.[2] That love affair carries over into ordinary negotiations. Often to get them off the ground, you have to unfreeze the situation by making the status quo less attractive.[3] The pressures you exert raise the cost of business as usual. As the other party weighs her choices, she begins to see that things cannot remain the same. She will be worse off if she doesn't deal with you.

These pressure levers run the gamut from outright threats to gentle prods and must be used carefully. Blurting out a threat to go over your boss's head is likely to escalate the tensions and might get you fired. Sometimes you can get your point across simply by letting the other person know that you *can* increase the costs to him or her. You don't necessarily have to act on that warning. Once he suspects that the current arrangements are going to change whatever he does, he is likely to be more willing to negotiate. That way he ensures that he has a voice in any decision. Alternatives can also be used as a pressure lever. If the other party seems reluctant to meet your demands, you make sure he knows you have other options that do.

Issue a credible threat. Threats are the most obvious means of forcing the other person to admit that maintaining the status quo is not an option. A threat commits you to a course of action if the other person does not respond in a particular way. Threats can be a powerful tool, but to apply real pressure, the threat has to be real. You must be prepared to follow through on it. If your bluff is called and you don't, you are the one who will be worse off, not the other party. The negotiation tips in your counterpart's favor if you issue an ultimatum on the minimum salary you will accept and then quickly revise that figure downward at the first sign of resistance.

Abby was more than ready to act on a threat. She and her reporter fiancé had planned an idyllic getaway in the Bahamas before he left on assignment for the Middle East. Abby wanted the long weekend to be perfect and did not even shop around for a bargain. The couple paid top dollar for a suite steps away from the ocean. Both had pulled long hours in exchange for the time away and they arrived, exhausted, at the resort. Instead of being shown to their room, they were told the hotel was overbooked. They soon found themselves shuttled off to a dismal lodging house miles from the ocean. They stayed the night and flew back home the next morning.

An irate Abby promptly called her travel agent to complain. She wanted a full refund for the hotel and airfare. The travel agent just as promptly denied any responsibility. He had no control over the resort's booking policies. Nonsense, Abby responded. There was no way he could compensate her for the lost weekend, but he could make her whole financially. If he didn't, she was going to make sure other clients were spared a similar experience. Either she heard from him by five o'clock or she would file a complaint with the consumer protection agency and post a reprise of her weekend on the Internet. For good measure she also mentioned that her fiancé was a reporter and friendly with the newspaper's travel editor.

The travel agent couldn't have cared less about a complaint at the consumer protection agency. It would take years for the agency to get to it. But much of his business came from referrals. Any bad press would be a disaster. He didn't need until five o'clock to settle with Abby. He agreed right then to credit her MasterCard account in full. Had Abby's travel agent suspected she was bluffing, he might have tried to stonewall her, but he could not take the risk. His bookings might suffer.

Abby had nothing to lose by threatening the travel agent. That is not always the case. In most business situations you need to give yourself and the other person room to maneuver. You might couple a threat with a conciliatory move that makes it clear you would prefer not to go down that path. Rather than issue an ultimatum from which you cannot back off, you can talk about what you will be forced to do if your counterpart does not move on your demands. Say, for example, a coworker resents being assigned to your team and is being less than cooperative. You can threaten to go to the vice president, but cushion the warning with an assurance that you would prefer for the two of you to settle the problem.

Force a choice on the other party. Threats can be masked and issued subtly, but the risk of retaliation remains. Letting the other person know you have other alternatives carries less risk and can be just as effective in persuading her to negotiate with you. Once she realizes you are not captive to her plans or her schedule, she is forced to move on your demands. Karen leveraged her alternatives in order to push a boss who was stalling on her raise.

Karen had been promoted from administrative assistant to department manager, but without an increase in pay. Her old position was never filled, so she wound up doing two jobs. Karen didn't mind the long hours, but she resented the flat salary. Her boss, a nice guy, procrastinated on any decisions that might cause dissension. "He never makes waves. He's not a coward," she says, "but he avoids conflict." When she complained about her salary, he was sympathetic and agreed she deserved a raise. "I'll see what I can do." Every few weeks, he would reassure Karen. "Don't worry. I'm working on it." But nothing changed. Patience was not one of Karen's virtues. Already in a slow burn over the delays, she heard about a similar job in another agency.

After several interviews, she decided the other agency was not a place she wanted to work. The offer did, however, provide her with the leverage to unfreeze the talks with her boss. She told him an opportunity had come up that paid 30 percent more than her current salary. She preferred to stay, but only if he could match that figure. Given her boss's obvious tendency to procrastinate, she set a deadline. He had to let her know by the end of the week so she could give the other agency an answer.

Karen used her alternative to raise the cost to her boss of doing nothing. He could no longer delay and maintain the status quo. It was the prod (and the justification) he needed to argue forcefully on her behalf with his boss and with human resources.

Often the people you are negotiating with do not have complete authority to make the decision. They must squeeze the resources you want out of a superior. Rather than become embroiled in a contest with a higher-up, they take the path of least resistance. It is easier to stall and see how things play out. To speed the process along, you have to provide them with the ammunition they require to get what you want from their boss.

Make the consequences tangible to the other person. Big sticks like the one Karen wielded are often not at hand and might not work if they were. An indirect approach can exert subtle, less overt pressure and be as effective in the long run. Caroline had always been willing to pick up the extra work that needed doing around the office. Resources were tight, and everyone was stretched. Usually Caroline accepted the extra assignments gracefully, but she had reached her limit. She couldn't take on any more work without producing a shoddy product. When her boss approached her with yet another project, she was ready. She was not going to let herself be positioned as a slacker in the shadow negotiation. On her white board she had listed all her projects and their due dates. She was happy to take on this new work, but she wondered which projects he wanted her to drop or delay. The move immediately shifted the focus in the shadow negotiation from her dedication to her unreasonable schedule. She forced her boss to make a decision. Rather than give the assignment to someone else or delay Caroline's other work, he hired an assistant for her.

Peter, recently hired as director of engineering at a telecommunications firm, saw early on that delays in getting systems up and running were causing problems. He tracked the source of the difficulties to Alex, the chief engineer. Only by making the business consequences of Alex's performance clear to corporate could he convince them to take his concerns seriously.

Peter's boss had known Alex a long time; he had watched his progress from technician to chief engineer. Downplaying Peter's worries, he encouraged Peter to coach Alex. Peter tried, but despite his efforts, he could see no improvement. Worse, Alex failed to inform Peter when problems came up, and these were beginning to reflect badly on Peter. To get his boss to take his concerns seriously and negotiate the problem the chief engineer posed, Peter gave a presentation on the financial ramifications of the delays and poor quality. If things continued as they were, the division would experience significant losses. Once Peter's boss saw the consequences in black and white, he was willing to negotiate. They transferred Alex to R&D, returning him to the bench work where he excelled. When incentives do not get the other party's attention, you need to make these kinds of strategic moves to increase the pressure. Otherwise the other party will predictably remain satisfied with things as they are. By making the current situation less comfortable, you shake up the other person's complacency. When the other person realizes the costs attached to doing nothing, he or she will be far more receptive to negotiating with you.

Establish Your Authority When You Are Negotiating for Others

When you are negotiating for yourself with another person, you can direct your strategic moves to him or her. Once you establish your credibility, you are all set. But if others are involved in the decision-making process and you are speaking for them, there is another level of complexity to consider. Not only do you have to be credible in your own right, you must also convince the other side that you have the backing of the group you represent. Whatever incentives you hold out or pressures you bring to bear, it is impossible to get a negotiation off the ground if the other side questions that support. Generally, they consider negotiating with you a waste of time and prefer to deal with the real decision makers.

Whenever you speak for a larger group or represent your organization in a negotiation, the other side needs to understand just how much latitude you have to make a decision or commit your organization. No lawyer in his right mind will allow you to make changes to a joint venture agreement unless he is convinced you can act for your partners. He wants some proof. Your customer must know whether your boss fully approves of the precedent-breaking agreement you have offered. Unless he has that assurance, he won't care about the terms you offer, however attractive. He is going to entertain quite reasonable fears that the final agreement will be far less favorable once those with real authority get involved.

Secure explicit authorization. Certain elements almost guarantee that your authority will be questioned. If the other parties involved have never negotiated with you before, they naturally want reassurance about your ability to commit. Big differences in status, age, or background can generate unease and sometimes outright suspicion. For example, Dora, treasurer of a utility in the northeast, looked at an upcoming negotiation and knew she would have to establish her authority before any meeting took place. Dora's assignment was difficult enough. She was to extricate the utility from a partnership with a Kentucky coal company that had not worked out.

I was going to be negotiating our withdrawal with a bank chairman and the president of the coal company. They were angry about how the partnership turned out to begin with. When my CEO told them I was going to handle the negotiations, they took it as an insult, another example of their shabby treatment. They felt quite justified in being offended. I was young enough to be their daughter. They were from the South, I was a northerner. They were heads of their organizations; I was a couple reports short of being boss.

To establish her authority to negotiate the financial disentanglement, Dora drafted a letter for her CEO's signature. The letter was conciliatory, but succinct. Dora had been chosen to conduct the negotiations because she was the person in the organization who knew most about the partnership. She enjoyed the full confidence of the board and had complete authority to act on its behalf. As Dora suspected, the president of the coal-mining operation attempted to bypass her and called her boss directly. The CEO simply referred back to "his" letter.

By establishing her authority ahead of time, Dora got the negotiations off on the right foot. The others involved in the negotiation recognized that they had no choice but to deal with her. At times you will not have the clear and complete backing that Dora enjoyed, in which case you need to establish the authority you do have. Clarity here serves two purposes. You won't be tempted to overstep your bounds and promise more than you can deliver. And the other party has a better sense of what he can legitimately expect to negotiate with you.

Maintain the backing of your side. The ability to negotiate effectively often depends on perceptions, and when you are negotiating on behalf of others, the impressions that influence the shadow negotiation multiply. You must address your opponent across the table *and* maintain the continued confidence of your own constituency.[4] Real authority is not necessarily conferred by a title or a corner office. It comes from the continued support given your efforts and your approach. Without express backing from your side, the other parties involved invariably doubt your control and your ability to commit. Are you really leading the negotiation? Can they trust what you say?

Debra and her boss decided they could no longer postpone office renovations. They badly needed their space rewired in order to upgrade their systems. Since Debra had just finished a major project, the timing was perfect. She had the time to handle all the supervision of the changeover. But the engineering contractor was uncomfortable taking orders that involved intricate systems decisions from a woman. He kept calling Debra's boss on the pretext of sounding out his ideas. What he really wanted was authorization. Debra's boss thought nothing of talking to the contractor. He enjoyed discussing the new fiber technologies. It never occurred to him that he might be undermining Debra. Until she protested. So long as her boss took the contractor's calls, the contractor would cut her out of the loop and refuse to deal directly with her. Once Debra worked through this hidden consequence with her boss, he stopped taking the calls. Their united front also conveyed their commitment to the terms of the original contract. That front came in handy when problems developed with the project and the contractor wanted to make change orders.

Consider authorization an ongoing activity. Even when you can count on your side's full support, your authority will be tested in the shadow negotiation. If those involved in the direct negotiations sense that you enjoy less than enthusiastic backing from the people who count in your organization, they will pick up on these doubts and use them. The testing intensifies, and your own constituents, watching this performance play out, become uneasy. They begin to wonder whether you are the right person to manage the negotiations for them. Soon you are in danger of losing credibility on all sides. To break this cycle, you have to confront challenges to your authority as they happen.

Fran, director of human resources in a research center, moved to stop the erosion of her authority on both fronts in the aftermath of a merger. Soft-spoken, with a self-deprecating sense of humor, Fran radiated approachability—one of the reasons she was so good at her job. She was a great believer in consensus building, and she went into the talks determined that they not be adversarial. She saw them as an opportunity to build strong working relations.

> *Confrontation goes against my grain. With good will on both sides, I thought we could find a way to work together on the challenges we faced in meshing two very different cultures.*

Across the board, existing benefits at Fran's center outstripped those offered by their new partner. As head of human resources Fran was charged with working out the discrepancies. At the start, she had to set at rest suspicions within the center that she was not "tough enough" to stand up to the other side's team of negotiators. "Some of our people were openly nervous," she says. "Envisioning Bambi coming up against Rambo, they were afraid I would cave when the stakes got high or the pressure mounted and give away their benefits."

These doubts spread through the center's grapevine. Inevitably, they reached the other company's negotiators. Sensing little widespread support for Fran's collaborative approach, they began to distrust anything she said as nothing more than lip service, lacking any real force. Their lead negotiator was already gleeful about facing her. Now he became openly scornful of Fran, writing off her collaborative overtures as so much "Zen mumbo-jumbo."

Fran's ability to negotiate—collaboratively or otherwise—depended on her colleagues' confidence in her and her strategy. To gain their active support, she set up an advisory group with representatives from all departments, including human resources. The meetings of this group furnished Fran with ample opportunities to calm worries. When talks stalled, she explained why she refused to make a concession or what steps she was taking to restart discussions.

Fran next consolidated her authority to speak for the center. "I was getting challenges from the legal counsel and from my own boss," she says. "I couldn't work that way, constantly guarding my back." She went to the center's managing director and asked him point-blank: Who has the last word. He said she did. This request for explicit authorization became key. The director was on record as supporting Fran, and she was beholden to him to deliver.

As Fran discovered, an "official" assignment does not automatically convey the backing necessary to carry it out. Without obvious backing from her side, Fran would have lacked the legitimacy needed to negotiate the benefits schedule for the merged companies. To get that authorization, she moved to dispel worries within her company that she might be too soft for the job. At the same time, she put in place monitoring mechanisms that prevented doubts from resurfacing later during the negotiations.

Sometimes your credibility will be challenged when you negotiate, as Fran's was. Because this questioning is seldom set permanently to rest, it is essential to think about your authority in terms of the strategic moves that you can make—not just to establish credibility but to keep it. Explicit and ongoing authorization from someone with real power gives you visible support that means something to your own team. It also drives home a necessary point to the other party. Attempts to circumvent you and go over your head will achieve nothing. The other side must deal with you. You are in charge of the negotiations.

Enlist Support

At times, the strategic moves you make on your own fall short. The other side does not see sufficient benefits in what you offer and the costs you have raised are not high enough to force a change of mind. No matter what you do you cannot seem to attract his attention or get her to take your demands seriously. If you don't think you have the resources to move the negotiation forward on your own, you can call up reinforcements and enlist the support of others. Just by sheer numbers, strategic allies can add credibility to your cause. Their confidence in you is what convinces the other party to negotiate with you. When an ally's opinion counts with that person, the extra influence often tips the shadow negotiation in your favor.

The roles strategic allies play range from modest to critical. Their interventions can simply open doors for you. A timely phone call from a mentor adds a personal note to a letter of recommendation and can shift your résumé to the top of the pile. An opportune word from a well-placed friend can coax a larger check from a contributor hesitant to support your agency. As allies become more actively engaged, they alter the dynamics in the shadow negotiation even more profoundly. They become, in effect, strategic partners and broaden your impact, particularly if they complement your strengths with other skills or give you access to different spheres of influence.

Allies can also wield sticks you may not want to use and apply overt pressure on the other party. He or she may think twice about incurring a boss's displeasure, alienating a prominent figure, or disappointing a valued colleague or an important client. Resistance tends to evaporate when it carries a penalty.

When enlisting strategic allies, you have to consider two points. The most obvious is whether the potential ally actually supports you and how firmly. The second is the relationship he or she enjoys with the person you are negotiating with. Does he have the clout to make a difference? Does the other party value her opinions?

Use allies as intermediaries. Acting as intermediaries, allies can intervene in a negotiation. They can troubleshoot a proposal ahead of time and ensure that its hearing is biased in your favor. When you involve them in the early drafting stages, they have a chance to contribute to the proposal's final shape. Once their suggestions are incorporated, the proposal carries their stamp of approval. In effect, they become its sponsors. Liv's boss June served as a critic and buffer during Liv's work/family negotiations.

Liv started from scratch when she carved out a niche for public-interest counseling at a major East Coast law school. With the birth of her first child, Liv had shifted to a 70 percent schedule, trading flexibility to work at home for actual hours. Pregnant with her second child, Liv wanted to bring in a co-director to job-share with her.

Liv was not breaking new ground when she requested a part-time schedule. A job-share, on the other hand, would be a first. For Liv and for the dean who would have to approve the request, the stakes were higher. A job-share could jeopardize the counseling office, which was universally regarded as Liv's creation. At the same time, it could establish a potentially troublesome precedent in a milieu that was not particularly hospitable to creative work arrangements.

Liv's boss—June, an associate dean—would have loved to work half time. Identifying as she did with Liv's situation, she acted as a sponsor for Liv. She reviewed Liv's proposal, identifying points where it might provoke the dean's resistance. Just as important, June raised the issue with the dean. That broad-brush and informal discussion colored the dean's first impressions. He respected June and valued her judgment. Not only was he persuaded to consider the proposal, he took seriously June's warning that Liv would resign if something could not be worked out.

> It was very important to have a buffer between the dean and me. Eventually I had to argue my own case, but June prepared the way. I did not have to go into the dean cold. And I did not have to threaten him with leaving.

Intermediaries like June position you favorably before talks even begin. At a minimum, their confidence primes the other party to listen to what you have to say. Their support can be particularly important when you are not in a good position to do the negotiating directly.

Dan, a senior navigator in the Navy, faced a double problem when his ship's home port moved from Southern California to Washington. The captain's standing orders stipulated
watch rotations and specified that full teams had to man the
bridge during any maneuvers in sight of land or in the presence
of other shipping. In California, the ship would leave port and
head straight out to sea, clearing land at once and rarely seeing
another vessel. In Washington, it still operated where there was
little merchant traffic, but land was always in sight. Under the
current standing orders, the on-duty time effectively doubled
with the change in home port.

Any alteration to the standing orders required the captain's
consent. But Dan hesitated to approach the captain directly, as
he would be jumping several ranks and wondered whether his
suggestions would be taken seriously given his relative lack of
experience. In addition, Dan had a reputation for caring too
much about his people, of putting concerns for his own team
above the operational mission of the ship.

All watch bills had to be signed by the senior watch officer
and the executive officer, number two and number three in the
ship's hierarchy of command. Dan approached both with his
concerns. If his navigation team had to be at full force, he could
not stand watch as officer of the deck. This conflict made the
senior watch officer a natural ally since he absolutely needed
Dan on that rotation. Readiness, a prime concern for the executive officer, could be compromised by doubling rotation times
on deck, so the number two officer was open to brainstorming
possible changes in the standing orders.

Eventually Dan, not the executive officer or the senior
watch officer, argued the case for change, but these allies prepared the way. They not only helped him to anticipate possible

objections the captain might raise on certain points; they also mentioned to the captain the difficulties that the ship's new venue caused in the rotations. By the time Dan presented his solution, the captain already recognized that the problem warranted his attention. Dan's motivation and credibility never came into question, and only the merits of his solution were discussed.

Use allies as strategic partners. Certain allies are positioned—through personal relationships or status alone—to influence a negotiation. Others bring specific skills that complement yours and increase your value in the eyes of the other party. Anna, the executive director of a social-service agency in a depressed New England mill town, drew on allies for both influence and skills. Increasingly troubled by her agency's dependence on state allocations and the United Way, Anna was determined to broaden the agency's financial base. She was especially concerned that the agency secure sufficient funding for its expanding community health programs. Private foundations seemed the logical place to go.

> *I became a cheerleader for what my agency could do for the community. I had a specific agenda. I wanted to be known and respected in the private foundation world. That was where the new money was coming from in health care, and I wanted to establish my agency as a "credible vendor."*

Anna soon encountered a major stumbling block in this plan. The foundations were not interested. The agency's rapid growth made foundation officials wonder whether she and her staff could handle the larger budgets involved. She also suspected they weren't overly impressed with her. "I just don't come over as a player," she says.

Anna decided she needed to shore up her agency's image. A disconnect existed between what the agency could accomplish and what outsiders thought it could do. At first Anna was baffled. Then she realized her board could provide a bridge to the wider community and to greater legitimacy. To access professional strategic advice on health initiatives, Anna invited the head of the school of public health and a respected surgeon to join the board. To give depth to the agency's financial planning, she sought out two prominent members of the business community and put them in charge of overseeing the finance and budget committees.

Anna's new board members became strategic partners in the agency's expansion. Anna never went alone to critical foundation presentations. She always arranged to have the appropriate board member accompany her. These moves increased foundation confidence in her programs, and they began to work with her on grants.

Allies are important resources in the shadow negotiation. They can be critical when you encounter difficulties in establishing your credibility. Their support makes your incentives more tangible precisely because they can trumpet your value in a way that you cannot.

Use allies as sources of pressure. Allies are not restricted to working on the bright side, extolling your virtues and the benefits of negotiating with you. They can also bring pressure to bear. Their influence on the other party raises the costs of not dealing with you forthrightly. Not incidentally it is often easier for them to be the bearer of bad news. June, as an associate dean, could let the dean know that Liv might resign unless a job-share could be worked out. Had the comment come from

Liv, he would have given it far less credence. He might have dismissed it altogether as a hollow threat.

During an intense negotiation, it is easy to forget that other people besides you and the person you are negotiating with have a stake in the outcome. These stakeholders represent potential sources of influence. When your interests coincide with theirs, it is not difficult to persuade them to become vocal or exert pressure behind the scenes.

Roni deliberately sought out such a stakeholder when she negotiated a part-time schedule. While serving as director of development for the symphony of a large city in the Midwest, she was getting her master's in public policy at night. She found the pace toward her degree frustratingly slow. When her contract with the symphony came up for renewal, she proposed cutting back on her hours in order to finish earlier. The symphony's general manager responded with two options. One: Go on a part-time schedule until she completed her degree requirements. The general manager made this option contingent on her commitment to remain with the symphony, full time and in the same position (that is, for the same salary) for two years after graduation. Two: Leave the symphony when her contract expired.

Neither option was acceptable to Roni. She suggested other possibilities, but the general manager refused to discuss them. Not wanting to leave, but unwilling to commit to two years at a flat salary, Roni tendered her resignation. She then turned to the conductor. His plans for a series of celebrity concerts and a European tour hinged on securing corporate support, an effort Roni was spearheading. When Roni told him of her resignation, his concern was obvious. "My alliance with the conductor was a natural," she says. "I knew what a high priority he placed on fundraising at that moment."

Although Roni never requested the conductor's intervention, she was not surprised when he asked the general manager to extend her contract and allow her to work part-time until the corporate fundraising was safely launched. After talking with the conductor, Roni did not press her boss. Instead, she proceeded as if she were departing when her contract expired. She was actually waiting for the general manager to come to her. And he did.

Roni capitalized on her good relationship with the conductor. The mutual interest they shared in the uncompleted fundraising effort raised the costs to the general manager of her leaving. By accepting her resignation, he would jeopardize the conductor's good will. It is important to note how carefully Roni employed this strategy. She avoided the appearance and the fact of exploiting the conductor. At the same time, she protected the general manager from any loss of face. Neither he nor the rest of the organization was ever aware that she had gone "over his head." Rather than bring public pressure to bear, she gave him room to change his mind.

Certain stakeholders are natural allies. But enlisting their aid implies a quid pro quo. Your strategy must take into account their interests as well as your own. These do not always dovetail so perfectly as Roni's and the conductor's. Moreover, the issue of enlisting outside support often has a hidden catch-22. Calling on allies, instead of being interpreted as a sign of strength—that you have powerful people behind you—is read as weakness. You obviously need someone to bail you out or fight your battles. The danger can be real, but the benefits of such help so frequently outweigh the costs that it pays to consider ways of offsetting any negative impressions. By enlisting the conductor's support indirectly and informally, for example, Roni maintained the public impression that she was negotiating on her own.

Allies even the odds at the table. Strategically chosen, they set the stage for a favorable hearing. They also alter the consequences for the other party. It is not so easy for her to ignore you or for him to treat your demands casually when that behavior carries the added risk of offending people whose good will and opinions have long-term value.

Exert Control Over the Process

Incentives and pressures increase your influence over a negotiation. Incentives pull the other party into the negotiation. You demonstrate just what you can do and are doing for them. Pressures push them into dealing with you. They come to see that their situation will only deteriorate if they don't. You—what you offer or can cost them—are the focus. In this sense, incentives and pressures are highly personal and can generate highly personal reactions. The advantages you are demonstrating are your advantages; the threats, however subtle, are threats you are making. The allies defending or supporting you are your allies.

It is not always possible to use these direct methods. There may be personal reasons. The moves, even when they can be deftly employed, don't fit your negotiating style. Promoting your value seems too blatantly self-serving and exerting pressure too heavy-handed. Or, worse, you suspect the remedy will do more harm than good and provoke resistance or retaliation. These circumstances call out for a different approach. Rather than attempt to influence the shadow negotiation directly by holding out incentives and stepping up the pressure—moves that always carry a personal dimension for you and for the person you are negotiating with—you can center your moves on the negotiation process itself.

Process-oriented moves, while they do not directly address your interests, do directly affect the hearing those interests get. The agenda, the sequence in which ideas and people are heard, the groundwork you lay ahead of time—all these structural elements influence how receptive others will be to your opinions. When your suggestions surprise or shock, you can almost bank on a negative reaction. If a boss or coworkers think you are trying to manipulate them or surreptitiously gain an advantage, they will see any effort you make as a challenge. Working behind the scenes, indirectly, you can plant the seeds of your ideas so that no one is taken by surprise or put on the defensive. Before an agenda gets fixed in anyone's mind, you can build support for your ideas. You may even be able to engineer consensus so that your agenda frames the discussion.

Anticipate reactions. How you present your ideas can be as important as what you say. To make sure your suggestions get a fair hearing, you must pay attention to the process leading up to their presentation. The insights you glean from scouting information refine your reading of the situation and that knowledge can be put to work. Once you discover where and how your ideas are likely to encounter opposition and, conversely, what kinds of proposals generally meet with approval, you can shape the process to your advantage.

Harry, the director of a university research program, wanted to expand the fellows program both in terms of numbers and diversity. In the past most of the fellows worked in labs supervised by two faculty members. Since the current arrangement benefited them, Harry anticipated that the two would resist any expansion of the fellows program. He also expected that he would be challenged about the quality of the fellows and the willingness of other faculty to supervise them. Anticipating these reactions, Harry instituted an evaluation process that had all the faculty members assess the candidates. When names came up, he brought out the evaluation forms. He had also secured commitments from other faculty members to supervise the fellows. During the meeting, he handed out a grid that showed which fellows would work with which faculty members. By anticipating obstacles, Harry was able to structure the meeting so that his agenda could move forward. Sometimes, it is possible to move strategically, as Harry did, to reframe the process.

Over the past year, Marcie's group had taken on several large projects. To staff them, the group had recruited talent from other departments and added new hires. Their current quarters were cramped, with most people doubled up in cubicles meant for one person. Despite these crowded conditions, Marcie was not optimistic when the annual negotiations over space were scheduled. If past experience were any guide, a high degree of gamesmanship would govern the discussions. Extra room typically went to those who pushed the hardest or protested the loudest. The previous year Marcie had stated her actual needs and been penalized for her candor. The negotiations proceeded according to a hidden rule: to get what you wanted, you had to exaggerate your needs by at least 30 percent.

Marcie believed that there were real costs attached to this process. The company was growing at a rapid pace, yet with the other group leaders pressing inflated figures on the adminis-trator, she was unable to assess the company's actual space requirements. Several weeks before the scheduled negotiations, Marcie invited the administrator over for a tour of her group's facilities. As they walked around, the administrator could see that the group was bursting at the seams. But, more important, Marcie found out from a chance comment that the administra-tor was tired of the game that the other groups played. Not only could she not allocate space fairly and efficiently, she could not plan where future needs were likely to develop.

Sensing the administrator's frustration, Marcie proposed changing the process. Rather than allocate space in a series of discrete negotiations with group heads, why didn't they develop criteria for assessing need? They could come up with a formula that took the guesswork and gamesmanship out of the decision-making process. The administrator embraced the idea with relief. There would be heated arguments over the criteria, but it was a step in the right direction. Without any pressure on Marcie's part, she found herself chairing the committee that the administrator created to develop more objective criteria.

Marcie's work behind the scenes allowed her to take con-trol of a process that had previously put her at a disadvantage. The shift in process that she initiated changed the game. Not only had she put herself in a position to initiate a more realis-tic policy for space planning, under the new guidelines her group moved to another floor where it had almost twice as much room.

Plant the seeds of your ideas. At times people simply shut down. They don't listen. Whatever the reason, they screen out certain comments or certain people. Being ignored in a nego-tiation is not always a question of saying too little or saying it too hesitantly—a common diagnosis when people lose their impact in meetings. When ideas surprise or shock, they are likely to provoke negative, defensive reactions. Also, bargainers screen out the familiar. If they expect to be pressured, forcefulness too loses its impact. Maybe they have heard the speech before, or a close variant, and they stop paying attention. Working behind the scenes, it is possible for negotiators to influence a negotiation in ways that make it easier for ideas to be heard. Planting seeds of an idea ahead of time relieves the burden of pushing ideas once you're into a meeting. These seeds remain in the back of everyone's mind and become part of the agenda.

Pat was a talker and an aggressive one in meetings. In the past, her fellow managers had tuned her out during annual staff reviews—not because she was hesitant, but because they felt she pushed too hard. Being heard was no small matter for Pat or for the members of her department. Merit increases reflected the managers' collective assessment of what individual engineers contributed to the firm. They were also widely regarded as signs of whether a particular manager was doing a good job.

This year, Pat vowed, the performance reviews were going to be different. No effort on her part was suddenly going to transform her into a shrinking violet—she was too commanding a personality. She could, however, prepare the ground ahead of time so that she would not feel so compelled to dominate the review sessions. Over many lunches in the weeks before the reviews, she casually asked other managers about openings in their departments. On each occasion she slipped in a mention of her star employees, saying it was too bad they weren't available. They had precisely the skills and attitude the managers needed.

Once the actual reviews started, the other managers had already heard of her stars. That name recognition saved Pat from overselling. By lobbying for team members informally, Pat was able to make herself heard without belaboring her case—an objective that had previously eluded her. Preliminary work like this allows you to build receptivity where an aggressive or direct approach might offend. Once you have planted the seeds, however firmly attached others are to their own agendas, those seeds cannot help but influence their view of the situation.

Build support behind the scenes. Even when we seem to be in control of the agenda, that control is seldom complete. Individual members of the new product team need to be persuaded to go along with a development plan. A majority of the board members of a nonprofit organization must be convinced before they agree that the funding guidelines must be revised.

Generally these negotiations take place either in a meeting where the group makes the decision or in stages, through back-and-forth consultations. This process has a good deal of room for slippage, and it is risky to leave issues you care about to a process that you may be unable to control. Hidden agendas can surface unexpectedly. Groupthink can overtake substance so that consensus becomes a matter of who shouts loudest or whose voice customarily dominates. Or you may discover that a decision has been reached without your input.

Lobbying behind the scenes provides a potential antidote to these dangers. You can build consensus before matters come to a head. Backstage efforts provide opportunities to gather momentum behind your agenda. As that support grows, it isolates the blockers, making continued opposition harder and harder for them. Moreover, once agreement has been secured privately, it becomes more difficult (although never impossible) for a supporter to defect publicly.

Lynn, a public-health expert in her early forties, left a job in a large teaching hospital to become head of a struggling community hospital in a suburb outside Baltimore. Lynn moved quickly to establish control over the direction the hospital's turnaround would take, but she kept this private agenda to herself. Each department head thought his or her budget should be the last to be cut, and Lynn could not afford to watch months of valuable time being consumed by departmental infighting.

> *Before I came on board, I crawled all over the place. Once I got here, I met with key leaders of the board, the medical staff, and management in the first six or eight weeks. I did those all one-on-one. These sessions are time-consuming, but they are also what I call "clean encounters." When you are pushing an agenda, it's important that your initial interactions not be contentious.*

Lynn's private talks linked the multiple agendas in play with specific people. They provided her with a strategic map. She discovered where she would find support and where she was likely to be blocked.

Lynn paid particular attention to the order in which she approached people in her next round of talks. She began with the most supportive player—the medical chief of staff. Not only had he been instrumental in bringing her to the hospital, he had publicly backed the kinds of changes she envisioned. Together they came to a basic understanding on his role in the hospital's turnaround. Next she met with the vice president of finance and administration, who, she thought, would probably go along with her plan provided she had a voice in its development. Cutbacks would take a heavy toll on the nurses, however, and before Lynn approached the head of nursing, she worked with the chief of staff and the finance vice president to keep the burden on nursing to a minimum. She saved the head of surgery for last, anticipating that he would be the most obstinate. But by that time she had everybody else on board, and he had little choice but to go along with her ideas.[5]

Lynn's private talks, and the way she gradually built support, got the key players to commit, one by one, to her reading of the agenda before any opposing factions could develop. That danger was real. Had the heads of the various services coalesced, they could have blocked her efforts. Her "clean encounters" fixed the agenda for the hospital's turnaround on her terms. When the various parties considered their options, they did so within the framework she proposed.[6] Lynn's consensus building also positioned her as a fellow collaborator. Having built commitment privately, she did not have to rely on her formal position to dictate terms when the department heads met to work on the budget.

In today's leaner organizations, bargainers frequently find themselves negotiating without direct authority to impose their will on an agreement.[7] When you anticipate resistance, as Harry did, you can structure the process to defuse the challenges. You can move behind the scenes to foster agreement on objectives so the goals of the negotiation align with your goals, as Marcie did when she defused the established gamesmanship previously embedded in the process of negotiating office space. If you are concerned that your interests will be ignored, as Pat was during the performance reviews, you can plant the seeds of your ideas so that the other party will be more receptive to them.

Even when you do have the authority to control a negotiation, as Lynn did, exercising it preemptively may interfere with a longer-term goal—that of building cooperation and a cohesive team. Behind-the-scenes efforts draw others into the consensus-making process that takes place within any group negotiation. Not only do these "clean encounters" allow you to identify and deal with any resistance before it hardens, they ensure that your views shape any agenda that emerges.

STEP BY STEP: PLANNING A STRATEGIC CAMPAIGN

Any of these strategic moves will position you to advantage in the shadow negotiation and increase your influence over how the issues come to be weighted and decided. But your choice of moves must be made against a realistic appraisal of what you can legitimately expect to take on all at once. The more complex the negotiation, the less likelihood there is that it can be brought to closure overnight. A single strategic move seldom carries the day.

The negotiation can, however, be broken down into segments. What cannot be achieved in one giant step can often be accomplished through a series of strategic moves. Approaching a complicated negotiation in stages, isolating benchmarks, gives you manageable goals. Not all the resources you need to create incentives or pressure the other person to pay attention to you are immediately available. They must be marshaled over time by building credibility, support, and respect. Thoughtful and well-planned strategies combine multiple moves that create incentives, apply pressure, and exert control over the process. As your value increases in the shadow negotiation, so does the cost to the other party of not coming to terms over the issues.

To illustrate how strategic moves can be used, singly and together, we return to Fiona Sweeney and follow her as she negotiates the change in decision-making mandated by her boss.

Fiona's negotiations, if successful, would improve coordination between sales and production. With the current system of commissions, sales managers pursued any and all sales opportunities with little regard for the company's capacity to deliver. In turn, production was blamed for delays and cost overruns. Although the lack of cooperation hurt profits and left customers disgruntled, Fiona soon discovered that the attitudes behind it were firmly entrenched.

The formal culture at the company supports consensus decision making. The reality is totally different. Sales dominates everything, and the compensation system encourages short-term, opportunistic behavior. There is a disconnect between the official goals of quality and customer satisfaction and the informal operational realities.

Sales routinely ignored the company's procedures for coordinating with production and quality control, and neither Fiona's predecessor nor the head of production had ever challenged the sales managers on their decisions.

The sales managers had been running the business for a long time. Each was outstanding in his own right, strong-minded and competitive, with zero tolerance for weakness. All relished a good fight and were accustomed to winning.

Fiona viewed her assignment as a staged campaign. She had no authority to order sales and production to cooperate. She was new to the division and the players involved saw no reason to deal with her beyond their perfunctory interactions.

To encourage sales and production to work with her on improving coordination, she needed to be credible to both. "I turned myself into an asset by filling unmet needs," she says. "These efforts gave me visibility and started my relationships with the various departments off on the right foot."

First, Fiona made adjustments to the billing process that cut the error rate over a three-month period from 7.1 percent to 2.4 percent. The increased billing efficiency raised her standing with all the departments. Customers were no longer calling sales to complain about erroneous bills, and production had an accurate accounting of its output. The move also positioned her as a potential ally.

Next, she appealed directly to sales and made them aware of her impact on their daily lives where it counted most to them—their expense accounts. She reduced turnaround time on expense-report processing from forty days to three. This was a simple task in computer programming, but its results got the attention of the entire sales force.

Fiona also needed to raise the costs of business as usual for the sales division. The people in sales were more than satisfied with the current state of affairs. All the informal reward systems—and many of the formal ones—worked to their benefit. Having brought greater efficiency to the billing systems, Fiona started talking about a bonus system that penalized sales if the department oversold and production could not deliver. She stopped short of acting on this threat and merely floated it as a possibility.

At the same time she took steps to make the lack of cooperation from sales more broadly known. For over two years the company had been surveying its customers about satisfaction. Nobody paid any attention to the findings until Fiona started posting them on the cafeteria bulletin board. Comments began appearing in the employee e-mail system, and it soon became apparent that customer discontent was a major problem, not a figment of Fiona's imagination.

Having planted the idea that something would have to change in the sales department, she mobilized allies in production and quality control. Their departments were directly affected by what sales did. Every time sales made a promise to a customer, production had to adjust its scheduling and quality slipped. Fiona proposed forming an operations subgroup with the heads of quality control and production. "The three of us had different areas of expertise," she says. "Pretty soon a common agenda emerged and we had a real impact in full staff meetings." Together, they began to work to isolate sales in the staff meetings. In one staff meeting, for example, Fiona proposed that a low priority be assigned to orders that had not been cleared by the operations subgroup. Quality control and production roundly supported the suggestion. Fiona no longer faced the prospect of confronting sales on her own.

When Fiona's boss gave her the task of negotiating a change in behavior in sales, he more or less dumped the problem in her lap. If she succeeded, fine. If not, he avoided being drawn into a contest of wills with the fiercely independent sales division. But Fiona soon reached an impasse. To make additional headway, she required, if not the general manager's active involvement, at least his visible backing.

To build support with her boss, Fiona kept him apprised of progress on her primary assignment, all the time soliciting his ideas privately. Working closely with him ensured that she would not be second-guessing his intentions. As his confidence in her judgment grew, he began to send more tangible signs of his backing.

Whenever he was out of the office on a trip, he delegated general manager authority to me and required that I approve all exceptions to production specs. This caused howls from sales, but made the point.

Moreover, the general manager started to think that the change in decision making he wanted might actually be possible. He let key people know that he backed Fiona's proposal to base bonuses on profits, not revenues. This change would affect everyone, but especially sales. For the first time sales managers began to question how long they could conduct business as usual.

With the general manager's visible support (and the veiled threat of impending changes), Fiona was positioned to deal directly with sales. She joined the division's quality improvement team. The big project in development was a new pricing and profit model to be used as a sales tool.

I became the local guru on this model and made myself available to sales for consultation and support. They began to want me to be involved in their decisions.

Fiona's gradual moves brought sales to the table. The sales force now trusted her, but they also realized she had the resources to enforce changes in the decision-making process if she had to. Only then was she in a position to negotiate those changes with sales. By working incrementally, she was able to demonstrate the benefits of new systems and how counterproductive resistance was for everyone. Increased internal coherence, communication, and efficiency raised profits and tightened quality control. Sales actually made more money with improved quality, and production no longer had the burden of delivering on the unrealistic promises made by the sales force. Customers and the general manager were extremely pleased.

o   o   o

Strategic moves increase your influence in a negotiation. They work not only to bring people to the table but also to ensure that they take you seriously once you are there. But influence is not static in a negotiation or from one negotiation to another. Strategic moves begin before any exchange takes place and do not end when an agreement is reached. Present encounters exert an impact on the influence you carry over to future negotiations. Parity, once reached, is not always stable, and credibility cannot be taken for granted. Authority earned in one situation does not transfer automatically to another. A banker spoke to us of the persistent need to "prove up." With each promotion, credentials had to be established. This proof takes place in the shadow negotiation, where you manage the perceptions other people have of you.

As the stories in this chapter show, you do not have to be in a great bargaining position starting out. With strategic moves, marshaled collectively and over time, you can shift the dynamics in your favor.[8] Strategic moves position you in the shadow negotiation, but staying positioned is a continuous process.[9]

Chapter 3

Resisting Challenges

People have a disconcerting habit in negotiations. They don't stay put—at least not where your strategic moves aim to keep them. There is a simple reason for this. The strategic moves that you make provoke reactions. They are, after all, designed to increase your control over the direction the shadow negotiation takes. But you are not the only one engaged in strategic positioning. However much the other party believes that negotiating with you is in her best interests, she still wants to conduct the negotiation on her terms. Rather than sit idly by and let you define the choices available to her, she responds with strategic moves of her own.

This chain of action and reaction characterizes all negotiations. It is the way bargainers communicate with each other. Any strategic move you make aims to present your slant on things. It tells the other party not only where you come down on the issues but also what you think of his or her proposals and attitude. Predictably, the other person reacts to these signals. He naturally puts out arguments that bolster his case, and she tries to persuade you that you are not on such firm ground as you thought.[1] The other person may challenge your reading of the situation. The company chairman agrees that you deserve to be appointed to the executive committee. But two other top executives are also vying for the position. He would like to tap someone from marketing and you are the best candidate, but he needs to do some lobbying. Pressuring him just puts him in a bind. Why can't you be patient, a team player? A colleague criticizes you for being manipulative. What you consider an effort to build consensus behind the scenes she characterizes as an attempt to short-circuit open discussion for personal gain.

The strategic responses the other party makes can be probing tests to discover points of weakness or real threats meant to fluster or provoke. More often than not, they come at your expense. To gain the upper hand, the other person emphasizes her abilities or experience and implicitly throws yours into question. To make his proposal look good, he characterizes yours as unrealistic and impractical. She casts doubt on your motives. He hesitates over your qualifications for that new assignment.

Actions like these shift the onus to you. That is their intent. It is next to impossible to negotiate through any problem when the other party's moves make you the issue in the shadow negotiation. The mere suggestion that you are controlling, incompetent, selfish, or manipulative clouds the issues. But, even more important, it puts you on the defensive. As long as that suggestion hangs in the air, it plays havoc with the balance between you and the other person. Attention focuses on it and you are forced to defend yourself.

Moves to put you on the defensive can be subtle, vague intimations rather than overt intimidation, but they change the dynamic in the shadow negotiation nonetheless. Doubt creeps in and you begin to think you are not in such a good negotiating position after all. Pointed questions about the relevance of those two years you took off to do community service make you hesitate to push for the job you want in a top-flight law firm. On the defensive, you react defensively, governed more by the other person's actions than by your needs. Inevitably you lose any edge you might have. Once you are on the defensive in the shadow negotiation, it is difficult to reclaim the initiative when you talk about the issues. Better by far to avoid the trap in the first place.

What should you do to counter the other party's challenges? You can simply deny the charge, protesting that you are not pushy or controlling or manipulative. But that response just digs you deeper into a defensive hole. Attention remains on what you are or are not. You can always retaliate in kind—giving as good as you get, tit for tat. "I'm not pushing, you are stalling." But rarely do *countermoves* like these change anyone's mind. They make your position no more secure, and they often escalate the tension. Rhetoric heats, attitudes harden, and the exchanges slip into a cycle of "I am not" denials and "You are so" rebuttals. More significantly, countermoves can precipitate a battle of wills, triggering the urge to put a woman "in her place" or prompting a man to assert his dominance—precisely the reaction you don't want.[2]

So where does that leave you? If a counterattack is counterproductive, still less can you let yourself be backed into a corner. Strategic moves against you require a response. You must put the other party on notice that you are not going to stumble blindly into the defensive position he or she is edging you toward. At the same time, you need to respond in a way that creates space for an alternative place of your own making.

Rather than ignore the other party's move or retaliate, you *turn* it. You push back on the move and refuse to go where the other side wants to lead you. *Responsive turns* are acts of resistance, not reaction. Turns redirect the negotiation by reframing what is happening.[3] They do not have to be hostile protests or elaborate explanations. You can simply tell a colleague who charges you with manipulation, for example, that you were gathering as much information as you could before the meeting and ask whether he has anything he wants to contribute.

Turns help you parry moves against you and resist attempts to put you one down. But they serve more than a defensive purpose. They can recast the way the other person sees you. As you turn a strategic move, putting your spin on the situation and the issues, you also resist the image of you that the other party may be trying to impose. That image is meant to put you at a disadvantage. To bring the shadow negotiation back into balance, you supply a different reading of you, your issues, and the situation.

Moves and turns, as we use them, do not imply unethical practices. Bargainers test each other all the time. Though they often issue outright challenges, they are just as likely to try to wear the other party down. When the advantage of time rests with her, she stalls. If he picks up on weakness or inexperience, he begins to insinuate that you lack the competence, judgment, or authority to make a decision. She overwhelms with numbers or other resources. He withholds vital information. Equally challenging are moves that attempt to disarm by flattery or an appeal to your "better" instincts. All these moves stem from a quite natural impulse to retain control over the negotiation.

Once you recognize the motivation behind them, you can turn them.

Alice Mason used a full repertory of turns when she took over a newly established department and had to negotiate internally for its fair share of clients. Alice's new department was the brainchild of the vice president for sales. He wanted a separate sales group to target start-ups in the growing biotech field. To get Alice's department off the ground, $5 million in accounts had to be transferred from National Sales. No problems surfaced in the planning meetings. Without a lot of fanfare, Alice and Len Davis, the manager of National Sales, established reasonable criteria for the transfer and a deadline. Alice trusted Len. His easy-going personality was a good mesh with her reserve. She liked hearing his company war stories over coffee. When they went on sales calls or developed a presentation, she always learned a lot.

Then the real negotiation began.

ALICE: I've put together a list of possible transfers. You were going to come up with a list. Do you have that? We can see where we overlap.

LEN: We've been so busy. I haven't gotten to it yet. But I will. Give me a couple of days.

Repeated phone calls prompted no action from Len. The day before the annual sales meeting, when account assignments were distributed, Len finally gave Alice his list.

ALICE: These accounts come to only $2.5 million.

LEN: Yeah, I know. But I really don't think your department is ready for any more. Why don't we take this transfer a little slower?

ALICE: We all agreed to the time line, the $5 million goal. It's a little late to change the rules now.

LEN: Look, I'm doing this for the best. Your people can't handle any more right now.

ALICE: My people are really pumped up about working on these accounts. What am I supposed to do with them?

LEN: Don't get so upset.

Because the department was new, with few ground rules and no track record, Alice was ripe for testing. Len's moves made it clear to Alice that he thought he could force her to make concessions and accept half the number of accounts she expected. Time was on his side, not hers. She was already hearing grumbling about the delays from her team. When she objected to his parsimonious list, he implied she was being emotional. Len came up with a revised list two weeks later, but it was filled with what Alice suspected were dead accounts.

Len's moves challenge Alice on several fronts. He plays on her sympathy and her team's inexperience. He insinuates that she is not being cooperative when she doesn't go along with his suggestions. But his moves also cast doubts on her skill as a manager—whether she has the right temperament, whether she is ready to lead. He tries to position her as someone who takes things personally and is too emotional and excitable to see the big picture.

Is Len the bad guy here? No. He is doing what negotiators do—trying to maintain his advantage in the shadow negotiation. To give up more accounts than is absolutely necessary is a risky policy for him at this stage. The more accounts he keeps under his supervision, the happier his sales force will be. One of those accounts might be the next biotech superstar. When he tells Alice that her team is not ready for that many accounts, he is not playing dirty. He's trying to make sure the negotiation goes his way.

Alice must turn Len's moves. She has let him put her on the defensive. "It was clear to everyone that Len didn't take me seriously," she recalls. "He thought it would be pretty easy to overpower me or wear me down." But Alice has a few turns up her sleeve. As Len watches her turn his moves, one by one, it gradually dawns on him that he's not going to maneuver her into a defensive position. Alice not only pays attention to the strategic moves she must make, but begins to anticipate Len's moves and turns them before they gain momentum. Once he realizes that he is wasting his time trying to take over the negotiation, the shadow negotiation comes back into alignment, and they reach a solution that is fair to them both. But before the negotiation is over, she has used a full repertory of turns.

A Repertory of Turns

Strategic moves against you require a response. Often you don't have the luxury of time to plan the best response, and so it is essential to have some "turns" on hand that you are comfortable using. You can turn the other party's moves against you in any number of ways.

- **Interrupt the move.**
  Interrupting turns break the action. They give you time to get collected and think about how you are going to deal with any attempt to put you on the defensive. More important, by changing the pace, interruption allows you to exert control over a critical element in any negotiation—

its timing—and to halt any momentum that is working against you.

○ **Name the move.**
Naming turns make the other party's move visible. They let your counterpart know that you are perfectly aware of what is going on and are unfazed. Once the other party realizes a maneuver is not having the impact intended, he or she generally gives it up.

○ **Correct the move.**
Correcting turns offer an alternative explanation for what is going on or at issue in the shadow negotiation. Rather than accept the other party's take as given, you substitute a positive account of your actions for the negative one he or she is promoting to your disadvantage.

○ **Divert the move.**
Diverting turns shift the talk away from the personal. We are at our most vulnerable in a negotiation when threatened personally—when our motives or abilities are attacked. You disarm the move by diverting the focus from you as the problem to the problem itself.

shift from personal to problem [handwritten marginal note]

Turns differ in directness and intensity. Circumstances generally dictate which will be most effective to use. Past dealings and scouting information often give you ample hints on whether the other person is likely to attempt to put you on the defensive and how. And inevitably humor helps.

Interrupt the Move

However alert you are, the other party's moves can catch you by surprise. You expect the negotiation to follow a certain path, and all of a sudden it veers in a different direction. Surprise moves tempt immediate responses, but these are not always the best alternative. Unprepared, you may not be able to come up with the appropriate turn on instant demand. Instead, you react defensively. You can avoid a defensive countermove by buying time. When the other party's move throws you off balance, take a break.

Interruptions stop the action. They prevent you from being swept up in a momentum that may not be going your way. After a break, you and the other person never pick up in the same place psychologically. You have had a chance to recoup and your counterpart no longer enjoys the element of surprise. Interruptions don't have to be long. Sometimes just getting up for a cup of coffee or walking over to the flip chart changes the dynamic. Other times a definite recess or a complete change of pace is in order.

Take a break. Even a brief interruption can rob a surprise move of its effectiveness. Sitting quietly for a moment can give you time to think of an appropriate turn. A hasty response can be reconsidered over a cup of coffee. Papers can turn up missing in a file, requiring a short intermission. A trip to your office often provides enough time to assess the new turn of events.

Carla had just been appointed head of her company's market review committee. Ellen, another member, had actively campaigned for the job and a residue of bad feeling remained. To start her tenure off on the right note, Carla invited all the members to a get-together session. They were in the middle of discussing how to proceed when Ellen rushed in. Apologizing for being late, she began to pass out copies of a four-page memo. Skimming the elegantly typed pages, Carla saw the outlines of a market-review strategy. "Ellen may not be chair, but she's certainly acting like she is," Carla thought. She smiled at

Ellen. "What a lot of work," she said, and then picked up her mug. "Anyone else want a refill?"

To a person the committee members got up and began to congregate by the coffeepot. When they sat back down, Carla told Ellen that the committee had not made so much progress as Ellen had independently. They had yet to identify the approach they wanted to take, let alone the priorities. Perhaps, Carla suggested, it would be better to consider Ellen's memo when ideas had been discussed a bit more.

Carla's interruption accomplished several things. First, it gave her time to collect her thoughts and think about a response. But it also had an impact on the process. She resisted being rude to a member who had obviously put in a lot of effort. At the same time, she prevented that work from dominating the discussion. Without her interruption, the committee's attention would have been locked on Ellen's memo. Carla's interruption had another, more subtle effect. Because she did not cut Ellen off, but rather tabled discussion of her ideas, she signaled to the other committee members that no one individual would control the sessions.

Call a time-out. At times surprise moves create more than a minor setback. Without warning you find yourself facing new players or discover the game plan has changed. A brief break may not give you enough time to get collected or figure out what to do. Moreover, it may not be dramatic enough to change the situation. You still have to contend with the additional players or the new set of rules. To turn these more serious surprise moves, you may have to suspend the negotiation temporarily, rescheduling to a later date and a different place. Not only does this turn give you more time, it creates an opportunity to make sure that the next round in the negotiation takes place under more hospitable circumstances. Gina, the retailing entrepreneur from Chapter One who religiously prepares for any contingency, once cut short a major meeting with potential investors when they caught her by surprise.

A midwinter storm made the flight from Boston both harrowing and late. When Gina finally landed in Minneapolis, she was tired and rattled. She was thrown even further off stride when she walked into the conference room and faced the entire investment committee. The crowded room, Gina realized, was a good sign. Clearly her company had sparked the committee's interest. Despite this encouraging thought, she found the united front intimidating. Although annoyed with herself for being cowed by such a transparent tactic, she immediately cut short her presentation. "I'm asking you to invest in a concept," she concluded. "To talk terms, you need to know what we are selling. That's more than chairs and sofas. It's a lifestyle. Now that we've had a chance to get acquainted, why don't we meet next month at the store?"

Outnumbered and robbed of any chance to scout information on the additional players, Gina did not feel prepared to field questions. Recognizing the danger, she deliberately interrupted the session. That interruption removed Gina from the inquisitorial spotlight and ensured the next meeting had a setting she could control. The shop, she knew, would show to advantage and on her own turf so would she.

There are times when a comment or observation so disturbs the negotiation that without a break the process could be derailed. James was in the unenviable position of implementing a staffing system that would force unit directors to justify their head count. Anticipating resistance, he met individually with the unit directors on the plan's details. Everything was in order before the critical meeting—or so he thought. The discussion was moving along nicely until the R&D director spoke up. "Look, James," he said, "we all know that this new system is stupid. We know how to run our businesses—this is just another new new thing that's supposed to tell us what to do." James thought he had an agreement with the R&D director, but this surprise comment now risked splintering support for the new system. James ended the meeting. The break gave James time to work behind the scenes to maintain support for the new system and to work with the R&D director on his staffing concerns.

Change the pace. People often use time and momentum strategically. They enforce artificial deadlines to pressure you into accepting a proposal before you can puzzle through the implications. Knowing that you are working against a deadline, they capitalize on your tight schedule to press for concessions, trading promptness for benefits. To prevent your schedule or artificial deadlines from driving the negotiation, you can slow the pace.

Bargainers can deliberately create a sense of urgency. Wait, they imply, and you will lose out on an opportunity. These moves—as common in boardrooms as in bazaars—are intended to force a decision. By turning them, you keep control over your decisions rather than let the other party set the timetable.

Jill was transplanting her antique shop from Connecticut to SoHo. She had her eye on a storefront her real estate agent had listed. She promptly stopped by to meet the owner. He told her the location was great with a lot of traffic. He was retiring; otherwise he would never leave. Jill was barely out of the store when her cell phone started ringing. It was the real estate agent. The space had stirred a great deal of interest. It would be gone by Monday. All his other prospective buyers were ready to take the space as-is. He did not want her to lose out.

The more the agent pressured Jill, the more suspicious she became. "I like what I see," she finally said, "but I need time to do some more legwork. My architect won't be able to inspect the shop until next week."

That inspection turned up major problems. The space needed to be rewired to be brought up to code and the roof had to be replaced. Those "other buyers" failed to materialize, and Jill negotiated a substantial reduction in the purchase price.

Before you slow or pick up the pace in a negotiation, you have to satisfy yourself that time is being used as a tactic. You must be relatively certain the deadline is artificial and be willing to live with the consequences if it is not. Jill, for example, gambled that the agent would not be pressing her so hard if he had other buyers in the wings. The risk of buying the building without professional advice offset any possible disappointment in losing it. Consequences in organizations are not always so easy to ignore. Clients or colleagues may resent what they consider stalling or undue pressure.

> Alice, not expecting the negotiations with Len to be difficult, used interrupting turns to advantage. She took frequent breaks to check her frustration and to put a damper on his temper. The moment Len started to raise his voice, she got them both coffee. If the break did not restore his usual affability, she ended the session. She declared a time-out whenever Len tried to overpower her with numbers. If he arrived at a meeting with his entourage trailing, she rescheduled so that her team would be available as well.
>
> Increasingly aware of Len's stalling techniques, Alice also took steps to reestablish her control over the

pace of the negotiation. Once Len tendered his meager list of accounts, he continued to stonewall. She broke the logjam by updating the sales vice president on their progress. She sent a factual progress report via e-mail to him and Len. The report prompted action from Len. After a token resistance, he agreed to talk about interim targets beyond the $2.5 million on his list.

Turns require a cool head. That is why interruption is such an important tool, particularly when you suspect that you are about to lose any control over the negotiation. Not only does an interruption break the momentum, it allows you time to regroup and consider what other responses you might have to make.

Name the Move

Naming turns attach a label to the other party's move. Just the act of naming lets the other person know that the tactic is transparent. As a result, naming turns deliver two direct messages. They show that you are not naive about common negotiation tactics and that the particular ploy is not working. You recognize both the tactic and the reason it is being used against you—and unsuccessfully at that. Naming must be carefully executed. The turn needs to be directed at the behavior, not the person. Otherwise it can degenerate into name-calling. You want to turn the move, not turn the other person off.

Naming turns run the gamut from a joking aside to a serious challenge. But for a label to be effective you have to apply one that the other party recognizes and accepts as valid. That realization forces him or her to reevaluate the behavior. Bargainers are quick to jettison tactics that gain them nothing or show them in a bad light. They also discard tactics that generate unintended effects or get in the way of what they want to accomplish. Naming turns prompt that process along.

Reveal the move's ineffectiveness. The other party generally intends a move to have an impact. By pointing out a move's ineffectiveness, naming deflates the move. Tactics meant to make you feel defensive are not much good if you don't get defensive. By naming the move, you let the other party know it's not working. However clever or disguised the tactic, you see through it and remain unruffled. Gloria, a media executive, was negotiating television rights to a hot property. After trying for several days to reach the elusive literary agent on the telephone, she finally succeeded. Before she could say hello, the agent started screaming abuse at her, attacking her competence and her experience. She was surprised that he would jeopardize a lucrative deal for his client, but whatever his motivation, she could not let his attitude go unchecked and set the tone for the negotiation. "I called to start talking deal points," she interrupted. "Obviously you are having a bad day. Why don't I get back to you?"

Several days later Gloria learned that the agent had attacked her to buy himself time. He did not yet control the television rights to the property. He had gone on the offensive to stall. But Gloria's naming of the situation meant that when they did negotiate, she would not be doing so from a defensive position. Naming, used in this way, puts the conversation back on track. The turn effectively says there are better ways to deal with each other.

Using humor can blunt what might otherwise be seen as an attack. Pietro was primed for his performance review. A senior researcher for a large international NGO (nongovernmental organization), he was determined to use his review to push for more responsibility and more visibility. The NGO recruited internationally for its scientists. Despite this talent pool, Pietro thought he could match his credentials with anyone's. He had had a great year—producing a report on a major grant project, publishing several peer-reviewed papers, and exceeding the goals he had set for himself. Aware that reviews with his boss had not gone that well in the past, Pietro was determined to make this one a success. He wanted to use his excellent performance as a platform for promotion. Pietro's boss looked over the list of accomplishments and commented, "It seems like a pretty average year." Pietro knew he had to defuse this putdown to have any hope of coming out of the review with the responsibility and visibility he was after. With a smile on his face, he named what he thought was happening, "Looks like you're trying to lower my expectations." His boss, caught off guard, denied the motive, and that denial restored the balance in the shadow negotiation.

Expose the move's inappropriateness. Some moves are out of bounds. By naming questionable moves, you make the other person understand that certain behavior is unacceptable. What's more, the behavior doesn't reflect well on him or her. Rough tactics sometimes call for tough labels. The label you choose must fit the action. You want the other party to realize how serious you consider the breach. When someone crosses a line, he or she has to know it.

Jen's community health center had been pivotal in restoring pride to an inner-city neighborhood. Money was scarce, and Jen watched her budget like a hawk. When *60 Minutes* first floated tentative plans to schedule a segment on inner-city revitalization around the center, Jen was jubilant. The construction union, however, immediately recognized a pressure point. If the network producers got wind of any unresolved labor problems, they might scuttle the program. The threat of picket lines alone would force Jen to make the center's construction projects all-union jobs.

The union officials considered the intimidating moves business as usual. Jen called them blackmail.

> *I was very angry. The union needed to understand that I was personally disappointed; that we as an institution were disappointed. I was not going to downplay that. They had violated a trust I thought we had. I wanted them to understand that we understood their game; that we disrespected that game; that I disrespected them and their shortsightedness. The head guy from the Local, who lives in the area, had tears in his eyes after I finished talking to him.*

By calling the union accountable for its actions, naming its behavior, Jen turned the move. Caught in an opportunistic play, the union officials backed down. Jen's naming forced them to recognize that their tactics, rather than giving them an advantage, hurt their cause.

Jen's turn worked because her label fit the situation. She knew it and the union knew it. Success in naming unacceptable behavior depends on whether the other party recognizes that he or she has crossed a line. If she considers her actions just part of the normal give-and-take of any negotiation, she won't change her behavior. She will merely see you as an unsophisticated or inexperienced negotiator, unaccustomed to the rough-and-tumble of the real world.

Highlight the move's unintended consequences. The naming turns we have discussed so far show the other party the ineffectiveness or inappropriateness of a move against you. In these situations, the bargainers know full well what they are trying to do. You just point out that they are not succeeding or should have thought twice before making the attempt in the first place. But bargainers are not omniscient. They do not always anticipate the impact of their moves, and their actions sometimes produce effects they never intended.

With the best intentions in the world, people still make mistakes. Their moves may have consequences they never planned, and those consequences can be named. Sometimes, the other person is actually trying to be supportive as he pushes you in a direction he wants you to go. He doesn't bother to discover how you feel about that particular destination at that particular moment. It never occurs to him that you may be less than sanguine about the shape his support takes.

Cynthia, a partner in a national consulting firm, had a mentor who felt compelled to micromanage Cynthia's career. The most senior woman in the company, she had shepherded Cynthia through several promotions. She wanted Cynthia to succeed and do it quickly. She kept up the pressure, not noticing that she did not micromanage Cynthia's male colleagues. If they wanted to spend more time with their kids, fine. If they argued that their current assignment should be extended, that was all right too.

Cynthia, on the other hand, never remained in any assignment long enough to catch her breath or get to know the people. She had just come off an exhilarating and exhausting year when her mentor announced that she had another choice job waiting. "This opening could not have come at a better time," she said. "It's very visible and will really stretch you." Cynthia already felt stretched to the maximum. "I cannot take on new responsibilities and a relocation right now," she thought.

Cynthia was caught in a classic double bind—afraid to say no, yet reluctant to say yes. No one turned down a promotion in her company. The opportunity might not come around again. If she wanted any control over her life, she had to turn her mentor's pressure to accept.

Cynthia could have named her mentor's actions in a number of ways. She could have pointed out that her mentor treated male subordinates differently, but she would never accept that label. Instead, carefully steering clear of the personal consequences of the promotion, Cynthia named the professional implications for her. Her rapid rise had stirred resentment. Her colleagues did not see her as a leader, they saw her as a protected person. If Cynthia was to take on the leadership role her mentor wanted for her, she needed time for reflection and opportunities to develop relationships with her colleagues. Cynthia's mentor appreciated her thoughtfulness and her candor. She wanted to promote Cynthia, but she also wanted to keep her. She dropped the idea of the promotion, shifting instead to what Cynthia wanted to do next.

Naming turns in situations like these flow from a good-faith assumption that the moves are misguided, not malicious. In spelling out those consequences—naming them—the turn enlightens. It allows the other person to see the distance between what they think they are doing and what you think they are doing.

Characterize the move as counterproductive. Naming a move can also show the other person that a particular negotiating habit or technique accomplishes nothing and may actually create additional obstacles. Sometimes negotiators make moves that have become second nature to them. They operate out of habit and never question the usefulness of their moves, even though they may be doing things that get in the way of fruitful negotiation. Naming behavior that has the two of you working at cross-purposes encourages you to find better, more effective ways of dealing with each other. Naming turns can be particularly effective in organizations where combative or aggressive negotiating styles stifle more collaborative approaches.

Linda wrote advertising copy in a small agency. Creative, with a fertile imagination, she was good at coming up with catchy ad campaigns. But whenever she presented her ideas to the senior account executive, he immediately began to pick them apart. Linda knew she was not being singled out. He treated everyone this way. Still, that assurance provided little comfort. With her ideas under constant attack, she could never decide whether they were being totally rejected or merely needed refinement. Exasperated, she finally asked the senior account executive if he noticed how he always played devil's advocate. From her perspective, a stream of criticism left no room to debate the merits of a proposed campaign. He was surprised at her reaction. No one had ever voiced this complaint before. Didn't she know that he would not bother to criticize if he didn't consider the idea worth some massaging? No, she said. When he started playing devil's advocate as soon as she handed him her copy, she could only assume that he didn't think much of it.

Once his role in their negotiations was named and Linda's reaction to it identified, they were able to see how their behavior interfered with their real task. His blanket criticism gave Linda no way to separate important conceptual comments from the details. Going forward, they agreed to reach consensus on a campaign's concept. Then he would have free rein to criticize as they discussed the execution.

Naming requires some coolness in the moment. Give yourself a moment before you respond. Charlene Barshefsky, the U.S. trade representative during the Clinton administration, used this principle to good effect when she took some time before naming a Chinese negotiator's move as inappropriate. During a difficult session in critical talks on intellectual property rights, the Chinese trade representative leaned menacingly across the table and said: "It's take it or leave it." Barshefsky waited almost a full minute before responding. "If the choice is take it or leave it," she replied, "of course I'll leave it. But I can't imagine that's what you meant. I think what you meant is that you'd like to me to think over your last offer and that we can continue tomorrow. I hope you understand that what you're putting on the table is inadequate, but I'm going to be thinking tonight about what you suggested." Ambassador Barshefsky named the threat as counterproductive, but in a way that saved face for her counterpart. The next morning they apparently had a productive session.[4]

> Alice took advantage of opportunities to name Len's stalling maneuvers. One presented itself when he handed her his first list of accounts.
>
> ALICE: These accounts come to only $2.5 million.
>
> LEN: Yeah, I know. But I really don't think your department is ready for any more. Why don't we take this transfer a little slower?
>
> ALICE: That's not the problem. *(laughs)* Fess up. You just don't want to give up any more accounts.
>
> LEN: Not at all. I'm doing this for the best. Your people can't handle any more right now.
>
> ALICE: Come on, Len. You and I both know that's not

the case. These people were handpicked to get the new department off and running. That's big on everyone's agenda right now.

In this brief exchange Alice lets Len know that she doesn't accept what he is saying. Her people aren't green or untrained and her experience is not the problem. He thinks he can get her to accept fewer accounts if he holds out long enough. In naming his move, she pointedly reminds him that the new department's success carries a high priority within the company and with their boss in particular.

Naming turns rob the other party's move of its intended impact and force him or her to reconsider its usefulness. The turn can put a stop to inappropriate ploys. By exposing counterproductive tactics, it can also precipitate a more substantial change in the way bargainers deal with each other in the shadow negotiation.

Correct the Move

Negotiators use strategic moves for a purpose. To bring you around to their view, they throw doubt on anything that supports your perspective. Subtly and sometimes not so subtly they challenge the underpinnings of your demands in the shadow negotiation. They dispute the merits of your arguments and your ability or right to make them. These moves are meant to make you wonder whether their rendering is not the real one. What had previously seemed clear and reasonable no longer appears so obvious. Maybe, you think, my proposal isn't so great after all. I should have put more time into it. Maybe this is the wrong time to ask for a raise. With the budget so tight,

I'm being greedy. Maybe, you concede, the other person has a point. Busy behind the scenes gathering support, you did delay open discussion. Once the other party persuades you to see what's wrong with you or your proposal or something you have done, it is an easy slide to get you to back off on your demands.

These moves often cast you in the role of an unworthy adversary. The other party exaggerates a weakness here or misinterprets a motive there. These attempts may be deliberate, but then again they may not. It's simply easier to downplay the requests of someone who is inexperienced, emotional, or too demanding. You turn these moves by directly addressing the faulty characterization. It does not matter if the unflattering image is consciously imposed or accidentally applied. How the other person sees you conditions how she or he deals with you. Correcting turns unmask distorted impressions and strip away qualities that are being falsely attributed to you. They revise misinterpreted motives or misunderstood attitudes. All these misperceptions, unless corrected, reinforce a bargainer who wants to whittle away at your demands. Correcting turns are not defensive. They go beyond simple protests and denials. They restore balance to the negotiation by elaborating on just what's right about your rendering and why.

Shift the focus to the positive. Not infrequently the other party jumps to conclusions based on the most cursory of impressions and then acts on them—to your disadvantage. Turns that correct flawed impressions of you begin with the faulty image. You need to ask yourself where it is wrong. Often you can trace the cause to inadequate or outdated information. Impressions drawn from previous negotiations may need to be revised. A boss, for example, may need reminding that you have outgrown your apprenticeship and that his earlier image of you no longer applies.

Correcting turns are particularly useful during job interviews where skepticism exists about your credentials or the appropriateness of your experience. At thirty-eight Leonore was a senior vice president in charge of human resources at a Texas bank. Frustrated at the way her skills were being underutilized, Leonore began looking for another job. "Nothing frosts me more," she says, "than when people assume, because I am a woman and in human resources, that I don't have any business savvy."

Her first interview started off disastrously. The bank chairman barely gave her time to introduce herself. He then fired questions at her about how she handled problem employees. When he ran out of steam, he complimented Leonore on her "people skills." Unfortunately, he observed, the demands of a commercial bank required more expertise from its human resource managers than an ability to deal with difficult people.

> *As soon as I could get a word in edgewise, I did. I answered all the questions he should have asked me. I told him how I reduced teller turnover from 82 percent to 15 percent. Then I proceeded to long-term medical benefits. I explained how I saved the bank $250,000 the first year and over a million the second when I renegotiated the insurance package with the carriers.*

Leonore went from being dismissed to being desired by correcting the banker's misguided impressions. Her version of who she was piqued his interest, and *she* began questioning *him* about the job.

Leonore's experience points out how important correcting turns can be when you don't know the other person. "Most people," she argues, "don't understand how to interview."

> But that becomes your problem once you are in the room. You have to get over the automatic assumption that it is your fault when an interview goes badly. The interviewer may not have a good idea of who you are or what you do. That's correctable.

Correcting turns don't necessarily ensure that you get the job or whatever else it is that you want. They can, however, restore balance to the shadow negotiation so that you and the other person can figure out whether some agreement on the issues is possible.

Supply a legitimate motive. Most people want others to consider them fair and ethical in their dealings. Moves that question your motives attack not so much your competence as your values and character. What you consider honest self-interest or a justified objection gets characterized as underhanded, opportunistic, or self-serving. Asking for that raise is labeled as greedy. Pushing to get more people assigned to your team is called shortsighted. Disagreeing with plans for the new product launch is characterized as self-serving resistance. Nor do these aspersions need to be explicit. A hint is often enough to damage your confidence and your position. By casting your actions in a bad light, such a move pushes you into defending them. No one wants the other person to think badly of him or her. Barbara found herself in this quandary when another woman implied that she was being insensitive to a working mother.

Barbara, a cross-country track coach in her late twenties, had led her team to the state's annual championships that spring. The athletic director, recognizing the team's potential for the coming season, hired an assistant coach. For the last several years the team had rented a house at the New Jersey shore for preseason workouts. Just before the team was to leave, the new assistant coach proposed that she bring her five-month-old daughter along. Barbara rejected the proposal for what she saw as legitimate reasons. Two adults had their hands full keeping a group of teenagers in check and focused without one of the coaches being distracted by a baby. "That will be difficult," Barbara said. "We have to be on our toes all the time."

The assistant coach immediately accused Barbara of putting unnecessary roadblocks in a working mother's way. "I felt terrible," Barbara recalled. "I began to suggest ways we could make it work—hiring a babysitter, asking another coach to come along." The assistant coach, impressed by Barbara's willingness to work on a solution, saw that Barbara's response was motivated not by a bias against working mothers, but by a concern for the logistical problems. "She finally admitted," Barbara said, "that it was stupid to hire an extra person just so she could go along."

When the other party casts aspersions on your motives, it makes it difficult to stay in the negotiations. You can't help but feel attacked. That is often the purpose behind the move. You don't want to stay in that situation—but avoidance isn't the answer, either. Rather than retreat, you turn the view around. Barbara, by coming up with ideas, corrects the negative explanation of her decision that the woman put forward. The possible arrangements she suggested not only showed that Barbara was flexible, they offered convincing proof that her original response to the proposal was legitimate.

Counter stereotyped images. Not all strategic moves can be turned in the moment. Sometimes they require a concerted campaign, particularly when they rest on untested stereotypes. Gender, race, age, or professional status often slip quietly into the shadow negotiation. A Generation Xer is not committed to work. A Latino salesperson won't succeed in certain territories. A woman has priorities and responsibilities at home that make her a less productive employee, less flexible or available. Many entrepreneurs battle these assumptions when they seek capital to launch or expand a business. Their businesses are "risky"; they are "risky." They lack business savvy and are too emotionally involved to make objective decisions. Undercapitalized to begin with, they don't have the collateral to back up a loan. Certain of these objections can be overruled by the facts. The bias behind them must be turned.

Maryanne's West Coast catering business was a success almost the moment she opened the doors.[5] The firm's imaginative menus attracted immediate attention in the press. Within months local media ranked her operation among the city's top catering services. Maryanne was delighted with the reception. She loved cooking, she loved her clients, and she loved putting great parties together. She soon needed to expand her operation to accommodate her growing list of clients. With a $125,000 loan, which she believed she could easily handle, she could take on more staff and buy additional kitchen equipment.

Despite Maryanne's track record, she quickly ran through her prospective lending sources. Then the last loan officer on her list turned her down. "I cannot approve a loan just because you make the best puff pastry in town." What, Maryanne asked, would change her mind? A business manager, the loan officer shot back. "I need to be sure you can repay the loan. I don't have that confidence."

Maryanne recognized the reasons behind the rejection. The loan office did not want to lend money to a cook. She was a risky proposition. While her cooking got rave reviews, nothing in her loan request suggested she was equally adept at managing money or that the business was solid. She needed to change those impressions. Would the loan officer reconsider, Maryanne asked, if she had proof that her business could comfortably handle the monthly repayment schedule? Forced into a corner, the loan officer had to agree.

For the first time, Maryanne asked her largest clients to commit to specific levels of work a year in advance. Demand for her services was high, she argued. Without a commitment, she could not guarantee that she would be available. She managed to secure enough pledges to satisfy the pickiest of lenders that she could cover repayment of a $125,000 loan. Maryanne then set about making her loan request more "professional." With help from a friend, she installed a financial accounting system that she could manage easily. Then she bought some desktop publishing software and redid her loan request, discarding the pretty pictures and replacing them with detailed financial projections.

Her banker began to see Maryanne not as a cook but as a businessperson. The revised loan request went through without a hitch. Instead of defending herself against the unfavorable biases in the banker's lending policies, she turned them, but it took some time.

Len was a master at putting Alice on the defensive. His moves reinforced a simple theme: She did not deserve more accounts; she was too emotional and too inexperienced to handle them. Exasperated, she put out a counterproposal to Len. She would accept his list, but only if she could have thirty days to identify and discard dubious accounts. Len refused.

LEN: You cannot have it both ways. If you want the accounts, you have to take some risk.

ALICE: I'm perfectly willing to take the risk as long as it's based on some decent information. And that's not what I'm getting.

LEN: Okay, okay. How about you take these (*quickly ticking some items on his sheets with a pencil*). And I'll keep these?

When Len tells Alice she is not a risk-taker, she does not contradict him. Rather, she corrects a faulty impression. Her appetite for risk depends on good information. Her turn takes the personal sting out of Len's comment: She is willing to take risks, but she is not so naive as to take foolish ones. When Alice turns this move, she revises the image of her as a weak manager that undergirds Len's rationalization for holding back the accounts.

Correcting turns help ensure that the other party sees you in an accurate yet favorable light. They stop moves that the other person may use to justify holding you or your opinions in little regard. In effect, correcting turns restore respect to the shadow negotiation. That respect is a precondition for successful negotiation. Without it, you have a hard time convincing another person to take you or your needs seriously.

restore respect

Divert the Move

Emotions run high when you are made the problem—whether it's some imaginary inadequacy or something you did in the past or something you want to do now. You can always take a break to recoup and gain some perspective. You can try to turn the move by correcting the other person's perceptions. But you can also deliberately step back, take the personalities out of the equation for the moment, and move to the problem.

Shift the conversation. Diverting turns shift the attention from the people to the problem.[6] Rather than confront a personal challenge directly, you channel the conversation to the problem at hand. In effect, you refuse to admit that you might be the problem.

Howard, manager of research at a small but growing investment firm, diverted a personal attack launched by the head of the firm's investment committee. Differences of opinion had arisen over the firm's growth strategy. Some managers favored dealing with high-wealth individuals, the firm's traditional business, while others wanted to move into the institutional arena. The conflict came out into the open during a meeting Howard had called. He had been getting complaints from his researchers. They were being asked to work on institutional projects. Since the requests would cut into their primary research responsibilities, they wanted some direction. As soon as Howard raised the issue, the head of the investment committee accused him of "empire building." Rather than credit the charge with a response, Howard shifted the conversation. The firm had procedures for interdepartmental coordination. Howard wanted to know why they were not working.

This shift brought the focus back to the immediate problem. It also made clear to the head of the investment committee that Howard's problem—far from being "empire building"—was symptomatic of a larger issue that needed the attention of the firm's management committee.

Diverting turns shift the conversation to the substantive issues being negotiated. When you focus on the issues and have ideas on how to deal with them, those solutions become the subject of the conversation, not you. The other party can disagree with the ideas in your proposal, but can no longer make your expertise, competence, or behavior the problem. If you suggest ways of being rewarded for a job well done that won't strain the budget, a boss has difficulty keeping up the pretense that you are being greedy. A coworker who is harboring past grievances may be persuaded to put them aside if you come up with a plan to avoid tensions in the future.

Personal attacks are often easy to read and turn. It's clear when someone accuses you of empire building. Other challenges to your credibility or motivation can be far less obvious. Sometimes they are not even intended to harm. Frequently you negotiate with people who know you or have known you in another guise. Maybe you have just been promoted. In the past, you were a silent observer in negotiations, an assistant taking notes. Now you are leading the team. Or you work in a family-owned business where almost everyone remembers what you looked like when you lost your baby teeth. These multiple or overlapping roles confuse the other person. Does a colleague suddenly stop seeing you as an assistant once you have been promoted? Does a father cease being a father on the job when the employee happens to be his son or daughter? Because people find it difficult to shift gears, they revert to old habits. Their moves push you back to roles they are comfortable with. Rather than address these constraining moves directly, you can establish credibility in your new role by engaging the other party on the problem at hand.

Trina was thinking about going to work for her father in a family-owned business. "My family is Greek, very close and very traditional. My father is a wonderful man," she stressed, "warm and kind. But he's also very much of the old 'father-knows-best' school. He's a meddler. If I was going to work with him, I had to be convinced he would listen to what I said, let me make my own mistakes, rather than just telling me what he thought I should do."

Trina wanted to join the family firm for several reasons. She could use her education and experience to help the business. Customer service, her specialty, had always been a problem. She could lighten some of the burden her father had been carrying since her uncle's retirement. And she thought she might have more flexibility. She was planning to go back to school to get an MBA.

Serious negotiations had just begun when Trina learned she was pregnant. Her father worried that she could not handle a baby, school, and work. (Given his dibs, he would have preferred that she stay home with his future grandchild.) Whenever these concerns surfaced, Trina deflected them by focusing on the business issues: her needs for generous health benefits and a flexible schedule, his concerns about what she should be paid and possible charges of favoritism from his long-time employees.

By turning the moves that her father made to position her as a daughter, Trina was able to negotiate with him as a prospective employee. He agreed to let her coordinate her hours with her school schedule and do some work at home. In exchange, she accepted a cut in pay. To finish her degree, she would take an unpaid leave for a semester, but the company would reimburse her tuition.

Look ahead, not to past mistakes. Negotiations that have a history can get bogged down in that history. Bad experiences or uneasy relations focus attention on past wrongs instead of future solutions. The discussion faces backwards, tempting the bargainers to justify earlier deeds or disclaim misdeeds. You may recognize the part you played in what happened in the past and push for less in the current negotiation. The other person may try to lay all the blame on you. To divert moves of this kind, you acknowledge the past and move on to the present problem.

For example, relations weren't good between the neighborhood association Susan headed and the town's administration. When Susan went to the mayor's office to talk about the association's annual fair, the mayor launched a volley of objections. He's looking for a scapegoat, she thought. He doesn't want his office to take the blame for last year's fiasco. He wants to pin it on us. Admittedly, the association had been disorganized, but the administration had also been lax in its police and traffic support. The weather had been beautiful and no one expected such a huge turnout.

Susan worried that the mayor might punish the association by raising the cost of extra police details or, worse, by refusing to renew its permit for the event. She had to get him talking about the fair, not past mistakes. "You are absolutely right, Mr. Mayor," she said. "No one wants a repeat of last year. That's why I wanted to talk to you before we started our planning. Let's see what we can do to get it right this year." Had Susan not diverted the mayor, she would have spent the next half-hour defending the association against the mayor's attacks.

Not only can you be held personally responsible for past events, you can be blamed when a negotiation begins to sour. To prevent hostility from growing over a particular issue, you can divert the discussion and turn to a less divisive issue. One politician, the chair of an influential committee and one of the few women in any position of power within her state government, told us, "Whenever we hit a rough spot, the anger and frustration were directed at me. If that started to happen, I shifted gears and took up another item on the agenda." Often when everyone at the table has managed to agree on less troublesome points, they are more inclined to tackle the hard issues with open minds. The progress generates confidence and they stop seeing you as an impediment.

Substitute a better idea. Those with less power often find their legitimacy or the authority they do have challenged. The moves can be subtle: a raised eyebrow, the failure to pick up on an important point, a covert (and dismissive) glance at a watch. No matter how much forethought a bargainer has put into establishing his or her credibility, these unexpected moves can undermine it.

Allison, a psychologist, was negotiating a contract with a large auto manufacturer to provide workshops on sexual harassment. She arrived for a meeting and was greeted by a new company representative. The woman she had been dealing with had been involved in a serious car accident. Since the woman was going to be out of commission for several months, the company, anxious to move forward on the harassment seminars for legal reasons, had asked her boss to take over the negotiations.

Allison soon discovered the atmosphere had chilled. The new man, dubious about the harassment seminars in the first place, immediately started revising the contract terms. The company did not need a full-blown course, only enough to kick off an in-house effort. How much was that? Allison inquired. Well, he was not sure. Why didn't they play it by ear? Instead of making a lump-sum payment, they could pay workshop by workshop. Allison objected to this idea. Her firm designed the entire sequence of workshops. If the company could sample one or two and then cancel the contract, her firm would lose money. "Look," the company negotiator came back, "this is not a big deal. Take it back to your boss. I'm sure it's okay."

With that move, Allison's authority to negotiate the contract evaporated. She restored it with a diverting turn. She did not bother to dispute the inference that the decision was not hers to make. Instead, she put on the table a solution to the payment problem. "Why don't we work out some penalty for cancellation right here? This is not the first time this issue has come up. I've developed a formula that's fair to our clients and to us. Once we get started, I'm sure you will want us to continue. That gets expensive for you if we bill on a flat workshop-by-workshop basis."

Allison's turn accomplished several objectives. She forced the discussion back to the issue—how her firm would be paid and what was fair. But she also established her credentials in a concrete way. She ignored the aspersions cast on her authority and then offered up a demonstration of her ability that robbed them of any weight. She brought her past experience and expertise to bear on a solution. She'd encountered this problem in the past and had dealt with it successfully. Allison's story illustrates an important point. If you want to divert a move away from the personal to the problem, it is best to have an idea about how the problem can be solved.

Alice used a diverting turn after Len complained that his people were pressuring him over the lost commissions.

LEN: Cut me some slack here. I'm getting a lot of pressure from my people. They don't want their commissions hurt.

ALICE: No one does. That's the reason behind my group. While we work on the developing accounts, you can concentrate on the established ones. It's an opportunity.

Alice did not respond to Len's obvious appeal for sympathy. That would have put her in a no-win position in the shadow negotiation. If she took on the role of understanding colleague, she would not be able to push Len on the accounts. If she didn't, she risked coming off as unfeeling and inflexible. Nor could she simply reply in kind—protesting that her team was just as mad as his.

Rather than "cutting him some slack" or launching a counterattack, she directed the talk to features that made the new arrangement an opportunity for his team. Since the loss of revenue, not the specific accounts, was the real issue for his team, she suggested that she and Len work together on a scheme to ease the transition. The commissions could be phased out instead of coming to an abrupt end. To ensure a smooth turnover, management might even be persuaded to compensate both sides for a period of time.

This diverting turn broke the impasse in their negotiations. Len dropped his attempts to wear Alice down and took up her suggestion of a phased transition in the commission structure.

Diverting turns bring everyone's attention back to the issues and prevent a bargainer from getting sidetracked by the other person's psychological maneuverings. The shift from the relational elements of the negotiation to the problem can be subtle, perhaps nothing more than a suggestion that it's time to get down to business. It can also precipitate a change in process from one of claims and counterclaims. Originating in a need to divert a personal challenge, the suggestions that such turns produce can take on an energy of their own and yield creative agreements.

A Caveat: Turning Demeaning Moves

Almost everyone we interviewed intuitively understood the dynamic give-and-take of negotiation. They expected to be challenged and tested. They had their fair share of experience with the "dirty tricks" of negotiation. Although few had been caught in the crossfire of a good-cop/bad-cop routine or seated with blinding sunlight in their eyes, they had more than a passing acquaintance with bullying or intimidating tactics.

Most advice on negotiation recommends that bargainers ignore such heavy-handed tactics. It is far better, the argument goes, to take the high road and refuse to participate on the same level.[7] This advice ignores a special brand of intimidating moves: the explicit use of raw power to dominate. Demeaning moves exploit vulnerabilities and expose the fault lines in the shadow negotiation. Gender, status, sexual orientation, ethnicity—all are fair game. Whatever the target, the intimidation plays on weakness and uncertainty to enforce subservient or conciliatory roles. In a startling exercise of presidential power, for example, Lyndon Johnson once remained calmly seated on the toilet while carrying on a policy discussion with a group of senators. The bathroom surroundings certainly did nothing to elevate the debate. The location was selected solely to underscore Johnson's power to talk whenever and wherever he chose. The senators were hardly in a position to challenge his ideas in that setting.

Not all demeaning moves are so extreme, but all are qualitatively different from the usual challenges you must turn. Demeaning moves dredge up tired stereotypes that erase individual distinctions. They call attention to a woman's body, making her the sum of her physical attributes rather than her abilities, and they ridicule missing alpha male qualities. They belittle with words and evoke hidden fears about the "other": the hot-blooded Latino, the violent black, the shifty Chinese merchant, the distracting Lorelei. As a result, demeaning moves carry different implications. The bargainer bears the brunt of a familiar or denigrating remark. If, as common advice suggests, bargainers opt to take the high road and ignore the demeaning behavior, they may reinforce the very stereotyped perceptions they need to turn. No response *is* a response. Unless contested, the label sticks.[8]

Casual assurances of "nothing personal" often follow demeaning challenges. If the targets react and get angry or flustered, that's their problem. There is something wrong with them, the perpetrator asserts. But these attacks *are* personal. They take place in the shadow negotiation and aim squarely at the bargainer's "appropriate" persona. They are meant to keep the target from getting out of line or stepping further out of line.

Demeaning challenges are often cloaked in friendly language or compliments, which makes them doubly difficult to turn. Kicking up a fuss after a bit of flattery seems churlish.

Raising an eyebrow at a tasteless joke can appear humorless or mean-spirited. The black account executive, praised for his performance on the basketball court and in the bedroom, is put in a no-win situation: metaphorically castrated if he objects and reinforcing latent stereotypes if he doesn't. If the bargainers let moves like these go unchecked, they participate, by their silence, in their own diminishment.

To turn a demeaning move, you have to *disrupt* it. The turn must stop the move cold before it gathers any momentum. Unless demeaning moves are disrupted, they automatically put you in a one-down position and set the tone for the rest of the negotiation. Finding the right balance is tricky. Too much disruption keeps attention on your reaction. The offending party realizes he or she has managed to rattle or annoy you. Too little disruption, and the attempt at censure goes unnoticed.[9]

Many factors come into play in choosing a response to a demeaning move. You must gauge not only the severity of the challenge but the comfort level you have. In environments with little toleration for exploitative behavior, you have more leverage, but you still must choose from a wide range of possible responses. Turns of this kind are as personal as the moves they counter. Success depends to a great extent on delivery—wit, inflection, an arched eyebrow. A humorous or mocking retort elicits a different reaction from a stinging rebuke. Few negotiators like to look foolish, and an ironic twist or sarcastic comment often exposes the absurdity of demeaning behavior better than a rapier thrust.[10]

One thing is certain. You need to think about how you are going to handle these challenges ahead of time. They *will* come up, at one time or another. Demeaning moves are unnerving precisely because they usually require instant turns. They must be turned on the spot. You seldom have the luxury of taking a break in order to figure out a great comeback, let alone an effective turn. Giving some thought to your possible responses prevents you from being caught off guard.

Before a major sales presentation, a young accountant hears a stage whisper: "She can run my numbers anytime." That sotto voce commentary is not a compliment. It is a deliberate move to put the presenter in her place, a woman's place. A Latino, recently promoted at his investment bank, hears not-so-subtle rumbling about affirmative action and the reward of mediocre performance. Having learned from experience to be prepared, the accountant had a retort handy. "Would you repeat that. Yes, you in the red tie. I couldn't hear." The Latino casually mentioned the recent merger he arranged that sealed his promotion. Suggestiveness and innuendo, they find, don't survive repetition. The accountant and the investment banker had other options available as well. Any of the turns we have discussed would work, provided they were produced quickly enough.

Interrupting Exclusionary Moves

Moves don't have to be overt to be demeaning. Sometimes they simply relegate you to the sidelines in a negotiation. Not just your comments but your presence becomes inconsequential. The conversation before a meeting never leaves Saturday's golf tournament, in which you did not play, or the Stanley Cup playoffs, which don't interest you. Talk drifts to upcoming college reunions and people the speakers know. Having worked your way through law school at night, you have no way to participate. What makes these moves so damaging is that they can set the tone for what follows. When actual discussions get under way, people talk through you or over you.

You cannot call a time-out when confronted with a demeaning move. Interruption must stop the action. Interrupting turns are particularly effective against exclusionary tactics. Unless you break an exclusionary pattern, you will continue to be invisible even though you have an important stake in how the negotiations turn out. One of the best stories of interruption we heard came from Dot, who was head of workouts for a money-center bank. She used irony, laced with humor, to cut ritualized and exclusionary bonding short. This low-key approach served her well.

> Bankruptcies, or potential bankruptcies, are frightening and publicly embarrassing to the principals. Their life's work is often threatened. Egos need to be massaged.

The negotiation in question involved restructuring the debt of a major retail conglomerate. "The combative gamesmanship started before the participants had finished their coffee," Dot recalls. "As the only woman in the room, I became a nobody, a phantom on the sidelines." She listened for a while, then rummaged around in her bottomless pocketbook. With some flourish, she pulled out a bottle of bright red nail polish and started applying lacquer to an already perfect manicure. Silence gradually descended. Dot looked up and smiled.

> "Any time you're ready, boys."

Her invitation brought the conversation to a halt. The irony was unmistakable. She controlled the money, and *she* was ready. The group got right down to business.

Dot's use of irony to interrupt is effective, but does it work for everybody? Early in your career, when you lack experience or authority, polishing your nails during a staff meeting is likely to be interpreted as poor judgment rather than ironic commentary. Dot's turn cannot be separated from her position. She is a leader in these negotiations. But the general principle holds. The key to interruption is a dramatic or humorous remark that stops the action. Teresa, an intern in a city hospital, interrupted a dispute over her patient's care. She watched herself being shut out as the discussion turned into a duel between the surgical and the medical residents. They fired questions at her for information but otherwise she was invisible. After a few minutes, she broke in. "You guys going to arm-wrestle all night?"

Brad, a research analyst, got caught in the crossfire between two powerful managers at his firm. Even though they were arguing over the conclusions to his report, he was ignored. Quietly, he got up and fetched a pair of scissors. While the dispute raged, he began to cut the pages of the report in half. Finished, he handed each of the managers a sheaf of mangled papers: "That should settle it." Brad's Solomonic intervention stopped the managers in their tracks. After all, it was *his* report they were dissecting and *he* would have to do the recasting.

Naming Hostile Moves

Interrupting an exclusionary move stops the action. In naming the move, you not only call a halt but also let the other party know that you recognize the move and that it is unacceptable. Naming sets limits. These limits are important to establish. Every bargainer has a personal threshold of tolerance, and the other party needs to be made aware of yours.

Naming offensive or intimidating behavior must leave the performer with no comeback. Otherwise, it can provoke an even stronger retort or prompt a bland "who me?" response—an incredulous or wounded look, a mystified denial.

Annie, about to negotiate a contract important to her struggling travel agency, knew ahead of time she would be dealing with a tough negotiator. "But, hey," she says, "the contract was worth an hour or two negotiating with an unpleasant personality."

> With car and hotel commissions as well as airline tickets on the line, Harry, this one man, was all I needed to end my short-term cash flow problem. He had a reputation for being a bully, but I figured I could drop the account later if he was too difficult.

To prevent Harry from gaining the upper hand, Annie planned to keep him focused strictly on the business issues. The strategy worked. Harry liked her proposal. Annie had seen nothing of the hard-nosed Harry she'd heard so much about. Pleased, she relaxed her guard.

> "By the way," he sneaks in just as he is about to leave, "you are rebating 3 percent of your commission back to me."

Besides being financial suicide and wiping out her profit margin, rebating commissions was illegal. If Annie were caught, her $75,000 performance bond could be revoked and her ticketing plates canceled. Annie remained cool and reminded Harry that rebating was against the law.

> "Wake up, bitch," he says. "Your competitors do it all the time."
>
> I just shook my head. I could see he was getting annoyed that he couldn't provoke me.

Caught in the moment, there was no way for Annie to gauge whether Harry was serious about taking a cut off the top or testing her. She knew only that what he was asking was illegal and that he was using offensive comments to intimidate her.

> I am nose to nose with this man, so stressed I'm afraid I'm going to start crying. "Get the hell out of my office," I tell him.
>
> The office goes deadly silent. Then Harry's face turns purple, and he begins to twitch. Soon Harry is laughing so hard tears are streaming down his face. I wanted to kill him.
>
> "Babe, you were great," he says gleefully. "Whoever would've figured a little girl like you would have the balls to tell me off?"

This rhetorical question provided Annie with her first opportunity to let Harry know she was onto his game. She named his behavior, but did not stop there. Rather than reveal how much his performance offended her, she complimented him on it.

> He made a move to give me a hug and I put out a cautionary finger that stopped just short of his chest.

"Impressive, Harry. You're very good. You got all the information you wanted. But I passed the test. A repeat is not necessary, okay?"

Annie poked fun at Harry's intimidating moves. Instead of taking what he dished out, remaining a passive target, she "turned" herself into a critic of his behavior. Her message was clear. "I'm onto your game. Don't think you are going to get away with it the next time."

Correcting Undermining Moves

Often the demeaning moves most difficult to turn are those that bring negative stereotypes to the surface. Confronting the bias directly only serves to legitimize it. No one readily admits to personal prejudice against minorities or working mothers. They almost always have examples on hand that buttress their prejudice. "I can't depend on him [or her] to be there in a pinch." Rather than counter arguments like these, you expose the bias behind them. You are not the exception to the rule. The rule itself is wrong. In using a correcting turn, you not only set yourself apart from the stereotype, you also prompt the other person to question the stereotype.

Jane's group leader caught her where she was most vulnerable—her dual role as a working mother. When she was in the office, she was there 110 percent, but the time she blocked out for her family was sacrosanct. Everyone in Jane's department knew she came in early and left promptly. One morning she was checking her e-mail and discovered a message from her group leader. Weekly group meetings in engineering would now be held at 5:30, Wednesdays. Jane assumed the group leader had forgotten her schedule and dropped by his office to remind him. The weekly gathering was the only time the group got together. If she couldn't attend, she would miss the project updates.

> JANE: Late afternoons are not good for me. Can we change to an early morning meeting?
>
> GROUP LEADER: Not necessary. You have to get home to the kids. Just write up your notes.

"Not overlooked," Jane thought, "inessential—not exactly the ideal employee." At that moment Jane did not care whether the head engineer was deliberately promoting that view. She could puzzle through motives later. She needed to set him straight about her commitment to her work before his attitude took root and her fellow engineers picked up on his cue.

> JANE: Sure you don't mind?
>
> GROUP LEADER: Of course not. Your kids need you at home.
>
> JANE: Gee. I thought you needed me here too. Guess not. Back to the kitchen for me? So much for progress.
>
> GROUP LEADER: For Pete's sake, I assumed you'd be more appreciative, one less meeting. We'll go back to the regular time.

Jane used a self-deprecating humor to turn a move that headed her toward the "mommy track." Moves like these are among the most difficult to turn. Often they stem from careless or unquestioned assumptions and are made unwittingly, without malice. Their effect, however, is not quite so harmless. They work off and perpetuate stereotyped generalizations that immediately put a bargainer at a disadvantage. Jane's boss was probably not even aware that he was applying a gendered standard. Correcting turns chip away at these stereotypes. Generally the other person learns something about bias in the process.

Diverting Harassing Moves

Moves that draw attention to physical appearance can be embarrassing or downright annoying. They are most often directed at women, but not always. Short, fat, bald—any physical characteristic can make someone the butt of jokes and the target of harassing moves. Such moves, because they hit so close to home, are also difficult to turn. You don't want to come across as being overly sensitive. On the other hand, you cannot let an inappropriate remark linger in the shadow negotiation, unchecked. The issue you focus on in diverting demeaning moves is *their* content. Exaggerating that content and showing its absolute irrelevance turns the demeaning move. It would be fruitless to point out that you can be bald and still think at the same time. The diverting turn comes in demonstrating that appearance has nothing to do with the business at hand and then segueing to the issues.

Grace, an intellectual property lawyer who could easily pass for a model, has become a master of the strategic one-liner.[11] When she went into a meeting to finish up the last details of a contract, both men in the room, one of whom she had not even met yet, immediately referred to her appearance.

First Jack tells me how stunning I look. Then this new guy Frank turns to Jack and says he understands why the negotiations have taken so long. Then Frank gives me an exaggerated wink. You get jerks like this from time to time. I never let that nonsense go. As soon as the words were out of his mouth, I turned a cold shoulder on him and said to Jack: "He's a real charmer."

Frank's implication was obvious. With a distraction like Grace around who could blame Jack for not paying attention to business? Grace silenced Frank. Without making a direct reply, she cut him out of the conversation and addressed his partner. The exclusion was calculated. She took the papers out of her briefcase and began discussing them with Jack. If Frank wanted to deal with her, he had to stop his "charming" observations and start talking about the contract.

o   o   o

Demeaning moves must be turned. Left hanging, they undermine you and your ability to negotiate. When you don't respond, you kick yourself later and that regret can eat away at you. But there is always a risk that any response to a demeaning move will provoke retaliation or amusement. To succeed, turns have to disrupt the offensive behavior. That means the message must be delivered in a way that its audience understands. Some bargainers rely on nonverbal signals. A raised eyebrow, an exaggerated sigh, or a roll of the eyes leaves little room for a verbal rebuttal. Just having a comeback makes it easier to take these challenges in stride. Often you don't have to use it. Knowing you have a turn at hand translates to body language and that is often enough to get the message across.

MAKING MOVES, MAKING TURNS

Negotiations are commonly viewed as a set of offers and counteroffers, proposals and counterproposals. They are also a sequence of moves and turns in the shadow negotiation. Everyone wants an edge in a negotiation. Bargainers maneuver constantly to gain an advantage. How you are heard depends on the deliberate moves you take to position yourself and the equally considered turns you use to respond to strategic moves against you. Left unchecked, moves against you tip the balance in the shadow negotiation and make it difficult to promote your interests. If your interests don't get a good hearing, it is unlikely that you will be satisfied with the agreement, either.

Both moves and turns establish your place at the table. They are the tools of an effective advocacy. Moving strategically you force the other person to take you and your demands seriously. Turning challenges that would undermine you and your demands, you maintain the balance in the shadow negotiation. In the process, you lay the foundation not only for acceptable agreements but also for creative ones.

Part Two

The Promise of Connection

Building a Collaborative Relationship

Chapter 4

Laying the Groundwork

In an early movie, *The Hustler*, Paul Newman plays Fast Eddy, a young pool sharp who gets bested by Jackie Gleason's Minnesota Fats. Fast Eddy can handle the cue stick. That's not his problem. He's simply no match for Minnesota Fats's ability to read him. Some three decades later, Newman reprises the role in *The Color of Money*. Still a wheeler-dealer but now down on his luck, Fast Eddy pins his hopes on a newcomer with a natural talent. Fast Eddy has learned a good bit about pool and life in the intervening years, and he tries to pass on some of this accumulated wisdom to his cocky protégé: "Pool excellence is not about excellent pool. . . . You gotta be a student of human moves. You study the pool moves. I study you. You pick up the check every time."

In a certain sense, Fast Eddy's advice applies to negotiation, not just pool. The strategic moves and turns you make all aim to get you where you want to be—and that is not being left with the check. But a single-minded concentration on your agenda takes you just so far. As Fast Eddy says, "You gotta be a student of human moves." When you are dickering over a car or trying to sell your condo, the bargaining is pretty straightforward. There is a buyer and a seller, and the issue on the table is money. Each of you has an incentive to make a deal if the terms are right. The car salesman needs to move inventory to reach his monthly quota; your pickup has developed an ominous rattle. The couple likes your condo, and you want to get settled in your new place. There are limits to how hard or far anyone can push. Neither of you can hold out for a windfall. If the salesman tries to gouge you or won't budge on price, you can always go someplace else. The *Yellow Pages* lists plenty of car dealerships. On the other hand, the car salesman won't cut a deal with you if he is going to lose money and the couple looking at your condo won't pay more than they consider fair.

The moves and turns you use to advocate for your interests enable you to strike the best bargain possible in these transactions. But as the bargaining moves further away from marketplace haggling, the shadow negotiation becomes more complicated. Needs and interests are no longer so obvious, and the outlines of a good agreement are not always visible. The other person's statements may conceal as much as they reveal. A negotiation over a production schedule can mask a hidden need to look good to the boss or to take time off without admitting to family pressures. To negotiate all the issues in play, you need to create a climate where hidden agendas like these can be brought out into the open. This requires connection.

People come together to settle differences, but how they feel about themselves and how they are treated determine how willing they are to work through those differences. Think about what happens when someone makes moves that put you down in the shadow negotiation, when he or she trivializes your needs, dismisses your concerns, or probes only to find an advantage. You feel frustrated, angry, or insulted—definitely not in the mood to communicate candidly. The same thing happens to the other people involved in the negotiation. When they feel undermined or unappreciated, they typically react by trying to turn the conversation in their favor, not by engaging in a collaborative discussion. Inevitably, communication chills and choices are cut off.

You prevent this reaction from taking hold by building a relationship with your counterpart and deliberately looking for connections between your interests and his or her needs. The sense of connection you can then establish changes the tenor of the shadow negotiation. The effort begins with an open mind—thinking of the person you are negotiating with not as an opponent or as a means to serve your ends but as someone who can illuminate the situation and has insights that may differ radically from your own. Deliberately narrow the distance between you and the other person, opening the lines of communication, and you increase the odds of becoming partners in a joint endeavor rather than contestants in a competitive enterprise.

CONNECTION CAN BE COMPLICATED

We stress the skill required to manage the relational dimension of negotiation because too often empathy or concern for others is treated as an inherited or natural disposition, not an acquired one. It's considered a predilection you either have or don't have. Folk wisdom also tells us that women are inclined to emphasize relational needs and men individual criteria in their dealings with other people. These attitudes can percolate through the shadow negotiation, complicating the dynamics and creating misperceptions about connection. Even though establishing connection takes hard work and considerable skill, connection itself is often linked to a "softer" feminine approach.[1]

A fallout of this common misperception is that men *and* women may avoid efforts to get connected. They see in connected moves not the strength that comes from employing relational skills but a weakness that can lead to demands for concessions and to accommodation. "Accommodating" bargainers are often expected to give in for the sake of peace. Aware of this risk, even negotiators inclined to be collaborative can overcompensate when the stakes are high. Afraid of being taken advantage of, they can dig in their heels and become unnecessarily rigid or inflexible. They may hesitate to use their relational skills simply because they worry that their efforts may backfire. Similarly, bargainers who read only signs of weakness in connected overtures can be in for a surprise when the concessions they were expecting fail to materialize.

The notion that connection leads to concession or accommodation blocks real engagement in two ways.

○ Differences never get fully aired or appreciated when one party expects the other to sacrifice self-interest or feels obliged to do so.

○ Collaborative overtures can be misconstrued as signs of weakness rather than components integral to reaching solutions that all parties consider fair.

Both traps are self-defeating, but there is a simple way to avoid them. You can engage in a dynamic kind of relationship building that is inextricably yoked to successful advocacy. Connection and advocacy do not cancel each other out. On the contrary, one does not happen without the other. To build a relationship with the other person, you don't have to forget your interests or rein them in. Quite the opposite. You connect in a negotiation by engaging your counterpart, not by giving in to demands just to make him or her feel good. When someone tries to back you into a corner in the shadow negotiation, you need to turn that move before you can get connected.

Avoiding connection and digging in your heels is not the answer either. It is a defensive response that leaves you on the defensive. It makes no sense to jettison relational skills simply because others might try to use them against you. Why not use those skills to engage your counterpart and move the negotiation to a place where neither of you needs to be on the defensive? If need be, you can always check attempts to convert interpersonal skills to a liability with a strategic turn.

Getting Ready to Listen to the Other Person

As we prepare for a negotiation, our focus is naturally on ourselves—what we want and what we need to do to better our chances of success. But there is a danger in this single-mindedness. We can become so engrossed in our take on the situation that we lose sight of the person we are negotiating with—except as a means to our ends or as a stumbling block in our way. Once into the negotiation, it is inevitable that we process whatever happens through that filter. A certain deafness sets in. We edit out what we don't want to hear and listen to what is said with a fixed script in mind. We make attribution errors that have us ascribing good intentions to ourselves but not to others. We create self-fulfilling prophecies. Expecting the other party to be overbearing or ineffectual, we interpret his or her behavior as overbearing or ineffectual.[2]

We think nothing of it when playwrights, novelists, and filmmakers use the tension between different points of view to heighten the drama. Consider Iago's asides in *Othello* or the private half-musings of Hamlet. Each provides a selective lens for the action unfolding and the psychological dynamic. So, too, different perspectives drive a negotiation. Other views and other emotions, equally justified and probably as strongly held as yours, are always in play.

Any two people will give different (sometimes wildly different) accounts of the same event. Naturally when we tell our stories, we are the heroes and heroines. Our story puts our spin on the events, conveniently editing out facts that don't fit. Typically we cast ourselves as virtuous, always doing the right thing. What we want is always reasonable and well deserved. The other person is greedy, inflexible, or domineering, focused only on the short term. We have done all the heavy lifting, finishing the proposal or going the extra mile to satisfy a client. The other one is the free rider. But what is true of our stories is also true for the other person's. To influence others in negotiations, you need to accept that they are equally convinced of their interpretation. You may disagree with their slant, but it is never wrong in their eyes.

Approaching a negotiation as a compilation of stories carries a distinct advantage. Stories alert us to the challenge we face in hearing the other person. Each story is told from a specific point of view and never includes every detail. Stories are filled with gaps, laced with contradictions and puzzling inflections. As we listen to the other person, we learn from those gaps and contradictions. What is left unsaid, or said silently through body language, becomes as important as verbal comments. Stories don't trade in certainties. They deal with "maybe" and "what if," not statements of fact. Because stories admit no rights and wrongs, but depend on different but legitimate points of view, they weave together both the stream of feelings and the stream of thought that meet to make decisions in a negotiation.

Connection, as we use the term, is intimately tied to the idea of storytelling.[3] To listen to the other party and hear what he or she is saying, you must be open to what is being said—to your counterpart's story. Connection, like piano playing, takes practice, and negotiation has its own equivalent of "finger exercises." Figure 4.1 shows an exercise in circular questioning that can help you regard the other party's actions not as biased and self-serving, but as valid reflections of what he or she is thinking and feeling at that point in time. The sequence of questions moves through three stages. It starts with you—what the situation looks like from where you are sitting, how you are feeling, how you got there. Then it circles round to the other person's story—how he or she might view the situation and might be feeling. Finally, it considers the ways in which those accounts might be linked.[4]

The purpose of the sequence of questions is to break the hold a hardened viewpoint can have on your thinking during a negotiation. As you consider a situation from various perspectives, you force yourself to entertain other explanations for why people might be acting the way they are. With a more complex story line, it is easier to see how those behaviors are linked. Often common concerns emerge with unexpected clarity, while differences in priorities become the building blocks of an agreement.

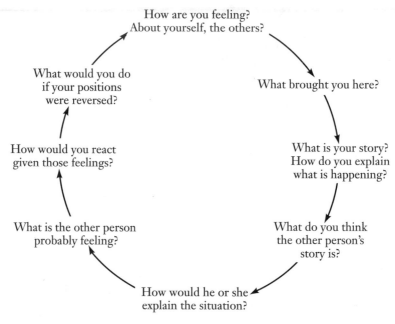

How are you feeling?
About yourself, the others?

What would you do
if your positions
were reversed?

What brought you here?

How would you react
given those feelings?

What is your story?
How do you explain
what is happening?

What is the other person
probably feeling?

What do you think
the other person's
story is?

How would he or she
explain the situation?

FIGURE 4.1 **A Circular Exercise**

How Circular Questioning Works

Conventional wisdom on negotiation has it that negotiators pursue "enlightened self-interest" when they take into account the needs of others. This is the notion of doing good for your counterpart *and* doing good for yourself. But enlightened solutions require enlightenment. Just as effective advocacy begins with you, with a positive attitude, connection emerges from a willingness and a curiosity to hear your counterpart's side of the story. It grows out of a belief that agreement depends on the wider understanding that comes from free exchange. This conviction grounds how you relate to the other party. It forces you to suspend belief or at least resist drawing premature conclusions—about the situation or your counterpart's motivations.

Alison Thomas, an account manager in an advertising agency, picked up the telephone. Her new client was on the line. "Look, Alison," he demanded. "What is going on? I've just spent half an hour I don't have talking to your creative director about the television commercials. I thought you were handling the coordination?" Alison temporized and tried to recover lost ground with her client.

Agency policy dictated that all client communication go through the account executive. Alison was furious that the creative director had circumvented her and approached the client directly. The account had been difficult even before Bob's interference. "The client manufactures drills and handyman tools. He's down to earth, without an aesthetic bone in his body. From the first, Bob's artsy approach made him nervous." Alison headed for the studio to call Bob on his behavior. He was out on a shoot, so she left a message on his voice mail that she wanted to talk to him ASAP.

Alison, working in a creative but highly competitive environment, always kept a wary eye out for encroachments on her turf. She had learned from experience that she needed to react if her authority was challenged or undermined. This time she realized it was probably a good thing Bob was out of the office. Otherwise she would have yelled at him, touching off a spiral of denials and counteraccusations. To cool down and get to a point where she was collected enough to deal with Bob, Alison went through a systematic re-storying of the events leading up to his phone call to her client. Alison's imagined walk-through of what had happened put her in a positive frame of mind where she no longer saw her relationship with Bob as irreparable.[5]

Step #1: Look at Your Story

It is important to start this re-storying process with you and your feelings. Sometimes you are relatively neutral, without much at risk. But in high-stakes situations, your emotions can run high. You may be so anxious or angry that you are ready for a fight. You may be so confident that you disregard the danger signals the other party sends. Or you may be so excited about the possibilities that you ignore your counterpart's lack of enthusiasm. These gut reactions color your impressions of any situation and clearly influence how you interpret the other person's actions. Unexamined, they can channel what you do in two ways: they tempt you to overlook what is missing from your account and they encourage you to proceed without testing whether your initial reaction has any merit.

Examining your own story in depth can reveal aspects you have been ignoring or refusing to see. Once you are aware of these missing segments, you have the tools at hand to do some self-imposed editing. For example, Kristen's firm had just received an unexpected assignment from a major client. The new contract was a plum, and she anticipated no problems in assembling the team she wanted. To her surprise, her initial overtures met with one excuse after another. One colleague did not bother with an excuse. "Sorry, Kristen. I've got too much on my plate right now. You'd soak up all my time." Somewhat taken aback, Kristen decided she had better think about what was going on before she reached the bottom of her list of candidates.

Technically and socially adept, Kristen took good care of her clients. Staff members were another matter. Whenever she heard grumbling about how demanding she was, she dismissed it as the sort of general complaint that goes along with working flat out. At first she rationalized the comments away. She set high standards and had zero tolerance for sloppy work. *There's nothing wrong with that*, she typically concluded. Now she was not so sure.

Kristen went over in her mind the difficult interviews she had had over the course of the last month—occasions when she had reprimanded subordinates to get them to toe the line or when she had been abrupt with another department head. She had an explanation handy for each case, but the list was long, way too long. She could not have had more tough situations than other department heads. "Chances were slim to none that I had inherited all the lemons in the firm or that every other manager precipitated the same confrontational responses." Suddenly it clicked for Kristen. She expected people to pitch in as members of a team, but she never treated them respectfully as colleagues. She expected collaboration on demand. She didn't negotiate. She issued orders.

Kristen's re-storying of her behavior opened her eyes. She began to question her easy rationalization of her demanding behavior. Setting high standards, she saw, did not equate with a dictatorial delivery. By shutting people out, not valuing their opinions or feelings, she cut herself off and gave her coworkers little incentive to work with her, even on an exciting assignment. "International consulting on this level is a results-oriented pressure cooker," she says. "At some point I guess I just absorbed a peremptory attitude by osmosis." As she began a second round of negotiations with potential team members, she knew she had to deal with the impressions she had inadvertently created if she wanted their cooperation. She could not change her negotiating style overnight, but she was now aware of the difficulties that her previous approach generated.

Kristen took a hard look at what she had inadvertently left out of her story. It is equally important to pay close attention to what you include. Emotional reactions influence your reading of any situation and need to be examined. Alison, for example, admitted how furious she was that Bob had called her client. This immediate response was, to her mind, completely justified. Not only had Bob gone against company policy, he had undermined her in the eyes of the client.

> At first Alison allowed herself the luxury of venting her anger at Bob. He had no right to contact her client directly. He always pushed ideas that were too radical for the client. She covered for him, but now he was going behind her back. He was a stickler, a perfectionist who complained regularly that he didn't have enough time or people. After winding down, Alison grudgingly allowed that she found Bob argumentative, particularly when backed into a corner. The only thing he cared about was winning another design award. The client's needs, the agency, policies and procedures—all came a distant second if they even registered on his radar screen.
>
> How did they get in this fix? After Alison got a grip on her feelings, she began to think about what landed them in this fix. Step by step, she reconstructed the history leading up to Bob's call to the client.
>
> *We'd had a meeting—Bob, the client, and me. The client's company was about to launch a national television advertising campaign and he wanted to talk about the first spot. Bob put up storyboards for a snappy video that was meant to cap-*

*ture the sleekness of the new product. My client liked the con-
cept, but worried that his customers would be turned off. He
was selling power tools, not CDs.*

*We met again when the rough tape was finished. Bob
was enthusiastic, really pleased, but the client remained dubious. Afterward he told me that he wanted the agency to work
up another treatment. I agreed right away. Satisfying the
client is our business. Bob hit the roof when he found out he
had ten days to produce another tape.*

At this point Alison also admitted that she might
have anticipated Bob's reaction to her lack of support.
"He always digs in his heels when someone criticizes
his designs. He gets defensive and argumentative."
Bob's actions, she felt, forced her to take sides. "They
put me between Bob and the client. The client was
lukewarm about Bob's tape and it's my job to keep the
client happy. There was no reason for Bob to expect
that I'd do anything different." Alison pulled no
punches in her examination. The new account was
important to her. She resented Bob's interference. She
looked bad to the client and to others in the office.

Connecting with your story, as Kristen and Alison did, gives
you a baseline. From there you are in a better position to separate your version from your counterpart's. Once you are clear
on your story—what is missing and what is legitimately
included—you can look for what is included in his or her version and what just might be missing.

Step #2: Look at the Other Person's Story

The tendency to get wedded to your own perspective is one of
the major barriers to effective negotiation. It's simply too easy

to become overly enamored of personal opinions. Operating in a closed world of our making, we tell ourselves we are right and the other person is wrong. We consider the merits of our position, but not theirs. We push our agenda, reiterating the same argument over and over. We explain our reasons and don't ask questions about theirs. Talking but not listening, we fail to pick up cues that what we are saying is not being heard. Over half of the information conveyed in personal interactions and on which we make decisions in a negotiation is nonverbal, yet we often fail to use these cues.

Taking a hard look at how the other person might view a situation often brings these overlooked cues to the surface. More important, as you consider his or her side of the story, you generally have to revise your initial explanation of what is going on. How people view a problem depends on *their* experience, not yours. Though you can never be completely sure ahead of time what that experience might be, you can make educated guesses about it as you prepare for a negotiation.

Josie, a big producer in an insurance company, had weathered a merger and postponed demands for a raise during the upheaval. When yet another new man arrived from headquarters to whip the department into shape, she decided it was time to become more vocal about a raise. Her request provoked a polite but temporizing response from her new boss. Bad experiences in the past inclined her to project them into the future and onto her new boss. Frustrated at being blocked again, she considered his reaction a stalling tactic. Then she began to wonder whether she really was hearing another version of the same old story. After all, even though her new boss was in a position to refuse her request outright, he had not actually said no. "If I were in this new guy's shoes," Josie thought, "I'd resent being pushed to act precipitously. I'd want some time to assess the problem."

While Josie was no less annoyed at her boss's reluctance to move on her raise, she was willing to concede he might have good reasons for his inaction. What she had been quick to write off as stalling might, from his point of view, be prudent management. By giving him the benefit of the doubt while he figured out what was going on, Josie not only got a higher raise than she requested, she opened the door for her new boss to talk about his plans for the department.

To reconstruct how a situation might appear to the other person, you must pay attention to more than the apparent and logical reasons behind his or her actions. Ed realized in college that he wanted to join a specific publishing and entertainment conglomerate. He worked in the Paris office for a senior VP during summer vacations. Although admitted to business school, he deferred a year and spent it working for the Chamber of Commerce in Morocco. Here he again forged links with senior executives at the company. Once at business school he invited the chairman to give a guest lecture.

By design and some pure luck, Ed was well known to upper management. He was hired after graduation, never having interviewed with the man he would be directly working for. Ed's boss, irritated at getting the top brass's fair-haired boy foisted on him, ignored Ed as much as possible once he started work. Ed sloughed off his cool reception; if he couldn't get information or a decision, he went over his boss's head to people he knew. Ed and his boss were caught in a vicious circle: the more the boss withheld information, the more Ed turned to his superiors.

Why should Ed have been surprised at his reception? He had meticulously engineered encounters with top management and never indicated the slightest interest in meeting the man who would be his boss. On the job, he dismissed the man as an annoyance to be circumvented. Ed's boss had good reasons to be wary. Ed struck everyone outside upper management as an opportunist who didn't particularly care whose toes he stepped on. But Ed was not concerned with the spin his fellow department members might put on his actions. Until his performance review, that is. Then Ed realized there were serious consequences in not trying to appreciate how his actions looked to his boss.

Events precipitate feelings about them, and those feelings are just as important to the other person's story as the plausible explanations you can find for his or her behavior.

> Alison, certain she was fully justified in her reaction to Bob's interference, turned the tables and began to consider Bob's position. "Bob may be a difficult person, but he is a crackerjack designer. He loved that original tape, and I'm sure it took the wind out of his sails when the client sent him back to the drawing boards."
>
> At this point Alison admitted that Bob probably did not appreciate her failure to back him up with the client. "He was 'high' on his design, already anticipating the awards he would win. I'm sure it put his nose out of joint when I didn't talk it up with the client." Alison, disappointed in Bob's failure to support her, could no longer deny him the same right to disappointment. This realization tempered Alison's self-righteous justification of her own actions. Bob, no doubt, was as mad as she was.

To get inside the other person's story, you must suspend your interpretation. This suspension is particularly important when it comes to his or her motives. You may have cast your counterpart as the culprit, but chances are good that he or she doesn't see the situation that way. In their stories, people do things for good and defensible reasons. To imagine what their explanations might be, try to think of the reasons that they might use to justify their actions. Since people rarely ascribe negative motives to their actions, this positive emphasis pushes you to imagine what the situation looks like from their perspective.

> After imagining Bob's reaction to being sent back to the drawing table, Alison began to develop some hypotheses about why he called the client in the first place. She even wondered what she might have done had she faced the same situation, what story she might have told from that perspective.
>
> *If I really liked my design, I'd be tempted to give it one last try. I'd know I should clear it through the account manager, but if she weren't available, I'd probably just go ahead. Then again, ten days might not be enough time to produce something decent. Quality might be compromised, and I'd want the client to know that.*
>
> Pursuing this train of thought forced Alison to concede that Bob just might have believed he was acting in the client's best interest by contacting him directly.
>
> *Maybe he thought I was new on the account and needed some help. Maybe he really believed that tape was terrific, the best design the art department could turn out. Maybe, since drills and machine tools are a guy thing, he thought he was a better judge than I. Maybe he was under the gun, feeling the time pressure. Maybe he tried to reach me and couldn't get through, but I doubt that.*

Thinking about possible answers to these questions, Alison began to suspect that Bob could have acted in good faith—at least in his eyes. His actions suddenly took on a different character. Maybe he was trying to help Alison, not to undercut her with the client.

When our actions bump against those of someone else in a negotiation, it is all too tempting to question the other person's motives. If we are operating with the best intentions, the other person, we figure, must be out to undermine us. But just as there are always two sides to every story, there can be similarly benign explanations for the motivations behind the other party's actions. Lingering suspicions about a counterpart's motives make it next to impossible to get to those underlying reasons. Until and unless events offer proof to the contrary, it is a good idea to assume that your counterpart is acting in good faith and is not out to undercut you. Otherwise you shut down communication and prevent any real understanding from emerging.

Step #3: Look for Links Between Stories

These final questions in the sequence help you understand the extent to which the other person's behavior may be prompted by your actions. He or she may be responding *to* you. Rather than pursuing some malevolent or unreasonable plan, the other party may be reacting to the way you are treating him or her. When we have a fixed idea in our head about a person's interests and concerns, we cannot help but process everything she says or does through that filter. We concentrate on what we think he should do, not what he can or wants to do. We quite naturally assume that he will act and react the way we would in a similar situation. This is the danger of "mirror-imaging."

State Department manuals, for example, urge foreign-service professionals to guard against interpreting data solely on the basis of their own experience. If they do, they risk assuming that one course of action is logical and likely only because that is the one they would pursue were they in the same situation.

Marjorie, who oversees joint ventures for a large pharmaceutical firm, kept a wary eye on a struggling marketing initiative in South America. Based on her numbers and financial modeling, she saw further deterioration ahead. Additional funding, she decided, was not warranted until the political and economic climate in the region improved. She began to push the head of operations in South America hard on cutting back. "Dick believed the currency crunch was a temporary setback," she says. "Although he agreed that revenues would be slow to materialize, he pointed out that we had invested significant sums in order to build distribution channels in the region. These would be put at risk were we to scale back."

Marjorie believed Dick was being less than candid about his real reasons for opposing the cuts. "Dick handled only South America. He didn't want his budget sliced. I, on the other hand, had overall responsibility for these distribution agreements and I, not Dick, would be held accountable for poor performance." At first Marjorie pressed her case on the grounds of corporate profitability. The two perspectives seemed mutually exclusive. "Then I realized that Dick was taking a longer look. Withdrawal during a crisis would jeopardize carefully nurtured relationships throughout South America." Until Marjorie and Dick actually put these different perspectives on the table, they were at an impasse. Once Marjorie revised her initial assumption that Dick was resisting the cuts solely to protect his power base, she could appreciate his long-term strategic objectives. Together they adjusted the program so that it would not present such a threat to earnings, but not so much that it imperiled future work in the region.

A disciplined look at a situation from various angles enables you to view the actions people take in a negotiation along an array of possible explanations. Actions produce reactions. They are linked and each usually has a plausible justification that must be drawn out.

> Alison's circular questioning led her to see the connections between the role each participant played in the negotiation. Bob, the client, and she had all contributed to the way in which events unfolded. With that understanding, she shifted from seeing herself as the aggrieved party to recognizing that everyone was implicated in what happened. Having looked for patterns of behavior and the reasons for them, she was able to understand that those patterns were determined in part by the premises and suppositions that constituted her map of the world and in part by what she could only imagine Bob's or the client's to be.

Narratives like Alison's are implicitly ambiguous. When Alison says "Bob *is* argumentative. He *is* undercutting me," she casts him in a single dimension. Bob's definition is open neither to debate nor interpretation. He *is*. When she starts to move to the realm of "maybe," into a narrative way of thinking, she uncovers various explanations not only for Bob's actions but for her contribution to them. She has shifted from a distancing detachment, a focus on what he did and laying blame, to viewing the event itself as a product of their interdependence.

Working out the plausible stories on each side of the table forces you to probe your initial reactions and find more charitable explanations for the other person's actions. You have to tell another story. Soon you reach the stage of maybe—maybe he means something else, maybe she has another reason for what she's doing. When you think about the good reasons for your counterpart's actions, you uncover previously hidden but sensible accounts that are possible for what he does or what she says. From there, it is a short transition to "what if"—what if I did something else? What if I gave her the benefit of the doubt and responded more positively? A single "what if" always contains the promise of additional options, other ways that the plot you construct together can play out.

How you solve your differences links with how you treat each other. Instead of concentrating on your own concerns and actions, you start to view the problem as a joint one, one that connects you both and for which you are both responsible.

Because Alison took time out to get in a connected frame of mind, she did not greet Bob with an attack or a lecture when they next met.

ALISON: You must have been disappointed about the first tape.

BOB: Disappointed doesn't begin to describe it. I was furious. That's why I called the client—to give it one last shot.

ALISON: That's what I figured, but it took some effort to get me there. Next time, let's talk first, okay?

Alison went on to recount the criticism she had taken over the phone from the client. Rather than bristle at the implied censure, as Bob usually did, he turned uncharacteristically sympathetic. Although he stopped short of an apology, he agreed to run any future problems he had with a client through Alison. That was enough for her.

∘   ∘   ∘

Good relationships do not occur in a burst of goodwill at the negotiating table. Atmospheres, attitudes, and habits often operate in the opposite direction. The question is not one of communication per se, but the kind of communication that takes place. When people negotiate, they tend to hold their cards close to the vest. Caught in a strategic communication game, they do not always say what they mean or mean what they say. Often they remain silent on what matters most to them as differences in status and role or past experiences put a damper on candor.

Efforts to connect with your counterpart encourage more open participation. The goal is to get people to share their experience with you so that you are not running blind on your own impressions. To negotiate on anything more complex than the purchase price of a car or the selling price of a condo, you need to understand the rationale your counterparts might have for the positions they are taking. But unless they have some signal, some confidence, that they are being heard, that you appreciate their concerns, they will be reluctant to share them with you. When the person you are negotiating with hears the communication going only one way, when all you are doing is telling and selling, he or she typically reacts by withdrawing or by making a defensive move or offensive turn. No one has a chance to recognize the mutual concerns that might exist. For those to emerge, you have to draw out the other side's story. It is not just information you are after. You want to build rapport and trust so that, together, you can engage in a dialogue. Many negotiations start out with opposing sides squared off. When you connect with the other person, you alter this dynamic. Being open to hearing him or her is a first step. The next challenge is to turn that positive attitude into action.

Chapter 5

Engaging Your Counterpart

It's easy to brainstorm about a problem—even a difficult one—once it's shared. The rub comes in finding ways to get to that point. For collaboration to take hold, your counterpart has to *want* to work with you. Reaching the point at which other people feel comfortable sharing perspectives takes concrete encouragement. You have to be prepared to shift focus from your needs and to draw out theirs.

The rewards of collaboration are great. In a truly collaborative negotiation, the participants engage in mutual exchange, not in parallel telling and selling. The mutuality of the interaction changes the negotiation. As we listen for the reasons behind the other person's concerns, we learn from what we hear. Often that learning is reciprocal. Issues begin to take on different dimensions when we understand more. Trust builds with the respect implicit in the give-and-take and the insights it offers. When the going gets rough, instead of getting tough, we pull together, not apart.

Usually people have solid reasons for taking the stands they do in a negotiation. They are not being difficult just for the sake of being difficult. They dig in their heels fearing they will lose face if they don't. They reject proposals out of hand not as a tactical maneuver but because that particular compromise does not come close to meeting their needs. What we interpret as recalcitrance or gamesmanship may be prompted not by the other party's stubbornness or competitiveness but by the conviction that we are not willing to compromise or listen.

However important it is to uncover these hidden fears or perceptions, unfortunately as negotiators we often get locked into habits that work against collaboration. Efforts that appear mutual on the surface are anything but when we pay attention to the other party's reactions only to test how far we can push. Collaboration does not get far when the give-and-take remains narrowly focused on individual demands. The negotiation becomes a balancing act. We probe the other party's reaction to discover the minimum we must give up to ensure that he or she does not go away mad and we still get what we want. These relational efforts may increase the odds that our demands will be heard and met, but mutual needs don't have much chance to surface. Being nice in an effort to manipulate the outcome is as transparent as being tough.

Even when you are genuinely interested in the other person's thinking and feelings, he or she may question your sincerity. Negotiators don't automatically assume that concern expressed about their doubts is real. They may construe a collaborative overture as a ploy to persuade them to go along with your suggestions. They need more than pleasantries to respond to your efforts. It takes some convincing, some active demonstration that goes beyond the perfunctory or the expedient, to override these doubts. You have to *show* the other person that you appreciate his or her point of view. There is a level of proof involved here. It is not enough simply to *think* you are being empathetic. Those thoughts must be translated into action, and that task can be difficult. Sometimes the other party puts us on guard and our defenses go up. The negotiation's outcome can be so important to us that its consequences for our counterpart slip out of focus. When his or her point of view pales in comparison to our worries, it takes a disciplined effort to draw it out.

A Failure to Connect

On February 15, 2001, news of a shakeup at WBUR rocked Boston's listening public.[1] After six years as the moving force behind public radio's *The Connection*, host Christopher Lydon and senior producer Mary McGrath were put on two-week paid leave, escorted from the building, and their computers disabled. The next day, in a show of solidarity, the rest of *The Connection* staff quit. Less than three weeks later, Lydon made the break permanent, saying he intended to pursue a career in a for-profit, independent production company.

There was no question in Lydon's mind where the blame rested. His reaction to the unceremonious forced leave pulled no punches: "We're angered. . . . Knocked out. Stunned. . . . It's a lockout and a shock." But he became considerably more expansive over his eventual departure.

WBUR broke The Connection *today instead of negotiating the future of the program with the people who created it. . . . We were willing to return. . . . Unilateralism and bad faith have marked the station's performance with us for*

many months culminating in the lockout . . . and the
announcement that they did not want to talk with us any-
more [Boston Globe, *March 2, 2001].*

Did station manager Jane Christo's unilateralism and bad faith cause the rupture, or was it Lydon's failure to connect with the station's goals and its view of public radio's mission? In her twenty-year career at the station, Christo had transformed its operations. And *The Connection* was a signature program, syndicated to over seventy stations in the National Public Radio network only the month before. There may be a kernel of truth in Lydon's contention, however. By all accounts, Christo was tough to work for, gutsy, demanding, and driven. Her high-school yearbook cited her aspiration to "own the world."

Lydon had his own problems. Sparring matches with management dot his résumé. As a staffer at the *New York Times* he butted heads with powerful Abe Rosenthal and left for WGBH, Boston's public television station, a year later, where he got into messy internal struggles in 1983 and 1991. Tom Winship, former *Boston Globe* editor and Lydon's boss during the 1960s, expressed little surprise that Lydon "worked himself into a big fight. He's a real ornament to radio and television. [But] he loves a good fight." Producer Rory O'Conner, who tangled with Lydon at WGBH, said: "Chris has a definite history of taking his producer and his ball and going home" (*Boston Globe*, February 28, 2001).

Both Lydon and Christo had much to lose if they could not come to a meeting of the minds. WBUR endangered a signature program if it forced out the host so closely identified with the show's image. Lydon risked a salary and a platform that showcased his talents.

The deal-breaker in the negotiation was Lydon's demand to share in syndication revenues. In a memo of July 27 that is addressed to "Dear Partner Jane," he lays out his claim:

We want to share with you, fifty-fifty, all new growth of "Connection" revenue. . . . Big new markets and new media and new revenue streams mean a new agreement with the people who invent the program every day [Boston Globe, *February 16, 2001].*

Christo balked over the possibility of WBUR and Lydon's group forming a for-profit company. Her objections were not solely that *The Connection* principals intended to keep a majority share. "I'm imbued with the whole public broadcasting . . . mission." All along, she believed, she had given the team "everything they want, all the support they want." Instead of an ownership position in a for-profit company, Christo offered Lydon and McGrath substantial raises as a show of good faith. If accepted, Lydon's salary would go from $175,000 to $230,000 and McGrath's from $100,000 to $150,000 with the possibility of an annual $50,000 bonus for both. The raise would have made Lydon the highest-paid personality in the NPR system, outdistancing NPR CEO Kevin Klose at $205,000, *All Things Considered*'s Robert Siegel and Linda Werthheimer at $141,234 and $136,761, respectively, and, in fact, Christo herself. Lydon rejected the offer, laying out his thinking in a memo dated September 20.

Mary McGrath and I see ourselves as Venture Broadcasters, not as Employees. Our ongoing negotiation with you is not about gratuities. It's about equity, about sharing risks and returns in this little startup of ours. We pull this program out of our hatbands every day. We work insanely hard [at] it. We've created something here. We know it's ours and we're going to insist on a partnership deal that recognizes our own-ership [Boston Globe, *February 16, 2001].*

But a selective memory is at work here. WBUR came up with the idea of *The Connection* in 1993; a staffer even invented the name. Lydon was only one of several journalists who auditioned for the job. Far from being "this little startup of ours," *The Connection* received no initial funding from Lydon. WBUR bore the development costs. WBUR gets fully half of its annual budget from individual subscribers, with under-writers and the Corporation for Public Broadcasting providing the balance. Should individual supporters, as "investors," also have a stake in the upside?

Despite the spin Lydon put on the events, his failure to connect played a critical role on multiple fronts. At every point he rebuffed conciliatory overtures or sent mixed signals. According to the *Boston Globe*, February 16, 2001, he qualified a statement that "we've had a blessed life at WBUR," with the observation that "an air of bullying and harassment and in-your-face stuff hangs over WBUR. There is an ugliness pulled out of the bad human resources bag to scare people." He followed up the statement "We'd like to work this out with Jane and WBUR" with the comment that he "wouldn't respond positively to the 'take it or leave it, my way or the high-way terms'" for a deal. Still, when forced out on paid leave, Lydon maintained that the situation was "emi-nently resolvable and obviously resolvable." In the end, it was not resolvable. "We've known all along that we weren't picking Jane Christo's cotton. It's our cotton." Rather than try to work with WBUR and Christo, Lydon positioned them as opponents, as plantation own-ers, with the role of indentured servant going to him.

On occasion, Lydon adopted a seemingly more connected posture, but the signals he sent in the shadow negotiation underscored the strong hand he thought he had. Public support tipped radically in his favor. Angry letters swamped Christo's desk and the Boston press. A month into syndication through the NPR system, was it likely that WBUR would jeopardize the program?

The situation deteriorated rapidly. Memos (quoted in the *Boston Globe*, February 16, 2001) volleyed back and forth between the principals.

FROM LYDON: find your [Christo's] note unresponsive and unhelpful. If you really want to get behind *The Connection* launch on NPR, let's see some first token evidence of support and let's see less of the nibble- - nibble, the stonewalling, the interference from middle managers . . . that [characterizes] the station's manner with us.

TO LYDON: Twenty minutes before you were scheduled to appear in a crucial hour of on-air fundraising, you told me [George Boosey] you would not do so. . . . You know that this was particularly inappropriate today since the first morning of an on-air fundraiser is vital. . . . On-air fundraising is part of your job description.

FROM LYDON: Your reprimand rings with more of the high-handed nonsense that I objected to in the first place. . . . You'll make it a two-way street with me . . . or there will be no street at all."

It turned out that there would be "no street at all," but that outcome might have been different.[2] Two strong advocates were at loggerheads, but it's safe to bet that neither Christo nor Lydon expected the negotiation to escalate so quickly. "Hanging tough" was not Lydon's only available course of action. Christo had made a substantial overture in the raise she offered.

Lydon, after all, would come out with a salary higher than hers. Rebuffed, she dug in her heels. To get Christo reconnected on their "mutual" problem, Lydon had to be the one to break the stalemate rather than expect all the overtures to come from the WBUR side. Instead, concentrating only on what he wanted and banking on the support of his vocal audience (and possibly other broadcasting alternatives he was pursuing), he continued to ignore Christo's obvious signals and cut any route to compromise.

APPRECIATIVE MOVES

Lydon had other choices. Through a series of connective overtures that we outline in this chapter, he could have moved both sides away from confrontational posturing. Appreciative moves draw bargainers to a place where mutual solutions can be found. All too often, especially in tense negotiations, we fail to hear what the other party is saying. Many techniques have been developed to prevent us from falling victim to this common habit. Active listening—a practice that involves paraphrasing what others say and using open-ended questions—helps. But although techniques like these are useful, they remain only techniques unless you genuinely believe that there is something to be gained from hearing more about the other person's point of view.

Appreciation is the key to drawing out a counterpart's concerns.[3] Despite the confessional trend in our society and daily exposés in the press, few of us are inclined to reveal much in a negotiation. The costs are too high. Any information we let slip, we think, might be used against us. But the reservation goes further than the rules of an information game. We expose something of ourselves as we share our perspectives and feelings. When they are disregarded or unsolicited, we feel diminished. Something meaningful to us, it seems, carries little weight. Appreciation lowers the costs of communicating by explicitly expressing the value you place on the other person's perspective.

Appreciation is tied up in notions of hidden value. An old drawing, a fine chest of drawers, a discarded toy in grandmother's attic all appreciate when someone recognizes their enhanced value. Appreciation is not limited to assigning concrete value to tangibles, however. It is also linked to a sensitivity to impressions and feelings. When you appreciate the other party's concerns, his situation, or the face she presents to the world, you open the negotiation to the nuanced perceptions that that person brings. Appreciation conveys the importance you place on these differing perspectives and the opinions, ideas, and feelings that shape them.

Just as you must position yourself positively in the shadow negotiation to be heard, you must also take steps to position your counterparts so they can tell their side of the story. By legitimately feeling and showing appreciation—for their situation, feelings, and ideas—you encourage them to elaborate, to fill in the gaps in your understanding.

- ○ **Appreciate the other person's situation.**
  Your counterpart has a better sense of her situation than you can ever hope to have. By openly soliciting her views, you validate them (and her). You show her that they are important to you and to how the negotiation comes out.

- ○ **Appreciate the other person's feelings.**
  How your counterpart feels about you and the negotiation

often drives his behavior. Those feelings are communicated through nonverbal cues as well as actual comments. Pick up on them and acknowledge the emotions that the other party carries into a negotiation.

○ **Appreciate the other person's ideas.**
If the other party puts out an idea, build on that contribution. Just holding the idea up for consideration shows her that you value what she has to say even though you might not agree.

○ **Appreciate the other person's face.**
Give your counterpart room to maneuver. No one likes to be backed into a corner with no visible or acceptable means of retreat.

Appreciation needs to be made explicit. Few of us would accept lightly the charge that we are insensitive to a situation or someone's feelings. But no matter how convinced we are that we appreciate our counterpart's predicament, unless we make him or her aware of that appreciation, doubts linger about the value those opinions or perspectives carry. So long as those doubts remain, the other party hesitates to tell his or her side of the story. Appreciation validates that story. When a bargainer's story is valued, when he or she is valued, a more complex account emerges.

Appreciation does more than produce useful information, however. It creates the context for mutual exchange. The tempo and the character of the conversation change. Subtly, sometimes imperceptibly, it moves away from defensive arguments and counterarguments to an inclusive discussion where everyone feels free to talk candidly about what they need from the negotiation.

Appreciate the Other Person's Situation

You can safely assume that your counterpart knows more about his or her situation than you do. Anthropologists have long been alert to the "local knowledge" that distinguishes one group of people from another. It is made up of customs and rituals and language, all those things that are simply accepted as part of the fabric of a culture and give it meaning.[4] Individuals have their own particular brand of "local knowledge," and one of your primary goals as a negotiator is to tap into it. The same words, the same actions, can carry quite distinct meanings for you and your counterpart. It is those meanings you are after. Those meanings help you understand the demands that he or she might be making.

How people see a problem depends on their experience. A dancer knows her world in a different way than a research physicist does. A marketing specialist's slant on a new R&D initiative may diverge dramatically from that of the project's engineer. These differences in perception matter when you negotiate.

Encourage the other person to elaborate. Everyone has a personal story to tell. You cannot disprove it to her, but she may come to revise it herself. Just as important, you can do no more than form a conjecture about his perspective unless he talks about it. To negotiate with others, you have to understand why they feel the way they do, not just how you think they feel. By encouraging them to elaborate on their perspective, you signal your interest in them. At the same time you create an opportunity to discover something new and unexpected.

This understanding is not easy to come by. The way we start a negotiation, our opening gambits, can shut down the conversation. Talking too much, we deny the other party an equal opportunity and ourselves the benefit of her "local knowledge." Even when we listen and question, pointed probing can scuttle communication so that his story never emerges. Unless we communicate a need to learn more—that is, actively encourage others to elaborate on their views—the discussion will continue to run along parallel tracks. Appreciation, at this basic level, offers the other person reassurance. It says it is safe to be expansive. Not only are his or her insights valued; the process and the outcome of the negotiation hinge on their elaboration.

Roberta, marketing director for a chain of foreign-language centers, more often than not encounters hostility when she first negotiates with center directors over corporate marketing plans. "The tension between marketing and teaching, between the local centers and corporate headquarters, is a constant in my work," she says. "Managers in the field generally come from backgrounds in education. To many, marketing smacks of commercialism. It's a pollutant, a danger to the quality of teaching and programming."

Not much about Roberta is intimidating. Barely over five feet tall, she's relaxed and keeps her calculator carefully hidden. But however casual her dress and warm her greeting, the center managers view her as an adversary when she arrives on site. Anyone from corporate, they assume, will force them to compromise standards so that the bottom line looks good. "They absolutely do not think marketing is something they *should* care about."

One week Roberta called at a center in the Southwest where the manager had not been using the new English as a Second Language (ESL) program developed at the head office. As soon as Roberta started to talk about marketing the program, the manager bristled. Rather than follow up on this reaction, Roberta asked if they could tour the facility. "I was there to help, but first I needed to get to the why—what about the program caused the problems for her." As they walked around, Roberta learned about the center and what was going on in the community. Only when they returned to the office did Roberta take up the subject of the ESL tapes again.

> *First off, the manager brought up her budget. With funds tight, she resented having to contribute to a marketing function that she couldn't use. When I pressed her on why, she told me something I hadn't noticed: Not a single Mexican appeared on the tapes, and her center works primarily with Mexican immigrants.*

Roberta, by drawing out the manager's story, discovered the complicated ethnic issues she dealt with on a daily basis. In turn, the manager learned that the ESL program could help her reach her community if it were revised along the lines she suggested. Until then the manager had remained silent, convinced that corporate would not be responsive to criticism from her. This negotiation, a common one between staff and line, established the ground rules for a working relationship. Problems that came up in the field affected both of them. But they each had something to contribute to their solution. They had to work together.

Respect the other person's objections. All too often you face a negotiating situation where the other party sees only negatives. Ironically, appreciating those negatives can turn the conversation around. Blaming someone *for* the situation chills any discussion *of* it. People can work on a joint problem. They generally don't feel so cooperative when that problem is defined as them. By steering the talk away from personalities to the issues, you make it possible even for people you see as difficult to talk about what in the particular situation causes them trouble. For example, a woman generally acknowledged to be impossible to deal with was blocking Donna, the CFO of an HMO on Long Island. "She could have doubled for a teacher I had in grade school—rigid, inflexible. Everything had a place and that was where she said it should be."

The joint endeavor Donna was proposing was in everyone's best interest. Donna's HMO had a new health center located at the airport and doctors who were not busy; the woman's insurance company supplied health coverage to airport employees and could increase enrollment. However rational or obvious the dovetailing of interests appeared on its face, both sides had to experience that mutuality.

> *Helen had been dragging her feet on doing anything to support us. I called her up, and she started right in. They needed this report and that report, all these other data. I felt like screaming. Instead I just said, "Fine, I'll get the stuff to you this afternoon." Then I set up a meeting.*

Donna orchestrated that meeting so that Helen would not be on the defensive. She started laying the groundwork for collaboration by preparing her own staff. Everyone had negative attitudes about working with this woman.

> *There was real history there. I knew it would be easy to overreact during the initial talks. Helen is legendary in the industry for stonewalling new ideas. The challenge was to be patient and not let any animosity surface.*

Brainstorming with her people about Helen's good reasons for objecting to the plan, Donna shifted their focus to how the situation might look to Helen. Everyone soon agreed that the major stumbling block was Helen's tendency to evaluate any suggestion in terms of the additional work involved. "She is," Donna says, "a person who will always, but always, see the glass as half empty." Any change was bound to make her life miserable and stretch her already overworked department.

Donna opened the talks by appreciating Helen's situation. By admitting right up front that they were asking Helen's department to do more work, Donna respected Helen's objections. She legitimized them, neither attempting to override nor to trivialize her real concerns.

Once we named this issue, brought it out into the open, she began to talk about the havoc the new program would cause in her department. We countered with concrete suggestions for evening out the burden.

How you treat people at the beginning of a negotiation often determines how willing they are to work with you. Bad feelings left over from previous encounters can chill the negotiation next time around. Donna met Helen as a manager dealing with a difficult problem, not as a difficult person. That positive signal provided Helen with an opportunity to explain the headaches that the joint venture could generate for her. Once she sensed the extent to which Donna appreciated and anticipated those difficulties, she shifted gears. Instead of raising further objections, she began to talk about possible solutions.

Lydon was determined to share in the revenues of a show that he viewed largely as his personal creation. Preoccupied with his "rights," he ignored Christo's concerns. To come to any understanding of why she was taking such a hard line with him, he could have probed for her reasons for preferring a stellar salary offer to any revenue-sharing arrangement. Lydon frequently cited *Car Talk* as a precedent for what he had in mind. Yet that precedent was one Christo was determined not to repeat and even there the circumstances were entirely different.

Car Talk was the brainchild of two WBUR volunteers. They formed a for-profit company that funded all development costs. Only subsequently did they enter into a contractual arrangement with WBUR to co-produce the show. Whereas public television abounded with examples of on-air hosts with ownership control (Charlie Rose, Jim Lehrer, Louis Rukheyser among the most prominent), public radio had yet to adopt the model. It was also a model that Christo resisted strenuously. She did not mind paying Lydon handsomely, but she considered turning over ownership rights to the show a violation of the public trust. Half of the funds for its development had come from individual supporters—and none from Lydon.

To have a dialogue about his precedent-setting idea, Lydon needed to see Christo and her concerns as legitimate. To her mind, Lydon was asking for the impossible. Revenue sharing ran counter to the mission of public radio. Unexplored, Christo's objections remained a deal-breaker. Had Lydon connected with her real concerns, it might have been possible to come up with solutions that served both their needs.

Negotiators have complex concerns behind their interests. Time pressures, conflicting responsibilities, a sense of mission, financial worries, physical or mental fatigue, fear—all contribute to their perspective. To the extent that appreciative moves can bring worries like these out in the open, you clear the air. The difficulties you are both experiencing, although different, can provide a bridge to connection. You are in the situation together.

Appreciate the Other Person's Feelings

The concerns negotiators have don't boil down only to their perspectives on the issues alone or to their take on the situation. Like Lydon and Christo, they are driven to their positions as much by their emotional reactions as by their objective concerns. Often it is impossible to separate the two, yet emotions supposedly have no place in negotiations.[5] Keeping one's cool is the name of the game. Emotional displays can be and are feigned for strategic effect. Actually getting emotional is another story. "Calm down, don't get so emotional" or "Get a grip" is not something anyone wants to hear. More often than not, the comment is meant to put you on the defensive.

In dismissing emotional messages or frowning on them, we miss out on important ways in which people communicate. We cut ourselves off from valuable insights into someone's experience. That information is useful, of course, but something else can happen when people share emotional reactions. Because emotions reveal important human dimensions, shared feelings can build a sense of connection different from that built by shared ideas, and can take mutual understandings to a new level.

Pay attention to the undercurrents. Emotional reactions can be expressed in many ways—by silence, by nonverbal cues, by cloaked signals. Sometimes people assume others will be sensitive to their feelings and then condemn them for being thick-headed or callous when they are not. After a negotiation takes a sudden turn for the worse, there is a common refrain. "She should have known how I would feel. I shouldn't have to tell her."

Everyone in a negotiation has concerns besides the demands they verbalize. By drawing out the reasons why they feel the way that they do, you come to a better understanding of what is going on for them. More important, you let them know that their feelings matter. This appreciation does not oblige you to give in to their demands. Responsiveness conveys a quite specific meaning: Any agreement will take their feelings and yours into account. By making them aware that you empathize with their reactions, you build the rapport necessary to work on the problem together.

Marsha, program director for a state agency, managed an internal supervisory staff in the state capital and a network of social workers based in major cities. Although she drew on a decade of experience as a field worker to develop the state's pioneering quick-response program, she was now viewed by those in the field as a bureaucrat.

> *To their way of thinking, field workers represent the "front line." They look down on those of us in administration. We are parasitic paper-pushers, effectively cushioned from any harsh realities or hard work.*

Resentment from the field came to a head over the reporting requirements that the agency imposed for the quick-response program.

> *One of the field workers stomped into my office and started blasting me about a new policy before I could say hello. She was primed for a fight and began ranting about why certain of the clearances and procedures were totally impractical in the field.*

Marsha just sat there, nodding occasionally. In the back of her mind, she sensed something else was going on. No one gets that upset about paperwork, however onerous or superfluous. Aware that the woman had just come off a horrendous court case, Marsha asked her about it. The woman talked about the child, how she felt she had let him down, not intervened early enough. After a few minutes, the woman took out a tissue, blew her nose, and resumed her criticism of the procedures.

Marsha built connection with the field worker by making it legitimate for her to express her regrets about the little boy. That appreciation bridged to the field worker's criticism of the additional procedures. Not all these objections were reasonable, at least not from where Marsha sat. In fact, two of the procedures would have helped in the child's case. But because of the shared emotions, Marsha and the field worker were no longer on opposite sides. They could talk about cases where the new protocols might be useful and those where they might be redundant or burdensome.

Emotions don't have to be shared in order to lead to an appreciation of the other person's situation. Undercurrents can be sensed and acted upon without the underlying emotions ever being made explicit.

Applying for a position with a consulting firm, Jim thought his résumé fit the job description perfectly. The three senior business executives interviewing him had taken early retirement from top-level jobs in banking and insurance to form a private consulting firm that would work with large corporations on 401(K) plans. They were looking for a young manager to handle operations.

I made my case forcefully, talking about new systems that could be used. The more I talked, the more resistance I felt. Then I realized why: I was a young whiz kid telling these guys how to run their business, as if they were computer illiterates.

Far from being technological novices, the group had considerable expertise; one of its members had been in charge of installing computer systems at a money center bank. "As soon as I traced the undercurrents to their source," Jim says, "I could deal with them. I wanted to work with these guys and let them know why. Their experience was a big part of that equation."

Pick up on nonverbal cues. A good ear can alert you to emotional undercurrents. It also helps to keep a good eye out. We reveal more about ourselves than we ever put into words. Hidden agendas are usually not verbalized in a negotiation. Our counterparts signal important clues to their reactions not by words, but by facial expression and body language. When you pick up on these signals, you let the other party know that you are paying attention with all your senses. The cues you pick up can also prevent you from escalating the tensions inadvertently.

Andrea, an admissions officer at a university in the South, was having difficulty with one department. The professors there short-circuited the admissions process by interviewing and admitting candidates on their own. As a result, admissions was stuck with incomplete or inaccurate files and cut out of the loop when the department's admissions standards were determined. Andrea needed to put new procedures in place.

Andrea, not much older than the undergraduates, armed herself for the meeting with the department members. Knowing she would be at a disadvantage by virtue of her age, experience, and academic credentials, she designed two forms. These, she believed, would solve the problem if the department filled them out for each student interviewed. As soon as she arrived, Andrea sensed the impatience in the room. The rigid postures, the perfunctory greetings, and lack of eye contact warned her to hold off on producing her forms.

It was a good call. The department members started the meeting with a litany of complaints about administrative paperwork. "The only answer the administration ever has," the chairman said, "is another form to fill out in triplicate. We started interviewing candidates on our own to avoid that." Andrea, all too aware of the forms burning a hole in her briefcase, never brought them out. Alert to facial expressions and body language, she jettisoned a plan that would have polarized the talks from the get-go. Instead, she requested that the department secretary notify her by e-mail of any upcoming interviews with prospective students so admissions could follow up.

Andrea took the professors' emotional temperature, but her appreciation remained as silent as the cues they sent. You don't have to probe feelings to demonstrate an appreciation for them. You can respond to them by changing your approach.

Christo and Lydon's negotiation became highly emotional. Most nonverbal cues are subtle, but neither Christo nor Lydon engaged in subtle maneuvering. Both questioned the other's intentions and so the rhetoric and the tensions escalated. Some exploration of the feelings underlying their stands might have helped. Lydon believed that he had made the show a success and felt slighted. Christo had every reason to feel her efforts on behalf of the show had been unappreciated. She went to bat for Lydon for an unprecedented salary, only to see him portray her as an unfeeling martinet.

Rather than treat the salary offer as inconsequential—essentially a slap in Christo's face—Lydon could have acknowledged that she had gone out of her way to find a solution. Later, after his enforced leave, he could have taken up Christo's offer extended in the press. "This is just giving them time to reflect. They need time to think." At this point, criticized to her superiors and attacked in the press, Christo probably felt angry and betrayed. Lydon could have paused before reacting and acknowledged the olive branch—admitting that he had been caught by surprise. Apology can be a way to get a negotiation back on track—but only if it is truly meant.

Negotiators usually send out abundant clues about their concerns. These clues have to be picked up on. Appreciating the other side's feelings, however expressed, shows that you are paying attention. Those feelings in themselves can open up a dialogue—they can be discussed. As you understand more, you may be forced to revise your assumptions about the other party's motivations and the reasons behind a particular set of demands or objections.

Appreciate the Other Person's Ideas

It does not take much to shut people down in negotiations. The other person puts out an idea and gets no reaction. The suggestion may be so sketchy or so tentatively offered that its possibilities elude us, but we discard it nevertheless. The rejection does not even have to be verbalized. A shrug of the shoulders or a hasty diversion to another topic is a sufficient signal. This rush to judgment affects a negotiation in two ways. Most obviously it limits the ideas on the table. A suggestion that is ultimately rejected can still spark other ideas. Equally important, people usually take it as a personal rebuff when their ideas are skipped over or ignored. Not only do they get offended, they withdraw, becoming much less likely to expose themselves further. Everyone knows what it is like to have an idea dropped, then appropriated by someone else, or ignored altogether.

Respond to the other person's ideas. No matter how casually an idea is thrown out, it deserves consideration. You want to encourage the other party to share his or her thinking. Showing appreciation for an idea, for the gesture that the other person makes in putting it forth, does not bind you to it. Such appreciation demands only that multiple ideas and possibilities be held open for consideration. Neither a yea or a nay, consideration says, "That's interesting, let's explore it." The idea is looked at from various angles, weighed. Picking up on another's suggestion shows respect not just for the idea but for the person doing the suggesting. That respect is often reciprocated, and everyone becomes more open to considering multiple possibilities, regardless of who puts them forth.

In the most difficult of situations, Betty learned how shared ideas can lead to connection. No parent in the child-abuse program she was running approached discipline in quite the same way. They did, however, have quite definite opinions and were not shy about voicing them. Many resented the court-ordered intrusion of people like Betty into their personal affairs.

Counseling sessions with parents were complicated for Betty. She was younger than most of the parents and had no children of her own. She had also been raised in a household where physical punishment was never used. Although living in Los Angeles, she was a Yankee from a privileged background. To downplay these differences and to get the parents communicating, she began her sessions by asking each parent to share with the others what trouble their kids had gotten into that week and how they had punished them.

> *Workshops with parents were extraordinarily difficult. We'd be talking about alternative ways of disciplining and a parent would state flat out: "I hit my kid. That's what my parents did. I'd probably be in jail if they'd lightened up. Kids need to know who's boss." Telling the parents they were wrong would have gotten us nowhere. The parents would hit the door and have to be forced back for another session. I needed to encourage them, to acknowledge how difficult parenting was, and to create possibilities for them to see other alternatives. I'd ask them to think about the benefits of spanking. But then I'd ask them to consider the advantages of other ways of disciplining too.*

Once the parents started talking, differences soon appeared among the parents, breaking down the barrier between Betty and "them." Using their own anecdotal accounts, she could help them see that a beating was not their only recourse.

Betty suspended judgment when disapproval was a natural reaction. Without that suspension, other alternatives would never have been considered. She supported the parents, neither criticizing nor accepting their behavior, and kept them connected by focusing on the task—becoming better parents. Now in medical school, Betty applies the same technique in her group tutorial. Every Monday morning the group meets to decide how to tackle the week's problem. The twenty members usually voice twenty opinions. "To me," Betty says, "this is negotiation—finding a way through the disagreements."

> *Some members of the group try to impose their views, cut off discussion. They say, "This is the way I see it, and these are the reasons." Pretty soon we have a war going on. It's better to say, "That suggestion is good for this or that reason, but what if we looked at it this way?" When suggestions are offered like that, no one has to go to the wall for their own views.*

Betty's appreciative interventions, with the parents and with her fellow students, help the group rethink their ideas in a connected way. By summarizing the benefits of a particular solution and linking it to other suggestions, she reinforces the group member's contribution, but also keeps discussion open to other alternatives.

Link the other person's ideas with yours. Betty's approach is similar to what Deborah Tannen calls "cooperative overlapping."[6] In many conversations, opinions or ideas are heard sequentially with everybody competing to be heard. By contrast, when cooperative overlapping structures the conversation, opinions are considered in relation to one another and get revised as the participants make new contributions. Each person builds on what went before. Everyone is both an empathetic critic of other people's ideas and a participant with his or her own opinions.[7] However definite these ideas may be at the beginning, they evolve through the exchange and commentary. The process is one of constant looping back, deliberately soliciting ideas from others, including them in the conversation, revising as you go along. In this sense it is quite different from brainstorming, where people invent options, throw out ideas, without making a decision. In an appreciative conversation those options and ideas do not remain distinct. Choices are not kept separate, to be selected or discarded. One idea builds on another.

John was called in to head up marketing at a mutual fund that operated in a special niche—responsible investing—when it ran into hard times. The fund would not buy shares of companies whose products compromised health or social standards—tobacco was high on the avoidance list—or whose operations benefited from exploitative wage scales abroad.

Before the recession, the fund had no trouble attracting investors. With the downturn, however, withdrawals began to accelerate, and several large institutional investors cut their stakes significantly. John had little experience with the investing population, but he knew marketing inside out. Aware of the resentment (and the fear) percolating through the fund since his hiring, he began a series of what he called "unstructured meetings." He asked the portfolio managers to come in with a suggestion of how to position their particular fund.

The first contributor stuck to her script. As fund manager for widely held industrials, she pointed out that many university endowments unknowingly held substantial positions in a company whose largest subsidiary was also the country's largest producer of pornography. The telecom manager followed up on this comment. A telecom company, also widely held, was the largest Internet distributor of pornography. Working around the table, building on suggestions, they assembled not only a list of target companies that endowments should avoid, but matched each with a potential substitute to recommend to their institutional investors. Gradually, a coordinated fundwide marketing approach emerged, one that was not the brainchild of any single participant or directed at his or her portfolio.

Cooperative overlapping can be equally effective in one-on-one situations. Nancy, director of managed care for a community health center, began to explore administrative steps to control costs. Her interest picked up when she noticed a rise in patient complaints about billing. Nancy soon found a computer glitch was the culprit. A simple problem, she thought, until she met with George, the resident in-house expert on information systems. "He was incredibly hostile. As soon as I said there was a minor problem, he shot back a sarcastic rejoinder. My comment told him just how little I knew about computer programming."

George was famous around the center for being difficult. He also loved his work. A perfectionist, he was not going to change the system just because she asked. If there was a problem, as Nancy claimed, he wanted complete documentation on the contracts. He clicked off all the data he would need to track the problem down. "What a great idea," Nancy replied. "Perhaps we could develop a form that includes everything you need and won't be too hard for my people to complete." George acknowledged that the suggestion had some merit and probably wouldn't take much effort. Still, he cautioned, he would want to do several test runs before making any changes. Nancy, who was just beginning to get a glimmer of the difficulties her "little glitch" might produce, immediately agreed.

Each learned something about the other in the process. George was pleasantly surprised at Nancy's flexibility and her willingness to admit that she did not have the answers. Nancy, in turn, was grateful to George for preventing her from tripping over her misguided impression that the difficulty was relatively minor and easily remedied. By actively soliciting your counterpart for ideas and taking them seriously, you give both sides something to build on. Those ideas become explicitly linked to your needs and evolve as they are explored.

> Christo and Lydon continued to conduct the negotiation in either/or terms—or, as Lydon put it, "my way or the highway." Lydon wanted ownership; Christo opposed WBUR's minority participation in a for-profit venture. But there were shadings between these two positions. "WBUR," Christo explained, "has never said they could not form their own company. However, WBUR will not form or fund their for-profit company." Lydon could have created room for mutual commentary by teasing out the idea embedded in Christo's remarks and building on it. If outright ownership would not work from her perspective, what would? This line of inquiry would have cost Lydon nothing and might have gone a long way to restore the trust and good faith missing in the negotiations. At the least he could have created an opportunity for Christo to put an idea on the table. By taking up Christo's tentative suggestion that the arrangements could be fluid within certain boundaries, he could have made it possible for them to move on and discuss just how flexible.

When we pick up on a counterpart's ideas or comments, we shift the negotiation from a yes-no, up-down decision to a process that weighs which ideas work best for everyone.

Appreciating the other party's suggestions, building on them, we break down the resistance to new ideas. With multiple possibilities rather than two mutually exclusive ones, we increase our chances of reaching agreement.

Appreciate the Other Person's Face

Image is a major concern for all of us when we negotiate. How we look to ourselves and to others who matter to us often counts as much as the particulars of the deals we make. In fact, these are seldom separate. "Face," a concept popularized by sociologist Erving Goffman, captures what we value about ourselves and the qualities we want others to see in us. Negotiators go to great lengths to preserve their face. They stick to their guns against poor odds simply to avoid losing face with those who are counting on them.[8]

Show respect for the other person's position. To connect in a negotiation, we need to be protective of everyone's face, not just our own. It's often easy to read what people think is important and what they value about themselves. If our demands tread on the other party's self-image—in front of a boss, a colleague, or even privately with us—they probably won't be accepted. Being sensitive to other people's sense of face does more than prevent resistance from developing. It lays the groundwork for trust. It says, in effect, that you respect what they are trying to accomplish and will not do anything to embarrass or undermine them, even if you can. This appreciation concedes nothing and often is the only way that the negotiation can move forward.

Sam, director of operations in a medium-sized business unit, had a new boss. During departmental meetings to negotiate project schedules and funding, Sam's boss constantly rejected his ideas. Soon it became a routine: Sam would make a suggestion and before he got the last sentence out, his new boss was issuing a categorical veto.

Frustrated, Sam pushed harder, only to meet increased resistance. Finally, he took a step back. His boss had transferred from finance and had no real experience on the operations side of the business. Perhaps, Sam wondered, he felt he needed to establish his credentials—or at least his authority. Rubber-stamping Sam's proposals might have seemed a sign of weakness, a loss of face in front of the new group he was to lead. From then on, Sam took a different tack. Rather than present a single idea, he offered an array of options and acknowledged that the final decision rested with his boss. Gradually, his boss felt less need to assert his authority and could respond positively in their dealings.

It's not only bosses who need to save face in negotiations; colleagues and subordinates do, too. Team members avoid peers who bump a problem upstairs at the first sign of trouble, making everyone appear incapable of producing a solution. Subordinates muzzle their real opinions once they have been belittled or dismissed by superiors. In the workplace, attention to face is a show of respect for another person, whatever one's corporate role.

Make it easy for the other person to retreat. Sometimes the people we are negotiating with back themselves into a corner. They dig in their heels and stubbornly cling to positions. They make comments they don't mean and do things they regret. All our antennae tell us that they want to retrace their steps but see no way to get out without appearing weak or indecisive. In these circumstances, protecting the other person's face means providing him or her with a way to retreat gracefully.

Lois was a senior researcher on a major study at a large university. Three years into the study, she and her fellow researchers were having trouble getting their original subjects to come to follow-up interviews on campus. Lois took her difficulties to the woman in charge of the study, who recommended that the researchers use home visits to conduct the follow-up interviews.

The new system worked. Follow-up rates increased markedly. There was a snag, however. Lois and the other researchers were constantly on the road and covering the extra travel expenses themselves. Lois, who considered reimbursement of these out-of-pocket expenses part of the study's obligations, went to see the study's head again.

> *After discussing the good results our home visits were getting, I mentioned that we had forgotten to talk about the extra costs. The researchers needed, of course, to be reimbursed for gas and sometimes for an overnight stay. Before anyone got further in the hole, I wanted to clear the matter up.*
>
> *The study director suddenly tensed up. Her hands were tied. Home visits were not included in the original study budget. The grant came through a federal agency, and she could not authorize any additional money.*

Lois appealed to the director's sense of fairness. The researchers, all graduate students, should not have to bear the additional costs. The new system should never have been put in place, she said, before the reimbursement issues had been straightened out.

Lois suddenly realized she was backing the study director into a corner. If Lois had been responsible for implementing the new system, the idea itself came from the director. "Look," she said, "I know you are in bind. Could you talk to the university's grant administrator? He might find a loophole in the federal regs or have other sources of funding he could tap."

Lois's appreciative moves did two things here that saved the director's face. She essentially inserted an objective third party as an intermediary into the negotiation. The study director could discuss "bending" the rules with a senior administrator in ways she could not with a postdoctoral assistant. The director never had to admit that her original suggestion was premature or ill advised. Lois also removed herself from the final solution, telling the director that she knew the problem would be worked out fairly. "The researchers were reimbursed for all their expenses by month's end," Lois says, "but I never knew where the money came from."

Having rebuffed Christo's offer of a substantial raise, Lydon needed to pay particular attention to her face. Instead, undercutting her with management and at NPR and attacking her management style, Lydon backed Christo into a corner. He circulated private e-mail messages and memos that embarrassed both WBUR and NPR. In a letter on the failed contract talks to NPR head Kevin Klose, for example, he characterizes WBUR as having a "system of harassment that calls itself management." Lydon's senior producer Mary McGrath yelled at Christo so loudly during a closed-door session that staffers in the adjacent office could hear. Not incidentally, these two incidents turned up as justification for the enforced February 15 leave.

Lydon's actions created no room for Christo to maneuver. Although he claimed that they needed "a new relationship," he restricted his thinking to contractual arrangements.

At the least, Lydon needed to exhibit—in action and words—that he appreciated the public embarrassment he was causing. Toning down the rhetoric might have helped. Resisting the urge to rally the troops in the press corps and his audience to his cause certainly would have eased the tension. As matters stood, any accommodation Christo might have entertained carried a substantial and public loss of face.

The cooperation needed to reach a good agreement doesn't have much chance of developing when the other party senses he or she is being backed into a corner. Typically the person reacts by digging in, as Christo did. By then, any compromise represents a retreat or an embarrassing surrender. But there is an alternative to going down that road. Overtures that demonstrate respect for a counterpart's face provide room for the other person to remain open to possible solutions or to back away without cost and with dignity intact.

LIMITS ON GETTING CONNECTED

For collaboration to happen, the connection needs to go both ways. Lydon intuitively recognized this dynamic in his comment that the relationship with WBUR's management would have to be "a two-way street." But he quickly tagged the observation not with a connecting overture, but with a threat—"or there will be no street."

Negotiators do not get connected by making concessions or by accommodating the other side for the sake of peace. Nor do they connect with everyone all the time and at the same level of intensity. It takes time and energy to build a relationship. There are limits to how willing someone is to go the extra mile; to devote the time as well as the emotional resources required. Not everyone wants to bother. Sometimes they are limited by their rusty or undeveloped interpersonal skills, other times by their lack of interest. First of all, not everyone can operate in a collaborative mode. The need to win, to beat down the opposition, is too ingrained to be overcome by even skillfully managed appreciative overtures. Second, the situation itself often offers no compelling reasons to make the effort. No points of mutual need emerge from the discussions. In other words, efforts at appreciation do not always result in a collaborative relationship, and it's important to know when to back off.

Resistant personalities. For a sense of engagement to develop that goes beyond superficial comfort or attentiveness, there has to be some reciprocity. Whether and to what extent a mutually respectful give-and-take can be nurtured is often difficult to judge. But for collaboration to have a chance, you have to begin a negotiation assuming that it is at least a possibility. If and when you discover that the other party is playing a different game, you can shift course to protect yourself. For example, Harriet, a venture capitalist on the West Coast, leans heavily in the direction of the collaborative in her negotiations—but she also knows when and where to draw the line.

Harriet, who has turned fifty, works in a field of aggressive deal-making dominated by male lawyers in their thirties and forties. "To put it bluntly, sometimes I stick out like a sore thumb." Early on Harriet recognized she could not and would not "play by the usual rules." In part, this decision was pragmatic. "I would be a sham; people would see right through me in a New York minute. But I get results—good companies, happy partners."

Trust, Harriet believes, is the glue that holds deals together. She works hard on establishing relationships. "My colleagues refer to a successful leveraged buyout as bringing home another pelt. I like to think of it as an addition to our community of companies." Harriet's collaborative approach does not always succeed. One negotiation crystallizes in her mind the difficulties she can encounter.

> *We'd invested heavily in a small company as a joint venture partner. When its software suddenly started to gain traction, the founder wanted to renegotiate the terms of the original agreement. Otherwise he would buy out our interest—and not for a very good price since the market was flat, if not downright depressed. The only way I could see to make him comfortable with the deal was for him to think I cared about him personally. I courted him. I tried to be there for him. I went to hear him give a lecture, flew to New York for dinner.*

Despite her courtship, the deal started unraveling. Harriet's boss cautioned her against being overly invested in the relationship or, as he put it, "profligate with emotional capital." Translating, Harriet took that warning to mean too much connection was unhealthy. Her involvement might be skewing her judgment.

As the entrepreneur stepped up the pressure on Harriet to cave in, Harriet redoubled her efforts to save the venture. In rapid escalation, they reached a point of no return. Harriet did throw in the towel, but not in the way that the joint venture partner anticipated. She gave up on connection. When he embarrassed her in public and in comments to her attorney, she took him to court. Nothing else was going to prevail over her client's need to best her and dominate the negotiations.

A tough bargainer, Harriet works through a collective "we" that demands parity at the table. This is part of the groundwork laid by strategic moves and turns. Getting connected requires something to connect with, neither an accommodating cipher nor a dominating opponent. It also demands a certain reciprocity from the other side. Finding none, Harriet took the only option left available to her.

> In parallel fashion, both Lydon and Christo were "tough" negotiators. Perhaps, given the personalities and histories involved, the negotiation was doomed from the start. But considering the stakes, it would have cost Lydon little to reconsider the potential damage done by casting himself as indentured servant to Christo's plantation owner. He didn't, and everyone lost out. The listening public was deprived of a vibrant personality, a signature WBUR show lost some of its luster, and Lydon gave up a prime job. The latter choice was Lydon's to make, but he might have made his way to a better solution had he given connection a chance.

Difficult situations. Sometimes the power imbalances are so great in a negotiation that they cannot be overcome with deft strategic moves and turns. Being responsive to the other side may be the only game in town. In these situations, appreciative moves are used tactically, not so much to engage the other party in mutual exchange as to get a hearing. In other words, appreciative moves become the tools of advocacy rather than of relationship building.

Jackie is an intensive-care nurse at a major teaching hospital. Daily she confronts hierarchical relationships that work against her being heard when she negotiates with senior physicians and residents about the postoperative care of patients.

> *One of my chief responsibilities as a critical-care nurse is to advocate for the patient. A lot of players are involved in caring for critically ill patients.*
>
> *They look after a specific aspect of the patient's care, and each generally has definite ideas about how the care should be handled. Negotiating among these differences is the most exhausting part of my job.*

Everyone in critical care is pressed for time. How Jackie phrases her concerns and times her approach determines how her suggestions are received.[9]

> *I had a recent case where I was convinced the patient needed a transfusion. Each time I moved him, his blood pressure dropped, and he was uncomfortable. Medication eased his discomfort, but it also caused his pressure to drop. We needed to get the patient stabilized, not just for his own good, but to move him off the ICU. Transfusion seemed the only route.*

The surgeon, however, opposed transfusion. "He shot me down but good when I suggested it," the resident informed Jackie. This history made it doubly difficult for Jackie to bring the issue up again with the surgeon.

*I knew I'd only get a few minutes with the surgeon to get
my story out. I had to engage him in a conversation explicitly and succinctly about the transfusion. I caught him on
the way to the Coke machine and asked him why he'd ruled
out a transfusion.*

The surgeon and Jackie had a mutual concern—the health
of the patient. They were both implicated in that outcome. To
the extent that she understood the surgeon's hesitation to trans-
fuse, the better off the patient would be.

*While the surgeon was waiting for the Coke can to drop, he
told me the patient himself was opposed to transfusion, and
he wanted to hold off as long as possible. I then voiced my
concerns, and he listened, between swallows. He still wanted
to wait, but we agreed on a plan of action. If the patient's
blood pressure continued to fall over the next four hours, he
would be transfused. This was a great outcome for me.*

At the bottom of the medical hierarchy, a nurse negotiating with a cardiac surgeon, Jackie responded to those dynamics and, in turn, made it easy for the surgeon to respond to her
concerns. That was probably the only way he would listen.
Timing and phrasing were as important to her success as her
actual proposal on how to handle the transfusion.

Jackie had to accommodate the surgeon to be heard. It was
his decision to make. Did the surgeon see Jackie differently
after their interaction? Would he respect her opinion more on
their next encounter? Perhaps, but only perhaps. Limits on
mutual engagement were woven into the relationship she had
with the surgeon and the one the surgeon had with her. In
unequal situations like these, appreciative moves can be used to

support your interests. They aim not so much to promote collaboration as to parry differences in status.

Where real inequalities exist, it is difficult to talk about connection. Bargainers with the least power are almost always the ones who pay the most attention to the other person's feelings and opinions. There is little reciprocity. They monitor the other side and then use responsiveness to get what they want. Connection, in fact, has been called the weapon of the weak. Perhaps that label accounts for Lydon's pronounced aversion. Certainly the balance of power was not tipped heavily in the direction of either Lydon or Christo.

Connection, however, is more than a weapon of the weak. Despite the uneasy relation between connection and power, connection can actually be used to create power in a negotiation—but it is a shared power. One of the key insights that comes from looking at the shadow negotiation is the impact relational skills have on the quality of an outcome. Without an appreciation of multiplicity, an ability to listen, or a capacity to suspend judgment, dialogue and discovery are next to impossible. Understanding how appreciative efforts can be interpreted or exploited does not lessen their value. They just have to be used with your eyes wide open. The benefits are too great to miss.

o   o   o

Connecting with your counterparts in the shadow negotiation involves you in a process of making them feel appreciated in all their complexity. Negotiators cannot be reduced to their issues alone. How they feel and how we feel influences how we work together. When others sense that their opinions and perspectives are valued and respected, when we understand something about what makes them feel the way they do, we encourage them to work actively with us, not to pull in the opposite direction.

Purposefully developing a sense of connection in the shadow negotiation changes the atmosphere. When bargainers begin to trust each other enough to share their stories, they are poised to learn from each other. In a collaborative dialogue, where connection has been made, arguments and counterarguments become forms of collective reflection. A mutual rapport, once established, multiplies the chances that you will be able to find creative ways to resolve your differences. But it takes work to engage your counterpart so that a shared purpose can emerge.[10]

Chapter 6

Getting Collaboration
to Work

Negotiations fall into predictable patterns. These patterns are
not hard to identify, and most of us encounter them more often
than we would like. First, there is the dance of concessions that
produces competing monologues. Each bargainer comes to the
table with his or her interests clearly defined and with fixed
arguments in mind. Suspecting that any disclosure might jeopardize their case, they hold back and give away as little as possible. They whittle away at each other's demands until eventually
they settle on a compromise, usually somewhere in the middle.

Then there are the abortive efforts at problem solving,
where symptoms are mistaken for their root causes. Bargainers
go round and round on trivial or secondary matters, blaming
each other for delays or a failure to follow through. However
involved or heated the talks become, the bargainers get stuck
in grooves and never explore together the reasons for the delay
or the inability to deliver. Because the root of the conflict

remains hidden or disguised, the underlying issues cannot be addressed. It's a lose-lose situation all around. No one feels satisfied. They have not really gotten to the heart of the matter or even been able to let off steam and air their differences.

Dissatisfaction like this rarely produces good or lasting agreements. "The clever thing to do," advised Mary Parker Follett, considered by some to be the mother of negotiation theory, "is not to let the negotiation drift toward two mutually exclusive alternatives—your way or my way." An either/or approach almost always leads to partial and disappointing results. There is a more promising although admittedly more difficult alternative. You can take steps to ensure that the negotiation conversation unfolds as a collaborative dialogue rather than an adversarial contest. The negotiation then becomes a continuous process of *relating* and *revaluing*. As you and the other person connect with each other, you both become aware of the gaps in your assumptions and have the means at hand to reassess them. Disagreements, rather than leading to a hardening of attitudes, form the basis for further inquiry.

Once engaged in a collaborative dialogue, it's often possible to generate solutions that would never have occurred to anyone independently. The reason for this is simple. When bargainers put their cards on the table, face the real issue, and bring everything into the open, they relate to each other differently. As Follett wisely pointed out, "I never react to you but to you-plus-me; or to be more accurate, it is I-plus-you reacting to you-plus-me. . . . In the very process of meeting, we both become something different," more receptive to that unknown that the other party knows. When we engage in dialogue instead of talking *at* each other, we learn from the exchange, and the boundaries of set arguments become elastic.[1]

Although good agreements come from an open process where the bargainers trust each other, the barriers against achieving that trust are considerable. Bargainers don't naturally trust each other. They worry that in revealing too much they will give the other person an edge. If, for example, you are candid with your boss about a project's problems, he may blame you. Tell the interviewer exactly what starting salary you want, and she may discount it and offer less. In fact, the uncertainty of negotiations prompts caution in divulging information, yet without some degree of candor it's difficult to talk about the real issues, let alone reach good agreements. This dilemma makes those familiar and dissatisfying patterns into which negotiations fall all the more understandable.[2] We humans are a suspicious lot when it comes to negotiation. Most of our models push in the other direction—toward strategic analysis that emphasizes differences rather than points of mutual concern.

When negotiators connect and become more candid, they often discover that the problem they were worrying about is not the root conflict, it's only a symptom of it. But any collaboration requires a good deal of effort. It takes active steering to reach a place where you and your counterpart experience mutual trust and rapport. To be candid with one another, people have to be confident that everyone is operating in good faith. They also have to be convinced that a less adversarial process can produce better results for them. Once they are comfortable expressing their concerns, secure that what they reveal will not be turned against them, they feel freer to discuss divisive issues. With conflict no longer avoided or suppressed, it is not so hard to work together on joint solutions. As everyone hears about what the others want, individual interests gain greater clarity through the dialogue and at the same time the linkages between those interests become more obvious. Both the problem and an individual's perspective on his or her stake in it evolve through the conversation. Bit by bit, incrementally, trust builds. The relationship that is formed through dialogue reinforces everyone's confidence that the problem can be solved together and expands their notions of what is possible.

Creating a place where dialogue can take place is part of the "invisible work" of negotiations.[3] It takes work to change the perceptions that people bring to negotiation and to cultivate a climate of openness and mutual respect. It takes work to keep a dialogue going when the other party's only inclination is to put demands on the table and press for a deal. It takes work to get everyone to own his or her part of the problem. This work has often been relegated to the backseat, pushed from prominence by the strategies and tactics needed to reach an agreement. Only recently have we become aware of how important this invisible work of trust building is to negotiation. Without it, commitment to a joint solution has little chance of developing and solutions remain, in one way or another, dissatisfying.

The invisible work of negotiation creates that "you plus me" that Follett talked about. Dialogue doesn't just happen. Trust and respect have to be nurtured before others feel safe in speaking their minds or want to bother. That takes some effort.

o **Work to make room for relationship building.**
   You have to give collaboration room to grow. The simple act of making other people comfortable goes a long way in ensuring that they will not be left guessing about how they will be treated. And, most important, by deliberately encouraging opportunities where experiences can be

shared, you create the possibility of finding a common
thread and a common language—a basis for actually
communicating with each other.

○ **Work to encourage participation.**
To get a collaborative dialogue off on the right foot and
keep it there, you must take steps to draw the other parties
into the process. That means managing the process so that
people feel involved and know where they are at critical
points in the process. It also means managing the process so
that people have the right information and a common sense
of what has already been achieved so that they can move
forward on the basis of shared assumptions.

○ **Work to keep the dialogue going.**
At times it is difficult to keep the conversation going. But as
long as you continue talking, there is a chance to come
together. It takes time for trust and rapport to be
established and for the other person's story to emerge. It
takes time for people to adjust to seeing things differently.
The steps you take to keep the dialogue going provide that
time.

○ **Work to get everyone to "own" the problem.**
For a counterpart to have a real stake in working with you,
he or she must recognize that the problem itself is a mutual
one. The work you do to create a shared history and to link
your issues with the other person's makes joint ownership
more likely. Only when your counterpart buys into the
problem with you can you explore mutual solutions.

Collaboration Is Not Easy
Kate Griscomb has faced multiple challenges in getting
collaboration to work. Kate, an English major with no
formal technical training, plies her marketing skills in

a high-tech company in Silicon Valley, and friction has been more the norm than the exception with the engineers in R&D who dominate the company.

The thirty-something mother of two characterizes the company culture as "pretty low key and nonconfrontational." Policy appears to be made by walking around, talking, catching people on the run. "The place is an informal, quirky democracy where people tend to settle in for the duration," Kate says. "People stick around for a long time, and they know they are going to bump into each other later at some point."

All is not so calm under the surface, however. Priorities have a way of being set at the top and filtering down, and R&D propels the company. Marketing seldom gets equal airtime. As soon as Kate is put in charge of launching an innovative medical software package, she notices a pronounced uptick in the friction between marketing and R&D. "This tension is not without cause," she says. Marketing decisions focus on the client, but in R&D the schedule rather than client satisfaction drives the decisions.

I'm always the bad news lady, screwing up the engineers' schedules. Everyone knows we could have a better product. But why should the engineers put their schedules at risk when they're what they are being measured on?

Kate envisions her role as being the client's voice in internal decision making, of bringing the client into the debate. What she can actually offer the firm's clients, however, depends upon a proposal's reception among the engineers in R&D. Wearing two hats, advocating for the linkage between the client's concerns and the company's goals, she trips alarms at two points. The first resistance comes from obvious and to-be-expected turf issues. Who has the final say, R&D or marketing?

The second is less visible and stems from the ambiguity of her role. The engineers in R&D wonder whose side she's really on—the company's or the client's, whose case she constantly pleads.

The issues are complex on both fronts. "This place has zero tolerance for discrimination. It doesn't matter whether it smacks of racism, or sexism, or ethnic prejudice." That said, Kate still points to problems.

The engineers in R&D just don't think someone from marketing can understand their problems. It's impossible to parse out whether that's because I'm a woman or because I lack the technical training.

Lessening the tension between marketing and R&D is Kate's number-one priority. Later installments of the story will show how the connected way in which she goes about that project has interesting ramifications for the entire company.

Work to Make Room for Relationship Building

How we think about a negotiation affects the solutions we are liable to come up with. Mental models tend to shape our actions. If we approach a negotiation as an adversarial or competitive contest, we think in terms of winners or losers. Bargaining over the price of a car or condo, we know the game and what is required of us. Our role is clear—we are either a buyer or a seller—and we play out a familiar script. Usually we don't care if we ever encounter the other party again. But this script is next to useless if our negotiation involves longer-term relationships or more complicated problems. We cannot perform as disinterested buyers or sellers. We need to engage our counterpart in a different process, one where we both acknowledge the stakes and the promise. That engagement, in turn, depends on reaching a certain comfort level with each other. Right from the start of a negotiation you can work to put the other person at ease.

Creating a comfortable space. When people are ill at ease with each other, suspicious of each other's motives, or intent on pursuing specific agendas, their exchange is constricted. A space—physical and psychological—must be structured that makes them comfortable. Negotiations, even among the most amicable players, can be charged with emotion and anxiety. Large sums of money, reputations, futures, and relationships are often on the line. To get a productive dialogue going, you first have to create an atmosphere in which friendly meanings attach to words and actions.[4]

The setting of a negotiation—both physical and psychological—has a subtle and sometimes not-so-subtle impact on its process. It affects the dynamics of the conversation. Both sides recognize that a setting can be manipulated to lessen awkwardness or increase tension. Where a meeting is held sends a signal about control. Seating people in low chairs or on the opposite side of a wide expanse of desk sets the stage for an attempt to dominate. Sitting everyone in comfortable loveseats conveys welcome. The same goes for psychological settings. When no one occupies the metaphorical head of the table, differences in status are downplayed.

Making people physically and psychologically comfortable establishes a baseline for behavior. At a very basic level, it lets people know how you operate and how they can expect to be treated. When they realize they won't be forced to sit with a symbolic sun in their eyes or left to squirm in the outer office, mutual respect becomes a given. This is not a question of whether you have the clout to make them cool their heels for half an hour. It's about the kind of negotiation you want to have. When your gestures show that you notice things about them and are willing to accommodate them, they signal your regard for them as people.

Marisa, a successful real estate developer in her late thirties, pays particular attention to setting in part, she says, because she is a "people person," but also to distance herself from the reputation real estate developers enjoy. "I want anyone I'm doing business with to know that we are not all unscrupulous."

> *People come in expecting me to be out to dupe them. I have to try to overcome this prejudice, and it's not easy. Almost always they are suspicious. One of our new tenants, a fashion photographer, wanted to paint his loft purple, but he started out making outrageous demands on a whole host of topics. Those other demands were just a screen to protect his real interest. He came on strong because he thought I'd automatically fight him on every point. You cannot get to the heart of things, to what others really want, unless they feel comfortable with you.*

Earlier in her career, Marisa admits, she frequently wanted "to cut to the chase. Get right down to business." But as Oscar Wilde wrote, "Experience is the name every one gives to their mistakes"—and experience has taught Marisa to be much more responsive to who is sitting across the table. Marisa generally starts out with the power balance tipped in her favor, but deliberately creates a perception of equal footing.

Are they sensitive to the courtesy of being called Mr. or Mrs.? Or distrustful of too much formality? Are they fastidious about their dress? If they are, I use the conference room instead of my messy office. Are they a forest or a tree person? Do they start with the big picture or the details? With the foresters I'll draw up an outline and not pin down too much.

By working to make the other person comfortable, you offer tangible proof of how you prefer to do business and lay the groundwork for the kind of negotiation you want to have. Marisa, for example, usually begins a negotiation knowing she is in control and takes steps to neutralize the negative impact differences in status can have on the negotiation. Her actions are symbolic gestures of inclusion.

Such symbolic gestures have many uses. Eric, charismatic and demanding, launched an effort to recruit trainees in the inner city for his high-tech firm. From a business perspective, this move made sense. The company had a vested interest in its talent pool. And the way Eric went about making that effort sent an unequivocal and connected message to his managers and to the prospective trainees. He personally interviewed the first half dozen recruits, but not on site. He took them to the local hamburger joint where the atmosphere and the dress were casual. Once they were comfortable with him, he arranged for younger staff to give them a Cook's tour of the firm's headquarters. The training program filled up in record time.

Kate's efforts to put the engineers in R&D at ease with her take another direction. She goes out of her way to meet the engineers on their turf. A wider gulf separates Kate's corporate office and the R&D lab than the two hundred yards of landscaped brick pathway between the two buildings. The engineers keep erratic schedules, often working into early morning and coming in late. Breakfast meetings in the marketing department's fancy conference rooms they write off as a corporate power trip.

Whenever Kate has something important to discuss, she does not schedule a meeting or pick up the phone. She walks over to the lab. Not only are the engineers more comfortable that way, she has a chance to see what is going on with them. Besides having spontaneous conversations, she picks up useful information from the cryptic messages and charts pasted on the walls and workstation dividers. These change daily and let her know when things are going well, when she can push and when she should hold off a day or so on a new wrinkle.

Establishing a "comfort zone" is more than paying attention to the seating arrangements and having hamburgers rather than a formal lunch in the company dining room. Whereas a strategic move might have you emphasizing differences, particularly those that highlight your control or status, connected actions seek to minimize them and draw the other person into a dialogue. You want to assure him or her that there is no need to be defensive or wary. The fewer elements of surprise the better. Defensive guards are not so likely to come up when others have some idea of what you are about and what they will encounter.

Creating space for rituals. Rituals bind people together.[5] Some are ceremonial occasions, with all the trappings of pomp and circumstance. Others provide quite unstructured and informal places for people to interact. From time to time, most people have a real need to doff their masks, to set aside the emblems of status and ceremony. The informal rituals of daily life—breaking bread, playing or watching a softball game, or just schmoozing—answer this need. They are times carved out of busy lives when people can meet simply as human beings unmediated by their differences. By mutual consent, defined roles get suspended temporarily in the shared experience of enjoying one another's company. As Virginia Woolf's Mrs. Dalloway puts it, dinner parties are a time to risk "one's own little point of view" for that "immeasurable delight in coming together," a time to "create" rather than "manipulate," to "combine" instead of separate.

The settings of informal rituals are places where dialogue dominates, where people can get to know one another beyond their professional or public personas. In formal negotiations, the exchange is constricted as people worry about what they might give away. Ritual occasions are more open. Not only do people speak differently in such situations, they also provide more details about themselves and discover points of connection. For many years in the garment industry, negotiators for management and labor would have a dinner right before collective bargaining began. Precisely because no one minimized the hazards ahead, they wanted a chance to encounter each other on a human level before the hard bargaining started. When they later met across the negotiating table, they had an enhanced sense of whom they were facing.

These kinds of informal rituals foster connection. A highly placed elected official we'll call Susan was brought up in a household where food automatically appeared as soon as any "big" issues came up or someone was out of sorts. The habit,

she says, is almost imprinted on her DNA. Even in her professional life, she brings out food whenever she feels the need for
a warming-up period or things get tense.

> *When we were hammering out the judicial reform, we
> were working around the clock. On Saturday mornings, I'd
> get coffee and donuts for everyone. I wasn't trying to be
> manipulative. By having lunch brought in or taking a
> break, you get to know one another very differently. It
> doesn't matter what the food is. So tell me about your
> daughter. She's going to be a vet? In my experience, those
> confidences change the dynamic in the room. Not 100 per-
> cent. But they help.*

They help by filling in the blanks, casting people in rounder
dimensions. We've all taken part in the sometimes frantic "do
you know" game played at the start of a negotiation with relative strangers. Informal rituals provide a more leisurely way of
finding points of connection.

In Susan's peregrinations around Capitol Hill and political
caucuses, she has observed a dramatic fault line in the way some
professionals view connecting rituals. For some, these occasions
are a natural extension of how they deal with people, and they
enjoy them. Others are more ambivalent. They balk at partic-
ipating because of the time it takes, time that distracts everyone from the real agenda. But they miss important
opportunities, she says. To illustrate she points to a small working group she chairs.

> *We start the meetings at 12:30 with lunch. Most of the
> members are always there, right on time. But one of mem-
> bers, a woman, often comes late.*

One guy had just taken his daughter on a golfing weekend for four days. He was all excited to tell us what he had done with her. This woman who has too much to do and skips lunch doesn't hear about the golf trip. She's probably the same age as the guy's daughter, and they would have a ton of places to connect. Later, if they disagreed, it would be a very different kind of disagreement, but she doesn't bother.

Susan's "professional" is all business. Her demeanor signals to everyone that she is basically uninterested in them as people. Asserting her independence from the group, she makes sure that if any informal linkages are made, they won't involve her.

She arrives with her yellow pad in hand and her list of ten or fifteen issues. All she wants to do is get through those items and then go on to the important things she has to do. She gets visibly annoyed if there is any personal chat. Everybody wants to get the deal done, but most realize the going won't be smooth unless each has a sense of where the other people are coming from. That's even more important when things get rough. She misses all that.

What is specifically missing is not just the time spent in schmoozing or at lunch. It is a willingness to suspend roles, to set aside the professional persona, and meet people without the buffer of a title or a particular piece of work that needs to get out the door. Kent understood this as he angled for a new leadership job in the regional office of his accounting firm.

Recently relocated to the office and with a new baby at home, Kent hadn't had a chance to get to know the regional manager. Before throwing his hat into the ring for the new position, Kent set out to spend some informal time with him. Golf would have been ideal, but Kent didn't play. He was, however, interested in community affairs, so he organized his firm's sponsorship of an event at the local Boys Hope Girls Hope chapter and enlisted the regional manager's help. With the event as a backdrop, they began to have planning lunches. These informal meetings were not the reason that Kent eventually got the promotion (nor were they the reason he took on the event), but they helped Kent and the regional manager get to know each other in a different way and made it easier for the regional manager to recognize Kent's abilities.

> Kate, recognizing the chill in her working relationship with the engineers, looks for occasions when she can take off her marketer's hat and interact with them more casually. The engineers are a tight group, brought together in part by their common rituals and in part by their idiosyncrasies. They share a particular addiction to junk food, a fondness for practical jokes, and a work ethic that merges with play.
>
> Each summer the "nerds" organize a lunchtime Olympics. People from all departments—from the mailroom to the CEO's office—get assigned to teams and play volleyball, softball, and Frisbee. Whenever she can, Kate now joins in. "I've gotten to be a real killer with the Frisbee, but that is beside the point. The object is to have fun." Kate has also started dropping in on the engineers' monthly "martyr-reward" ceremony at which they hand out a plaque for the department member voted most sleep deprived over the past four weeks.

Ritual occasions like these provide opportunities for people to let down their hair and see each other in different settings. Rapport cannot help but build as they step outside their usual roles and come to understand each other better. When, for example, Kate joined the engineers at play, she began to have a much better sense of the constant strain under which they worked and their need for an outlet.

Creating space for storytelling. It is commonplace during breaks for negotiators to connect with each other outside their roles. But rituals that enable us to know each other better do not have to take place off-line. People can also come together over the problem or the task at hand. Prompting opportunities for them to tell their stories helps that coming together.

A good many factors motivate people when they negotiate. They may throw themselves behind an issue or remain lukewarm for personal reasons. An outcome may be good for the company in the long run, but bad for their career in the short term. They may cushion their demands out of a need to protect a relationship. If we think about interests analytically, almost as an objective third-party observer, and shut out all but the rational or obvious, we can perhaps identify these factors, but only perhaps.

Stories are different from objective accounts. They fill in informational gaps, but beyond that they embellish the facts, giving them color, a context and a history. The power of stories is that they link the teller and the listener and provide the means of finding a common language and common values. Bargainers cannot recognize shared interests unless they can talk to each other and be understood. When people swap stories about their situation, they are talking about what they value as well as what they want.

Interests and values need to be distinguished in negotiations. They are often taken to be the same thing, but they are not. Interests are what we want and need. They can be translated with relative ease into a currency we can trade. Values, on the other hand, cannot be traded or compromised—and yet they often define what a negotiator holds most dear.[6] When we discover something about the other person's value system, we open a window on what drives his or her decisions. Differences in interests we can bargain over; differences in values require another order of understanding before we can work through them. We face this clash between values and interests in many communities. When a developer comes to call, conservationists concerned about urban sprawl and the bird habitat may not be receptive to any proposal, no matter how lucrative. Union members, on the other hand, may care more about jobs than about birds or an increase in blacktop.

Storytelling, when woven into a negotiation's fabric, provides a means for the participants to express not only their interests but their values as well. Both can bridge to good agreements. As people come to know each other in a deeper way, their understandings become less superficial. Generally, they are better able and more willing to tackle the difficult issues dividing them. Storytelling is not the norm in negotiations. You must incorporate opportunities for it or else generally all you will hear is a list of the other party's demands.

Building a storytelling framework is central to how some people negotiate. They consciously move the negotiation toward the narrative mode in order to increase the information everyone has at hand and to draw out different perspectives. By pushing for greater expansion and coming down on the side of multiplicity rather than simplicity, which storytelling does, they build into the negotiations a distinct possibility of a different ending, one not envisioned in the beginning.

Tamara grew up in a small eastern European town where children are weaned on folk tales. Now a health-care consultant in Cleveland, she works for the city's major teaching hospital. Over the past few years, Tamara has watched the area hospitals consolidate. Strategic partnering has real advantages. But, she cautions, wagging an admonishing finger, bigger is not necessarily better. "My mother used to remind us all the time that you cannot make soup from a stone. However good a potential merger looks on paper, in operation it can be a disaster." When Dr. Black, the head of her hospital, sounded her out on the possibility of a merger with City Hospital, she was skeptical. "The whole idea," she says with a throaty laugh, "reeked of problems."

The only thing the two institutions had in common was generic—they were both in the health care business. But the way they practiced medicine and delivered services diverged at every conceivable point. City provided a safety net for the urban poor in the blighted downtown area. Its plant was antiquated; its staff dedicated to service. Predictably, her teaching hospital prided itself on its research and its state-of-the-art facility. The differentials in pay were substantial across the board. Dr. Black was strong-willed and opinionated. The head of City matched him in stubbornness. They were, Tamara suspected, likely prospects for endless battles over turf.

When an excited Dr. Black outlined a broad-brush proposal, Tamara politely suggested he take several steps backward. "Slow down," she advised. "There are synergies here because our institutions have almost nothing in common. We don't overlap, but we don't talk the same language, either. How can we negotiate a merger and have it be successful?"

*We started, instead, by convening small groups of adminis-
trators and senior physicians from various services at both
institutions. Merger, even the concept, was never mentioned. These sessions were billed as get-togethers to discuss
health-care reform. Participants were specifically encouraged to talk about their history, what worked and what
didn't. At first, you'd have thought they all walked on
water. Gradually they opened up.*

When the possibility of a merger was eventually raised, the
turf issues and disparities in mission and practice remained, but
the participants' suspicions had, at the very least, been blunted.
"It doesn't matter what you are involved in," Tamara maintains.
"You still have to speak the same language. You cannot talk to
each other otherwise, no?" People, even busy doctors, she finds,
discover they can communicate more directly through stories.
They are able to build on similar experiences or the odd anec-
dote. "It's not too different from swapping war stories."

Sometimes others listen to stories with a jaundiced ear at
first. They hear them as self-serving accounts or question the
motives behind them. Bias is pretty much read into the tale.
That is, in part, the function of storytelling. It puts on the table,
or at least allows to surface in shadowy form, the negative personal assumptions people are making about each other. Understanding derives as much from airing these negative attitudes
as from learning more about specific wants or needs.

In the initial stages of Kate's negotiations with R&D,
the client, while more than familiar to her, was a relatively unknown commodity to the engineers. With
major responsibility for marketing the new product,
Kate spent most of her time translating the client's
demands to the engineers.

When I came to the engineers, I was usually asking for something that would throw a monkey wrench into their schedule. The request might make the product better or the customer happier, but it screwed up the engineers' timing.

Meetings to decide which "bells and whistles" on the client's demand list would actually be included in the product quickly split into opposing camps. "The marketing people did not understand why R&D couldn't just give the client what it wanted. The engineers kept saying no way. Suddenly," Kate says, "the reason jumped out at me."

I was so focused on my customers' concerns, I had started to sound like a broken record, not appreciating the incredible pressures R&D was under. We are measured against schedules in marketing too, but we have more flexibility. If marketing gets caught in a time crunch, we can let some of the pieces go. Engineering doesn't have that luxury. A more formal sequence is involved in designing a product and working out the bugs. When they get surprises, which almost always happens, those blips ripple through the entire project, causing delays and headaches.

With this realization, Kate reversed direction. Instead of pressing her concerns in the lab, she began to push the engineers out into the field. At a trial site, the engineers could talk directly with a client, without her serving as a conduit or a buffer. To help solve "her" problem, Kate converted what were two-way disputes—between R&D and marketing—to three-way discussions involving the engineers, herself, and the client. She brought the client's story into her negotiations with the engineers.

As soon as the engineers had a chance to listen to the customer, they started to understand it wasn't a question of bells and whistles versus their schedules, but what trade-offs had to be made. "When they came back from these visits," Kate says, "we were singing the same song, maybe not at the same volume yet, but we were getting close."

Difficulties still arise—and often. But because the engineers have come face to face with the client and its dilemmas, they no longer see Kate as a source of their troubles. She's someone with whom they share a problem that has to be puzzled through.

Making room for relationship building is a prerequisite for a collaborative negotiation. The other party must feel comfortable with you before he or she begins to accept that your commitment to a mutual solution is genuine. The invisible work that you do to provide the space for rapport to grow not only signals the tenor you want the negotiation to take, it also provides an opportunity to get to know each other better, whether you are sharing a coffee break or swapping stories.

WORK TO ENCOURAGE PARTICIPATION

Collaborative problem solving requires that people feel included and involved. Legitimizing their individual concerns is a prerequisite, but managing their involvement on an ongoing basis can still be a challenge. In complex negotiations especially, it is tricky to keep the parties engaged. All have different interests and concerns that can cause them to defect from an emerging consensus at any time. To prevent this splintering, negotiators need to manage the process so that its structure is clear and manage the agenda so that people know where they are at any given time. But to be in a position to intervene when the possibility of impasse looms, bargainers must have a mental map of the parties and where they stand.

Keeping the process transparent. Negotiations can get confusing. Sometimes no one knows where they are in the process or how they got there. Confusion like this breeds suspicion and can be just plain disheartening. Making sure everyone is equally informed and in the loop keeps them engaged. When people all have the same cut at the information, they are much more likely to trust the process and their fellow participants. Equal access to information goes a long way toward convincing people that nothing underhanded is taking place behind their backs.

Negotiations can also be chaotic, especially when things move quickly or take unexpected turns. If people leave a negotiation session and discover later that what was agreed upon was not at all their understanding, they feel duped or see themselves as the victim of a dirty trick. By circling back and reviewing your progress, you avoid misunderstandings about what has been said and what has been accomplished.

These connective steps build commitment to the process, but they also affect the content of the discussion. Everyone starts in the same place, inside the circle. Once individuals are drawn in as active participants, they become vested in the process and have a different stake in its success. The exchange becomes freer and more collaborative.

Information performs many functions in a negotiation. It can be a source of power or a defense against attack. It can also be the means of bringing people together. Sharing information is an act of trust. It tells everyone that there is nothing hidden. That's why Sarah manages the information flow in her negotiations so zealously. "When someone suspects he or she is not getting the whole story," she says, "participation becomes guarded." Sarah practices corporate law in a high-powered New York firm, where she specializes in putting together complex mergers and acquisitions. Although she deals only in friendly takeovers, time pressures are excruciating and tempers fray easily. "The kitchen," she says, "can get pretty hot. You don't want somebody flying off the handle or forging ahead when you haven't reached any real consensus."

Two points, she finds, are critical in any session: How it begins and how it ends. At both moments, she takes deliberate steps to make sure everyone is operating from the same assumptions. Before a marathon conference call gets under way, she calls a time-out.

> *Can we spend just a minute now that everyone is hooked in and see where Jim thinks this thing is coming out? Where Marcia thinks it's coming out. Where Al thinks it's coming out. I guarantee those are all different right now, and we need to be on the same page.*

Keeping everyone in the fold and the process moving are not easy tasks. When talks begin to stall, Sarah communicates her concern immediately. With what she calls "reality checks," she lets all the key players know that progress has bogged down, but is scrupulous about not attaching any blame.

> *If everyone starts screaming at each other about who is slowing things down, they will never be able to work together once we put the deal to bed. They're still in the courtship phase, and it takes a certain amount of patience. We'll get on the same page eventually. We may be a couple*

of chapters behind, but I'd rather spend a little more time.
You cannot assume anything, particularly consensus.

If all the participants need to start from the same working assumptions, they also need to come away from each session with the same notion of where they are. At the end of every session Sarah circles back, checking that everyone has matching impressions of what has been agreed upon. This practice reveals cracks in the consensus while simultaneously reinforcing what has been accomplished.

Getting on the same page, circling back and circling round, Sarah not only captures people in the process, she establishes personal ties and builds a sense of trust. Everyone knows they are getting the whole story. "This softens the ride when the negotiation is bumpy. Once they know they're getting all the information and don't have to be suspicious," she says, "there is nothing that brings people together faster than a shared sense of imminent disaster." Even with these steps, there are times when more effort is required to keep people involved and certain individuals on board.

Creating a trusting environment. Trust is not a given in negotiation. Indeed, most of the time, negotiators start the bargaining process with wariness. Before you can engage people in collaborative problem solving, you need to dispel that wariness so that a sense of trust emerges among the parties and comes to characterize their working relationship. But in a complex negotiation, not all parties are equally important. Some have the power to make or break an agreement. Others will likely follow along. It is important to map these relationships—who is likely to be an ally in your efforts and who might block a potentially creative agreement. Trust building with blockers takes work, because they automatically start out distrusting the process.

For example, Gregory faced entrenched opposition when he negotiated an acquisition for his bank. Gregory's bank, based in Denver, wanted to move into the growing Latino market and had its eye on a group of banks located in New Mexico. The Denver bank's reputation for predatory lending and overzealous closing of branches automatically aroused suspicion among community groups. Gregory had a brief window of opportunity to seal the deal, but the situation was rife with conflicting interests. For starters, powerful community groups made a series of demands. They wanted a commitment from Gregory's bank that it would change its lending practices and they also wanted a list of likely branch closings. The legal and retail departments in Gregory's organization rejected these demands on all counts. To make the deal happen, Gregory had to dispel the suspicion and mistrust among these disparate parties so that they could engage on the issues.

Gregory knew the community leader, Ileana, and sympathized with her stand. He also believed the acquisition created an opportunity for his bank to take a leadership role in the Latino community in New Mexico. So while he labored with the legal department to come up with acceptable language, he also worked hard to build a relationship with Ileana. He was in constant communication with her—they spoke almost weekly. She knew how to reach him at any time. He worked through senior management to get retail to share information on possible branch closings. He arranged for the managers of different business lines to come to the meetings with the community group to talk about their lending practices and to hear from the community.

All Gregory's work to create a trusting environment with Ileana paid off. Right up until the very end, despite multiple drafts from legal, there was no agreement on the language for predatory loans. Gregory kept at it, translating back and forth between legal and Ileana, until they were close. Finally, because he had established a good working relationship with Ileana, he was able to make a final appeal. "Look how far we've come—it would be a shame not to reach a deal now. I can't push the bank any further." Because of the trust he had taken the time to build, she believed him. Together they had broken new ground.

> Something, Kate thought, is out of kilter in the way we handle contract negotiations with clients. Engineering is responsible for getting the products to the client on time, but the group gets involved only at the tail end of the negotiations. With this insight into the possible cause of the engineers' frustration, Kate begins to engage the engineers actively in initial contract negotiations—when price and schedule are first worked out. She now e-mails the group as soon as a client requests a proposal. Rather than inundate the engineers with detail, she keeps these updates brief—what the client will be looking for and when. By alerting the engineers, she improves her chances of getting their complaints and suggestions before rather than after the fact. By keeping her actions transparent and by working to create trust, she makes it more likely that problems will surface early. The engineers, now full partners in the process, are also more likely to support her when she needs them.

Keeping the other parties involved increases their commitment to the process. Even daunting problems seem capable of solution when everyone feels they have a voice that will be heard and when the discussion unfolds within an emerging sense of trust.

Work to Keep the Dialogue Going

In real estate, location is everything. In negotiations, some people think, timing is everything. When Ann Douglas studied labor negotiations back in the early 1960s, she noticed that everyone seemed to agree when the time had come to settle.[7] At that moment the tone and tenor of the negotiation changed. People spoke faster. They didn't break for meals. Everyone focused on reaching a settlement, and generally they did.

The longer we stay in a negotiation, the more likely agreement becomes. People may just wear each other down and grasp at any out to escape. Or, having expended so much time and energy, they begin to think it is ridiculous to come away with nothing. The dilemma is somewhat akin to being put on hold on the telephone. The recording tells you calls are answered in the order they are received. You stay on the line, but agonize about when to hang up. The longer you are kept on hold, listening to Muzak, the surer you are that someone will pick up soon.[8] A similar conflict arises in negotiations. Do we continue to hang on or cut our losses? The longer we stay in the negotiation, the more that calculus shifts. Quitting becomes less and less attractive as an option. But time operates in positive ways as well.

Giving the relationship time to develop. Good working relationships are not built in a day. Bargainers can start out as wary adversaries testing and doubting each other. They may honestly believe that they have no other choice, given the circumstances.

But as long as they stay talking, there is always the possibility that their feelings about each other will change and along with them their take on the issues. What seems unreasonable at one point in a negotiation can be accepted without question at another. Given some time, relationships can develop that shift everyone's view of the issues.

For Diane, for example, issues became nonissues. Diane, a research biologist with a business degree, saw opportunity knocking when Howard approached her to join his struggling biotech firm. Too eccentric and too opinionated to fit into a corporate mold, Diane liked the idea of working with Howard. Equally appealing was the prospect of a smaller place, where she could exercise more direct control. Big, bold, and in a hurry, Diane is high-energy from her corkscrew curls to her staccato speech patterns.

> *Large corporations are not right for me. There are too many layers in the decision making. Particularly in biotech, the drug conglomerates can become the tail that wags the dog. Howard's small company seemed ideal. What's more, he needed me, or someone like me, desperately.*

Diane had worked with Howard before, both when she was a marketing vice president at a large pharmaceutical company and later when she went out on her own as a consultant. "As a scientist, he bordered on brilliant. As a businessman, however, he was a complete washout. One month to the next, Howard had no idea whether there would be money in the till to cover the rent," she recalls.

After taking a hard look at the company's revenue stream, the products on the assembly line and those in development, Diane was convinced she could reverse the flow of red ink and raise some working capital. "But," she quickly points out, "if I was going to take the risk of a turnaround, I wanted some of the rewards up front."

Diane's demands were stiff, but well within industry standards: the title of CFO, a 25 percent equity position in the company, and an annual salary of $150,000. "Howard freaked," she says. "What really sent him ballistic was the equity. I just couldn't understand his reaction. If I left within four years, he'd get the stock back anyway."

After several intense discussions, Diane began to get a clearer picture of Howard's real concerns—as opposed to the objections that he actually voiced.

> *Money was not important to Howard. He was paying himself a pittance, less than anyone else was taking home and only a quarter of what I was requesting. The only thing that mattered to him was the success of the firm. But he was in total denial. He could not admit that the company was going in the drink. He needed a business partner, but he was afraid to give up any control.*

The issue of stock was personal for Howard. To raise working capital, Diane planned to tap the venture capital markets. VC investments come with a hefty price tag—generally they take a 50 percent slice of the company and a seat on the board. Even if the turnaround were successful, Howard faced losing control of the company he founded.

> *After a few sessions I realized that I would have to backpedal. Working as a consultant for someone was not the same as being his or her partner. I was still an outsider to Howard.*

Diane shifted her target salary and dropped the equity demand altogether, deferring the difference as a future bonus. "Unless I could scrape together sufficient working capital to fund our expansion, the stock was worthless anyway. The company would fold."

The most important revision in Diane's demands had nothing to do with dollars and cents or ownership. She asked that Howard set aside lunches on Fridays to talk about where they were headed.

> *Howard was all set to have both of us write up a memo before each meeting. I quickly squelched that idea. I was afraid if we reduced everything to writing, we'd become captive of those ideas. I wanted these sessions to be more fluid, more a weighing of strategic possibilities.*

Diane's request prevented parallel monologues from developing. After a rocky start, Howard and she realized how complementary their talents were. Neither wanted to build a company and surrender control to their financing source. Considering the price of venture capital money close to extortion, Diane turned to her own networks and managed to raise all the necessary working capital through contacts in the scientific community.

Diane stopped viewing herself as Howard's lifeline, bailing him out of a dismal situation, and began thinking of herself as his partner. The perspective, now mutual, changed over time. Diane did not have to negotiate to catch up to her original demands. Before she began looking for a second round of financing, Howard voluntarily met them. "He no longer worried about losing control," Diane says, "or about my jumping ship."

Diane and Howard began their contract negotiations in a rather traditional manner—with proposals and counterproposals. Together, they developed a new story for the company and how they could work with each other. After that, the outstanding contract issues resolved themselves. What is interesting about their process is that neither of them lost anything along the way. Giving each other time, they both gained.

Stories need time to come out. Relationships need time to develop. By probing and pushing, you can discover where agreement might be possible and on what terms. You can also discover the differences are irreconcilable, but in that case nothing is lost. Talks would have terminated anyway.

Using lulls to work back channel. Sometimes the moment is not ripe for agreement. Diplomats and trade delegates speculate on this question all the time. When is it possible to negotiate? The theory is that until the other side needs to negotiate, they won't engage in serious talks and any effort to prompt action is wasted. The answer is only half right. You may not be able to come to agreement until the time is right, but you can keep the lines of communication open so that when everyone does get serious, you don't have a lot of catching up to do. This caveat holds for our everyday negotiations as well. When Francesca began negotiating a pivotal joint venture for her firm, the climate was chilly at best. But she kept her communication channels open and eventually the outlines of a deal became visible to all.

Francesca heads strategic development for a software firm. Recently its management decided the company would grow by acquiring promising applications rather than developing them in-house from scratch. Francesca targeted a small start-up that had designed state-of-the-art software that enabled working people to control their kitchens from their office computers. The CEO gave Francesca the go-ahead, but the in-house director of research was less than enthusiastic. He constantly questioned the product's commercial viability. "Officially he maintained the market was not large enough to justify the cost and the effort. Off the record, everyone knew he was opposed to any application his department had not developed internally."

Francesca retreated from actively promoting the acquisition. Instead, she began to work behind the scenes with the software designers at the start-up and with industry analysts. Gradually she drew the director of research into these discussions. This gradual approach paid off. The data Francesca had assembled, with the active help of analysts and investment bankers, all pointed to the application's potential. It could easily become a big winner. The director began to see that acquisitions like the one Francesca proposed, far from curtailing his department's authority, would actually give it a larger playing field. As soon as he started talking about how much they should pay for the acquisition, they were ready to get down to serious business and negotiate terms with the start-up.

Kate compares the process of maintaining an ongoing dialogue to taking a step into the unknown. When you are not quite sure where you are going, you have to trust each other. "It was actually easier, in some ways, dealing with R&D when we were on opposite sides of the fence. We each knew exactly what to expect."

Dialogue opens up possibilities, but even when people trust each other, they can find it hard to let go of old attitudes and step into the unfamiliar. And most people need time to recognize the benefits of changing old habits or established procedures.

Once Kate and the engineers really started talking, she realized that she was not the only one with a blind spot. Their boss, she concluded, was pretty much oblivious to the problems. As head of R&D, he was a force in the industry and one of the most confrontational negotiators in the company. Whenever Kate negotiated with him, it was always difficult. "He's funny and dynamic," Kate says. "Personally I like him very much. But we can reach a Mexican standoff with my being forceful and his being even more aggressive."

Because the new cooperation between marketing and R&D was so important and so fragile, Kate started inviting engineers on the development team to her meetings with their boss. For the first time, the head of R&D began to hear rumblings from "his" engineers, not from marketing, about the sacrosanct schedule. Privately, he considered his guys the best in the business and pushed them. They were perfectionists, and they delivered, usually on time. But now he began to wonder. Schedules were useful yardsticks, tangible and convenient, but were they the only measurement or even the right one for R&D? Things, Kate realized, were getting ripe for negotiation.

Given time, difficulties that seem insurmountable can disappear. Problems evolve into other problems. Even when significant differences remain, a growing rapport allows you to talk through them. Just keeping a dialogue going means that change remains a possibility.

Work to Get Everyone to "Own" the Problem

When we advocate for ourselves, we make strategic moves to give the other party ample reason to take our demands seriously. These carrots and sticks may bring him or her to the table ready to negotiate with us. They do not, however, guarantee that she won't fall into those old self-defeating patterns common in negotiation or that he won't see us as an adversary and push hard for his own interests. If we want the negotiation to take a different direction, one where collaboration and commitment to solving the problem together dominate, we need a process that puts our relationship with the other person on another footing. We need to take that additional step—toward discovering where and how we both need each other. If we can begin to appreciate how we need each other, then problems become joint challenges. They have to be worked out together. Neither side is responsible for precipitating a crisis nor able to solve it alone.

Looking for links in the problem's history. Typically when we sit down to negotiate, everyone involved has an individual take on the problem and the best solution, and these can diverge radically. The distance in these viewpoints widens when the problem itself is the result of something we have done in the past. Blame replaces dialogue as we try to lay responsibility for the problem on the other party, and he or she just as readily assumes it's our fault. It's tough to have a collaborative discussion when accusations are flying back and forth, even silently. To break this blaming cycle, it helps to reconstruct the history of the problem. Once we are clear on how sometimes inadvertent and quite innocent actions contributed to the present difficulties, we can begin to look beneath the convenient explanations, those hasty assumptions that pull against our seeing the problem as a common one that we can work on together.

Helen, a systems whiz who works for a large accounting firm, had her work cut out for her when she ran up cost overruns on a consulting assignment. To renegotiate her firm's fee, she had to bring the client around to admitting they had both contributed to the overruns. The conflict could only be resolved satisfactorily if they both "owned" the problem. "I'm not a bean counter," she says. "And at first I ducked the issue. I don't like to talk about fees. Besides, I was mad."

> *When we priced the contract, our figure was based on promises of all kinds of in-house assistance. This help never materialized. I had to assign extra people to the project, which put us over budget, and even then we could not finish.*

Annoyed by the lack of support, Helen plowed ahead.

> *The company's point man was a hard-nosed numbers guy who considered cost containment close to godliness. I knew getting paid for the additional staff was going to be a big problem.*

The project's first phase involved a diagnosis of the company's existing computer systems and recommendations for future software. Helen's analysis was comprehensive, but when it came time to present her recommendations, they were sketchy at best.

The VP liked the proposal, at least as far as it went. He took no responsibility for the cost overruns. Helen was the expert. She priced her team's services and would have to live with that figure.

> *He was angry. He was not about to take ownership of the overrun issue or discuss an extension of the contract. He said his own staff could have done the work for less money in half the time.*

Minutes into the meeting Helen realized two things: First, for him to see the situation in a different light, she would have to reorient the discussion, move it away from fixing blame for the overruns. Second, to be heard, everything she said or asked needed to be consistent with his view of himself as a savvy administrator in control of costs. That was the face he presented to others. Helen started by telling the story of the project from the beginning, using circular questions to draw him in.

> *At key points as I was describing my understanding of what had happened, I asked if he agreed with my account. When we got to the promised support from his staff, I wondered what he would have done had he been in my position. Although he bawled me out for not letting him know what was going on, he was starting to see my dilemma. Then I asked whether the original promise of assistance was reasonable, given his staff's workload.*

Working through the project's history, they came to a shared understanding of how one action set off another reaction. The cost overruns were neither her fault nor his. Both parties acted in good faith. His people were busy, but the assignment was also more complicated than Helen anticipated. Admission of mutual responsibility required both to take joint ownership of the problem. That acknowledgment pushed them toward a joint solution. They extended the contract, with more realistic cost parameters, and agreed to split the overrun charges. Common problems call for common solutions.

Posing questions that encourage the other person to rethink the problem. All too often in negotiations we don't put in the work that enables our counterpart to see the problem as a joint one. We tell her what is wrong and expect her to be persuaded by the elegance of our arguments. We take up a lot of space trying to convince him we are right and give him (and ourselves) little room to learn and reflect on the situation. As a result, the real problem gets defined within restricted and limiting boundaries.

Kim pushed those limits in a negotiation with her boss about procedures in their community hospital by posing questions that encouraged her to confront a problem she was studiously avoiding. New insurance guidelines mandated that the hospital could not collect fees even for minor procedures unless an attending physician was present. Kim's boss consistently turned a blind eye when these guidelines were ignored. Kim, in turn, worried that an audit would turn up the violation. The hospital's reimbursements would be cut and she would be blamed. Despite Kim's warnings, her boss remained unfazed.

> *The violations were both unsafe and illegal, but the guidelines put my boss in a tough spot. She's under pressure to keep costs down and at the same time is faced with regulations that make that impossible. Our expenses for medical staff would skyrocket under the new guidelines.*

The negotiations between Kim and her boss were poised for deterioration. Kim thought her boss was tolerating illegal, unsafe procedures. Her boss, on the other hand, dismissed Kim's concerns as nit-picking and self-serving. "To her, the chances of an audit were slim. The increased costs made the risk worth taking." Rather than continue to press her boss on the disaster an audit would cause, in a "tell and sell manner," Kim began to ask questions rather than state facts.

> *I started by asking her to assess the risks with me. Neither of us considered the probability of being audited particularly*

high. We agreed on that. But what would happen if we were wrong? What would be the consequences? As we went through them, we also agreed that they looked pretty bad. Not only would we be denied reimbursements, we would be savaged in the press and lose public confidence.

Kim's boss did not change her mind about the real problem overnight. She asked Kim to gather information on how the guidelines were implemented at other hospitals. That small step was a beginning. Gradually they began to look at the problem together, as one that affected them both but in different ways, and one for which they had to come up with a workable solution.

Asking for help. It seems simple enough on the surface. If you want someone to own a problem, ask for help. An appeal for help can be an important connective overture to bring another person into the process. But that is not always easy to do. Worries get in the way. The request might be construed as an admission of inadequacy, an inability to handle the problem.

Larry set aside these worries when he negotiated with his boss for more resources. The needed support would never materialize unless the division manager owned the problem with him. To get joint ownership, Larry asked for help.

Larry runs several information technology projects in his firm. Economic conditions prompted a corporate mandate to keep head count flat. Between increases in the number of projects and staff attrition, Larry knew his team would not be able to meet its commitments on time. He had several choices. He could try to slow down his projects or defer some of them. This was risky not only for the business but also for his career.

After complaining to some of his colleagues, Larry decided to negotiate formally for more resources. First he had to convince the division manager there was a problem. He created a presentation that described the extent of the problem. One chart arrayed the system functionality gains against head count. It demonstrated the progress that had been made in the face of decreasing head count. Another chart plotted the workhours needed to complete the projects over the next year against what he actually had available. It was clear that there was no way the work could be done. After framing the problem, instead of asking for more resources, Larry asked for help.

The division manager's first reaction was that nothing could be done. The rule on flat head count was firm. Larry asked the division manager what he would do in Larry's place. They continued to talk about the problem. The division manager came up with a novel idea. The next time Larry lost an employee, rather than replacing that person, he could contract out the work. That way they could get more project work done for the money invested. Larry had never considered contract workers; it was not something that had been tried in his division. The solution came from the division manager, but it would not have been possible without Larry's careful presentation and an explicit appeal for help.

> Kate knew from the start that she wanted to renegotiate the terms on which she and the engineers in R&D dealt with each other. Besides casting her as the bad news lady, the adversarial bickering accomplished nothing. What started as an effort on Kate's part to open a dialogue with R&D turned into thorough rethinking of departmental relationships and standards for performance.
>
> As Kate and the engineers began to experience the problem from each other's perspectives, they came to

realize they had been focusing on the wrong thing. The source of their difficulty was not the client, or marketing, or R&D. Within their company's seemingly easy-going environment, they uncovered a core inflexibility that caused trouble for everyone. Internal standards and rigid performance criteria made it impossible not to leave someone dissatisfied, usually the client and marketing. As long as the engineers were evaluated on output time, responsiveness to client demands would suffer. They asked the head of R&D for help. After listening to Kate and his engineers, he broadened the limited conversations to a company-wide debate. What was good performance? How should they measure it?

The people you negotiate with seldom experience an epiphany and suddenly own a problem with you. It takes work to bring them along with you so that they recognize their part. A sense of interdependence cannot be forced on them. It must emerge from a deeper understanding that you are both implicated in the problem and must work on its solution together.

o   o   o

Cumbersome and time-consuming, collaborative negotiations create a context where mutual concerns can emerge. When people connect in a negotiation, they relate to each other differently. Because they can appreciate each other's situations and concerns, trust can build.

How the conversation is conducted is as important as *what* the conversation is about. Collaborative agreement making moves beyond the sometimes one-sided strategic exchange of information. Each action, each comment, has mutual implications that must be appreciated. Expecting cooperation, not domination or a forced compromise, bargainers can be more open in their exchange. Differences can be considered from various vantage points, not battled over. With more mutuality built into the discussion, understandings deepen and open up multiple paths to agreement. That's what the invisible work of relationship building makes happen in a negotiation.

Part Three

Putting It All Together

Balancing Advocacy and Connection

Chapter 7

Crafting Agreements

Advocacy and connection go hand in hand. If effective advocacy enables you to claim a place at the table and garners credibility for you and your demands, the relational skills of connection define the engagement that takes place. You cannot ignore either, but where you put the emphasis varies from one negotiation to the next and within a single negotiation. The balance struck between them is often a matter of personal preference, and bargainers tilt in one direction or another. Experience teaches some negotiators to press hard for what they want and not give an inch, while others depend primarily on their ability to connect. Seldom, however, does any negotiation present a stark either/or choice between advocacy and connection.

The shadow negotiation is where masked attitudes and hidden agendas play out. The personal dynamic established there is defined by the strategic moves and connecting overtures you choose to use. But there is also an interaction between the shadow negotiation and the negotiation over the issues. This interplay affects the balance between advocacy and connection that you strike regardless of whether you personally lean in one direction or the other.

How advocacy and connection come to be blended does not depend solely on the person doing the mixing. Different circumstances and different issues demand different combinations. The mix will not be the same when you are haggling with a used-car dealer as when you are trying to negotiate changes in your department. The issues or problems involved impose their own discipline on your choice. So far we have focused on the impact that advocacy and connection have on the shadow negotiation. Now we turn our attention to the ways that the problem at issue affects your advocacy and relationship building.

When the actual issues at dispute are considered, as opposed to the relational aspects of the shadow negotiation, making an agreement is typically framed in one of two ways: as a contest to be won or lost or as a search for joint gains.[1] In win-lose negotiations, bargainers split up or distribute a resource. Usually a single resource is at stake, and money is involved in one form or another. Most of these negotiations end with some compromise. No one loses out entirely or wins everything.

This kind of bargaining is categorized as win-lose because the more one side wins, the more the other loses, and vice versa. When you buy a car, haggle for a rug in a bazaar, maybe even negotiate a salary, you are operating within this framework. We prefer to call the model not win-lose but *pushing*. As a label, pushing captures what actually happens in the negotiation. Each party wants to leave the table with the biggest share of the resources—whether that is the asking price for a house or the requested raise or an extra week of vacation. Since the resources to be divided are fixed, you want to push your agenda so that the final division goes your way. As a result, the balance in both the shadow negotiation and the negotiation over issues leans heavily toward the use of strategic moves and turns. You use the tools of effective advocacy to pressure the other party to make more concessions than he or she had intended.

Even in these pushing kinds of negotiations, relying only on the tools of advocacy can incur hidden costs. You may go into a bargaining session thinking you know the price you are willing to pay or be paid and the costs associated with victory. But winning, getting the best deal, depends on how *best* is defined. The full price on the table is often not limited to a single resource like money. Opportunity, goodwill, time, or the quality of a relationship may be at stake. In pushing, money or some other currency can be left on the table. As a matter of fact, one of the mistakes negotiators consistently make is to assume that they are dealing with a fixed pie and that their only challenge is to figure out how to split it.

When negotiation is defined as a search for joint gains, connective skills become more important. Joint gains come from making trade-offs that benefit everybody and leave as little behind as possible. In the parable of the orange we told in the Introduction, for example, the expanded solution becomes not the rind or the juice but the whole orange. Neither the rind nor the juice goes to waste, and both sisters get their needs met. Packaging is the term we use to describe this type of negotiation. Rather than push for what you want, you try to discover the different interests in play—rind or juice—and make a trade based on those differences. In other words, you come up with package deals. To discover interests and needs, you must connect at some level with the other person.

mutual inquiry

Based on our interviews with negotiators, we think there is a third type of negotiation—one we call *mutual inquiry*.[2] Mutual inquiry builds explicitly on the open relationships and trust forged in the shadow negotiation. Whereas pushing and packaging do not require fundamental changes in the relationships between bargainers to reach an agreement, mutual inquiry sets them in motion. As an empowered advocate, you are a full participant in the inquiry, and your invisible work of connection encourages the other person's full participation as well. Mutuality grows precisely because the relationships change in the shadow negotiation. With trust building on both sides, you and your counterpart can be more candid and learn from each other. Appreciation for one another's concerns deepens as the communication becomes more open, and this increased understanding makes it possible to see where individual interests intersect with common concerns. Bargainers who engage in mutual inquiry are apt to reevaluate what they want. In the process, they often redefine the problem itself.

There is nothing that automatically makes a negotiation one type or another. Buying a car appears to require only pushing. You want the best model for the lowest price. But things get more complicated once you have another car to trade in and financing options to consider. The visit to the car dealer now calls for some packaging. Negotiations with close colleagues gravitate to mutual inquiry. Yet when time is short and decisions must be made, pushing usually takes over.

Most negotiations can be carried out in different ways. You have choices in the process you pursue—pushing, packaging, or mutual inquiry—and in the balance you strike between advocacy and connection. Of course, the decision is not totally up to you. The other person may have a very different process in mind and shift in another direction. Then it may be necessary for you to recalibrate that balance.

PUSHING

Pushing is the strategy you need when you find yourself in a win-lose negotiation. You and the person with whom you are negotiating are adversaries. You are adversaries not because of how you feel about each other but because of the structure of the negotiation. Bargaining over a single commodity like money or time, what one wins, the other loses, and there is little you can do to change that. When you are negotiating a contract and the only issue under discussion is price, inevitably someone is going to come out ahead of the game—or think the other party has. That's true even if the resource in question is split down the middle. Everyone involved can still feel okay about the outcome, but no individual bargainer can ever be sure that he or she couldn't have done better.

In pushing, you try to cut the best deal possible for yourself, recognizing that all the while your opponent will be doing the same thing. The tactical maneuvering begins with opening offers. These camouflage real desires. No one wants to be the first to put his or her cards on the table, and people almost always ask for more than they actually need. In the back of your mind, you might be willing to settle for a 5 percent raise, but you initially demand 8 percent. Once that 5 percent figure gets on the table, it is the most you can hope to get. Starting high (or low, depending on whether you are a seller or a buyer) gives you an opportunity to learn more about what the other side wants without giving away much information about your own bottom line.

Opening offers lead to counteroffers and a series of concessions that typically get smaller until you reach a point where compromise is possible. After you have made your opening offer, you try to be as persuasive as you can about the merits of your position and stress the reasons why the other side's demands are excessive. You make your concessions slowly and reluctantly, all the time exaggerating their value. Any concessions the other side offers you treat as trivial and in no way a match for what you have put on the table. Power tactics such as bluffs and threats are common. Throughout the negotiation, you want to play your cards close to the vest. If the other party learns what you are really looking for, he or she may use that information to extract concessions from you. While compromise is inevitable in this kind of negotiation, you want to make sure you aren't the one doing all the compromising.

Pushing and the Tools of Advocacy

It is important to understand the rules of pushing. Otherwise you can end up with less than you deserve. Jessica, an architect, mastered the art of pushing to negotiate the best deal possible for her clients with a contractor. Jessica's clients in this commission were leasing new space for their art gallery. The three floors that the gallery would occupy had been gutted down to the studs. As part of the lease, the landlord had already agreed to absorb certain costs under what's called a build-out allowance. The more work Jessica got the contractor to include under the build-out allowance, the more money her clients would have left to spend on interior finishes.

Jessica preferred to rely on a small group of contractors whose work and word she trusted, but she had no choice in this negotiation. The contractor was married to the building owner's sister and came with the deal. She got her first hint that the negotiation would be adversarial when she overheard the contractor and his super joking. "No worries here, boss. Architect's not any bigger than a roll of drawings."

After reviewing Jessica's drawings, the contractor came up with a long list of items he categorized as extras that her clients would have to pay for. Jessica flatly refused. Her clients had signed the letter of intent on the basis of the landlord's verbal representations that those items would be included. The contractor protested. He didn't know anything about the landlord's promises. He certainly wasn't a party to them. Given the close relationship between the owner and the contractor, Jessica didn't trust his protestations at all. "I'd checked him out with other architects. Once I relented on any issue, it would be like opening Pandora's box. He'd push for concessions across the board."

Jessica remained firm. If that work wasn't included, she warned, her clients would think about rekindling negotiations with the owner of a building down the street. She also pushed the contractor hard on the cost of the finish work. By cutting out the padding on the "extras," she believed, they could easily reduce construction costs by $140,000. The contractor resisted, pressing for concessions on each line item. He claimed the contract was already too thin. One hundred forty thousand was impossible. Maybe he could squeeze out $50,000, but that was a long shot. Jessica, who was prepared for a prolonged battle, basically outlasted the contractor. She knew he needed to keep his crews busy, and this was a slow season. After two hours of haggling, all he said was, "Okay, but I'm not going to do a corner bead."

This negotiation—over a contract price—required pushing, and Jessica deployed all the tools of effective advocacy.

Going into the talks she knew exactly where she had leverage—and she used her information strategically. Well aware that the contractor would not want his crews idle, she held him to the owner's previous promises. She let the contractor know she and her clients had an alternative—leasing a building down the street. That signal raised the stakes for him if he continued to resist her terms.

But what about connection? What role, if any, does it play in these "pushy" negotiations? It turns out it can have a major one. Jessica looked good to her clients. She had negotiated a great price. But she had to watch the contractor like a hawk. She could not trust him not to cut corners. "That extra supervision time was the trade-off I made when I pushed only on price." The contractor's reputation and his behavior tilted Jessica toward using forceful moves and turns. "Making concessions on price was not going to get a first-rate job out of this man. Hanging tough on the price was the best protection I could give my clients."

Blending in Connection

It is possible to push in a connected way. You can advocate for your interests forcefully and still promote them in a way that makes it easy for the other party to acquiesce. Barbara, an assistant vice president for nursing, used connected pushing in a situation where price (or money) was also the issue. She negotiated a good severance agreement by showing her hospital's administrators exactly how they could give her what she wanted.

The community hospital where Barbara worked was downsizing, but for public-relations reasons wanted to keep the number of nurses that it laid off low. Barbara looked at the downsizing as an opportunity. She had been thinking about going to graduate school. Rather than wait to be laid off, she offered to resign provided she received a lump-sum payment that would cover a year's expenses at school. This was what she wanted, but she was well aware that the lump sum she requested would set a dangerous precedent for the hospital. The administrators would be bound to worry that other nurses might demand the same deal. So she was unsurprised when the hospital countered with an offer that halved her request and was roughly equivalent to what it would pay for outplacement services.

Knowing that the hospital needed to characterize any lump-sum payment in a way that did not create a precedent, Barbara proposed that the missing half be paid as a tuition reimbursement, a standard program for which she would be eligible if she remained on staff and did not leave voluntarily. The hospital administrators agreed that this suggestion was reasonable and went along with the proposal. Barbara was a clear winner here. She got exactly what she wanted. At the same time, she made the solution painless, even attractive, for the hospital administrators. They wound up paying her more than they intended, but the figure did not go beyond their obligations had she remained. Equally important, the solution allowed them to avoid bad publicity and sidestep a disastrous precedent.

Likewise, Alexander—manager of corporate purchasing for a drugstore chain—had to use connection if he wanted the local purchasing agents to buy into his new single-distributor model. When Alexander took the job, purchasing was handled separately by each store in the chain. The system was costly and inefficient, but Alexander's company had grown by acquiring local drugstores and leaving them to run their businesses more or less as they pleased. The local stores saw no need for change.

They knew the various distributors and had worked with them for years. Alexander knew they would resist a push to single distributors for various product lines.

Although Alexander could have used his position to impose his plan, he decided that it was more likely to succeed if he involved the local agents in the process. He stressed that it was in the company's best interest to adopt the plan, but he worked with the purchasing agents to develop criteria for selecting the distributors. He took his connected overtures a step further, however. Aware that abrupt change would be difficult, he brought together a committee of local purchasing agents to select the distributors and worked out a strategy to implement the new system gradually over an eighteen-month period. Participation in the selection process gave the local agents a voice in shaping the new system, while the phase-in gave them time to adjust.

Pushing has a taint associated with it. Most commentary on negotiation warns that pushing is not the best way to get good agreements and that it prompts others to use tough tactics against you. Nevertheless, being able to push effectively is an important skill for all negotiators. Some deals require it. Some people demand it simply to protect your interests. In the end, all deal making requires an element of pushing at some point in order to ensure that you come away with your fair share of whatever is being negotiated.

PACKAGING

In pushing, you stake out a specific position on an issue. You may demand, for example, a 10 percent raise. But you may be motivated by lots of reasons besides getting more money. You may want recognition for a job well done; your child-care costs may be escalating; you may feel you are losing ground to others who are paid more. Different interests like these provide the raw materials for packaging. By focusing on them, you broaden the discussion from a single issue. The idea is to create more bargaining room than generally exists when everyone sticks to fixed positions. You might not be able to get that 10 percent raise, but there might be other ways to compensate you that make up the difference—a bonus, a new office, a new title, more time off.

Gains are realized because the people involved in the negotiation are different and have different wants, needs, and goals. Some things matter a great deal to one negotiator but not to another. Preferences, capabilities, experience, and beliefs vary greatly. These differences can be converted into currencies of exchange and traded.[3] They can be used to construct options that sweeten the deal for the other party and satisfy you at the same time. If, for instance, something is important to Susan but doesn't really matter to Joe, Joe may be willing to give it up in return for something he really wants.

Mary Parker Follett gives us a nice example of how interests can be explored to come up with a creative package deal. She was sitting in Harvard's cavernous Widener Library, and one of the other readers had opened the window. The breeze was welcome, but it blew her papers all around. The solution? "We opened the window in the next room, where no one was sitting. This was not a compromise. . . . We both got what we really wanted. I did not want a closed room, I simply did not want the North wind to blow directly on me; likewise the other occupant did not want that particular window open, he merely wanted more air in the room."[4]

Packaging like this converts a negotiation from an adversarial contest over a single issue to a problem-solving activity. As different interests emerge, the prospects for new arrangements increase. Rather than fight it out over a single issue, bargainers work through various solutions until they come up with one that meets most, if not all, of their needs. The stark choice between the window closed or open gets set aside in favor of another option—opening a different window. Communications skills come to the fore as negotiators explore how their interests can be meshed in a package deal. Follett's solution hinged on the discovery that her Widener companion objected to a stuffy room but was basically indifferent on how to increase the ventilation.

Tilting Toward Connection in Packaging

The problem solving implicit in packaging works to the advantage of bargainers who dislike confrontation and are more comfortable using their ability to connect with people to work out a good solution. It is also the strategy of choice when pushing is out of the question, when the cost of alienating the other person is too high. For example, Janet manages the systems group, an internal support function, at a large pharmaceutical company. Because her group sells its services to the firm's many departments, negotiations over payment for those services are ripe for haggling over time and money. Janet struggles against being held captive to departmental calls for low pricing and fast implementation schedules. The department heads want the best system for the least cost, and they want it yesterday.

Janet's negotiations could easily turn into pushing contests, but for one thing: Janet's group provides a service to the company. She must maintain its profitability, but she cannot leave any dissatisfaction in her wake. To avoid this pitfall, Janet has become adept at developing creative packages in her dealings with the department heads. In fact, she has built her reputation throughout the company on her ability to make constructive trade-offs.

A good illustration comes from a negotiation over the updating of a unit's inventory system. Ted, the unit head, submitted a proposal to Janet's group, and over the course of several preliminary sessions Ted and Janet scoped out the work. They were now ready to begin the real negotiations over pricing and scheduling. Ted needed the system up and running as soon as possible, but was under pressure to keep costs down. Janet, of course, wanted her group to be paid a fair price for its services and would prefer more time. Her group was already stretched. As Janet and Ted discussed the project, their different priorities surfaced. Janet immediately recognized the makings of a trade. Since time was crucial to Ted and resources limited for her, she explored the possibility of Ted's unit paying a premium to get the system up sooner. With additional resources, Janet could assign more software engineers to Ted's project. She knew some of her staff would welcome the overtime. But Janet did not stop there. She suggested that Ted's people could do some of the routine preparation to keep the additional costs as low as possible.

In the end Ted chose Janet's first option. He agreed to allocate more funds to get the system up and running. Janet, in turn, committed two engineers to the project during the design phase so that the system was ready to go online in three months. They would then return to normal operations during implementation.

Package deals like these trade on differences in interests. The challenge in packaging is to peel back those interests, layer by layer. The information you discover enables you to continue to float options that satisfy you and the other party. Ted, for example, cared more about having the inventory system in place than about the marginal costs incurred in speeding the design work. The trick in packaging is to access this kind of information and incorporate it into your thinking. Effective advocacy may get your point across, but it is the connection skills you use that allow you to discover the specific packaging that makes a solution acceptable to the other party.

Sometimes the other person is reluctant to reveal much about his or her interests. If he assumes he is engaged in an adversarial, win-lose game, he is going to disclose as little as possible. Direct questions about what she wants can provoke a hostile response. Why do you want to know? Sometimes the other person is not sure about what he wants and what would satisfy him. Probing may only back him into a position he does not really prefer.

People's interests are complex, interweaving personal and career concerns. Usually they are reluctant to talk about them. When pressed, they often respond with a generalization. "We want to do what is best for the organization" or "I just want to be treated fairly." These amorphous statements are of little help in coming up with good package solutions. Because the comments are open to misinterpretation, they may actually hamper any understanding of what each side really wants. It is important to be as specific as possible in your probing of interests. You can ask general questions at first to break the ice. But answers to global questions like "Why are you interested in this issue?" or "What are your major areas of concern?" or "What are the key things you need from an agreement?" probably won't reveal much.

Targeted questions can produce more focused responses. "What about this particular option works for you?" generally gets you further than "Why do you want this agreement?" Less direct methods can be just as useful, however, particularly when the other person seems suspicious about the inquiry to begin with. Propose various scenarios and pose what-if questions that prompt the other person's opinion. Parsing those responses together often reveals which interests he cares about and which he may be willing to trade off.

Jacob realized that he would really have to probe interests during negotiations over a severance package. After his bank merged with a large commercial institution, it offered a generous severance package to people whose jobs were eliminated or whose new responsibilities did not compare to their previous positions. The first few months after the merger were chaotic. Jacob was first transferred to a different but roughly comparable position. A month later, however, he was reassigned to a more ambiguous position. Given the uncertainty in the aftermath of the merger, Jacob decided to return to school for his MBA and wanted to use his severance package to pay for it.

Jacob faced several challenges. He had a deadline of sorts. The severance package would only be in effect for eighteen months. He also needed his boss to concede that his new position was not comparable to the previous one. Jacob knew his boss's interests were complicated: All division managers were under pressure to reduce head count. In this respect, Jacob would be doing his boss a favor by taking the severance package. On the other hand, his boss had a key project that needed to be completed over the next several months. Were Jacob to leave, his boss would be caught shorthanded.

Although initial discussions were discouraging, Jacob did not give up. He sharpened his presentation about the comparisons between his current job and what he had done in the past. By understanding interests, Jacob was able to propose a package that met his boss's needs. What if he were to stay an extra three months, finish the bulk of the work on the project, and develop a transition plan with the rest of the staff? In return, his boss would agree to support his eligibility for the severance package. His boss was pleased with the proposal as it met most of his interests. Jacob stayed through the summer and enrolled in business school in the fall. He even got the outplacement benefit postponed until he finished graduate school.

Using Advocacy in Packaging

The skills of connection don't just uncover differences in interests you can use to put together creative trades; they can also alter a relationship so that options are considered and not immediately rejected. While these skills are of enormous value in coming up with a creative package, even a clever package deal can be difficult to sell. The other party may not agree that the package meets his needs and must be convinced that it does. The demand for effective advocacy does not diminish in packaging.

Sue Ellen had just been appointed executive director of the Center for Cross-Cultural Communications at a college on the West Coast. This was the college's first experience with such a program, and no one in the administration had a clear idea of what Sue Ellen should be paid. Sue Ellen, on the other hand, went to her first meeting with the new provost prepared to push hard for a specific salary level.

> *My colleagues and I had put a great deal of thought and planning into launching the center. Our financial worries were behind us. I knew we were about to get a huge grant from a foundation although the terms had not been finalized yet. I was really excited about the center's future. At my first meeting with the provost, my optimism just bubbled over. While I talked, the provost sat there. She just sat there emanating skepticism. She simply did not believe a word I said. I could picture vividly the thoughts behind that impassive face. I was exaggerating, attempting to put one over on her. No foundation would award that much money to a new, untested program. The university would end up financing the whole thing.*

At that moment any negotiation about salary was risky for Sue Ellen. She quickly realized that it would result in a bad deal for her. She tabled any effort to negotiate her salary and went to work without settling the money issues with the provost. Her friends thought she was crazy, but Sue Ellen believed she would do better in the long run if she proved to the provost that the center would be a success and that she would be a big part of that success.

Sue Ellen's ability to offer the provost a package deal, in effect, hinged on her credibility. Because the provost needed to have confidence in Sue Ellen's leadership, Sue Ellen moved strategically to demonstrate that the center would add to the college's prestige and that her contribution was pivotal to its success.

Everything I did—the lunches I had with her, the ways I raised funds, sought out projects—was aimed at proving what a good thing the center was. How terrific I was. She wasn't going to pay me what I wanted to be paid until she had some sense of the value she would be getting for her money. I also made it clear that I was not going to work without an agreement for longer than three months. That's the time I thought it would take to get everything sorted out at the center.

Once the grant came through, the provost's skepticism began to dissolve. Sue Ellen's advocacy allowed her to explore with the provost how the center's goals complemented the college's mission.

Sue Ellen used what she learned about the provost's priorities to formulate options on how she might be paid. Under one package, she proposed a low base salary and a sliding scale tied to the grants she received and the fieldwork and training programs she conducted. Under the other, she would be paid a higher salary that included a fixed fee for fieldwork and training. Sue Ellen was indifferent on the two options. She was not worried about putting some of her salary at risk. She knew she could attract research projects and build attendance for her training sessions.

Later the provost told Sue Ellen that being given the two payment schemes helped her focus on which would work best for the college. Once she was convinced of the program's viability and Sue Ellen's importance to it, the question for her became not what to pay Sue Ellen but how. She elected to go for the sliding scale. If the programs materialized, there would be additional revenues to pay Sue Ellen. If not, the college had limited its financial commitment.

Blending Advocacy and Connection in Packaging

Packaging like Sue Ellen's is a form of problem solving that builds options from differences in interests and priorities. The approach can change a negotiation from a win-lose proposition into one where joint gains are possible. But just coming up with a package deal does not ensure that the other party will agree. The elegance of the solution may not be enough.[5] Even creative suggestions can be met with recalcitrance, and this point brings us back to the shadow negotiation. Unless the other person recognizes the benefits of making a deal, even your most ingenious solutions will fall on deaf ears. For a package deal to be considered, you have to create a climate in which it will be heard as a proposal that improves the outcome for everybody.

Both advocacy and connection contribute in putting together a successful package. Strategic moves and turns provide incentives for the other person to listen carefully. At the same time, the invisible work of connection makes him or her more receptive to hearing your proposal and to providing insights into why he or she just might not think it's so great.

The essence of packaging is to uncover as much as you can about the other party's situation so that you can come up with creative ways of meeting both your interests. Although this seems obvious, it is not always easy to do. When a negotiation is viewed as (or is) a contest or the focus remains primarily on individual demands, pushing dominates. Even when the benefits of creative packaging are clear, pressure toward pushing remains. No matter how clever you have been, you still have to deal, at some point, with what's included in the package and what's left out. In other words, pushing and packaging call on effective advocacy and depend, at the same time and in varying degrees, on connecting skills.

Elyse discovered how finely advocacy and connection needed to be meshed when she was asked to take over a section of the magazine where she worked—with no additional help. She agreed to assume the added responsibilities for the magazine's next issue, subject to an important proviso. At the end of the month, she and the publisher would revisit the staffing question.

The meeting with the publisher turned into a masterful balancing of advocacy and connection. Elyse first concentrated on how difficult the past month had been. A long-time contributing editor accustomed to working on her own and handing her manuscripts on to someone else for production, Elyse suddenly found herself with more responsibility and control of a separate department. She had to decide which stories to run with what artwork, coordinate on all fronts, check that the ad revenues were sufficient, and make sure everything was ready by press time. She had too few resources at her disposal and the publisher had grossly underestimated the time she would have to spend coordinating the various departments. To continue, she insisted, she needed at least two additional staff members.

Then she switched tracks. She started to appreciate the publisher's situation. "The editor-in-chief had died suddenly, and the publisher was in a real bind." The magazine was rudderless on the editorial side, and the publisher was keeping a sharp eye on costs, fearing a drop in readership. "When I told him we all missed the editor, but he probably more than anyone, he began to open up." The publisher recognized full well that everyone was overloaded, but did not want to take on additional people at a time when subscriptions might drop precipitously. "Would I settle, he asked, for some part-time help in-house and maybe outsourcing the rest of the work?" The deal was a good one for Elyse and the publisher.

In each of these examples of pushing and packaging, a different balance is struck between advocacy and connection. Where the emphasis falls colors the shadow negotiation and, in turn, defines the agreement eventually reached. Strategic moves and turns keep your interests front and center and are basic to pushing. In packaging they continue to be important. They create the incentive for the other person to solve the problem with you. But connection plays an equally important and instrumental role. By exercising your relational skills you can fashion the particular package that has the best chance of being accepted.

MUTUAL INQUIRY

Negotiations involve at least two people, so they are by definition a mutual experience. But the way the process is actually experienced is not necessarily mutual. In pushing and packaging, responsibility rests with individuals to propose the deals or make the demands. In pushing, one side states a position and the other responds. The bargaining goes back and forth until some compromise or stalemate is reached. Self-interest also drives packaging. The negotiator in search of joint gains finds out as much as possible about the other side's interests so that he or she can enhance the package deal if further inducements are necessary. Package deals, if well constructed, leave everyone better off, even though some people may not do so well as the others. The burden in the shadow negotiation falls primarily on advocacy. Connection facilitates but does not dominate.

With mutual inquiry the balance shifts to connection. Inquiry in the context of mutuality is more than trying to solicit useful information about the other party's interests or bottom line. The process is fluid as those involved listen together, learn together, and make their agreements together. The learning that occurs transforms the dynamics at work. The focus moves from individual advocacy to mutual engagement. Interests and problems are defined as a collective enterprise, given meaning through the process. Solutions are worked out together, not proposed by individual participants to be either rejected, countered, or accepted by the others.

The need for effective advocacy does not disappear in mutual inquiry. You cannot engage in mutual inquiry unless you hold up your side of the mutual. But mutual inquiry moves beyond an instrumental concern for the other party, beyond enlightened self-interest. There is an expectation that everyone in the negotiation will be influenced by the others and be available emotionally as well as analytically. Mutual inquiry negotiations are fluid precisely because the participants expect to be influenced by one another's perspectives. They assume that something will be learned in the interaction. And, knowing more, they may change their minds not only about what would be an acceptable agreement but also about the problem that needs resolving.

Mutual inquiry builds explicitly from the relationships we develop as we negotiate. The process is rooted in the belief that there is only so much you can discover about another person's wants, needs, or feelings without his or her active participation. Questions are asked in ways that make it easy for people to talk about their situations, to tell their stories. Opinions are expressed not as categorical statements but as part of an ongoing dialogue that presents ideas for consideration and further probing. For many, it is only by talking through their needs and interests in a supportive context that they come to know what those interests really are.

Carrie headed public relations for a large mutual fund in Boston—until she was fired. This experience convinced Carrie that her financial and mental well-being depended on being in control and independent.

> *The real slap was that they fired me two months before my pension would fully vest. I promised myself that I would never again put myself in a position where someone else could mess up my bonus by a whim or kick me out without a single complaint ever being filed.*

There was a silver lining to her dismissal, however. She immediately started her own firm, taking several clients with her. Even so, being fired left an indelible mark. She wanted to be in control. She was not going to let an organization or other people have that kind of power over her. This determination shaped all her strategic decisions about her company. Then came a phone call from her major client. "Carrie," he said, "I'm paying you so much, you should be working for me full time. I want you to think about that before we meet next week."

Carrie sweated the week out. "I cannot do this," she thought. "I won't feel safe having only one client. That's just as bad as being at the mercy of a corporation."

Never before had Carrie discussed her motivations or reservations with a client. Whatever the cost, she simply produced what the client demanded. But this was not a matter of getting a client exposure in the *Wall Street Journal* or *Barron's*. This situation was personal and this particular client had given her a big boost when she most needed it. She felt she owed him an explanation for her refusal.

> *I told him everything. My history with the corporation, how unfairly I had been treated. I told him I simply could not put all my eggs in one basket, ever again.*
> *He nodded, then was silent for a while.*
> *"I didn't realize," he said finally. "I probably should have. Even if I could force this issue, which I clearly cannot, you'd be miserable. What really bothers me is that everyone knows how much I'm paying you. I need them at least to think I'm your most important client. How do we do that?"*

Rather than severing the relationship, her client offered an unexpected solution.

> *Did I think I could put in a separate phone line for him? I felt like asking him how high he wanted me to jump.*

Carrie's fears about being captive to one client blocked her ability to see any possibility of a creative agreement. It also muddied her reading of her client's motivations. "I saw the outcome in black or white. He wanted more control. If I didn't go along with what he asked, I was out. I didn't realize how much he valued my services." By letting her client in on her story, Carrie made her problem his. From a proposal (his) that could be either accepted or rejected (by her), they reached a place where there wasn't any his or hers.

The negotiation not only transformed Carrie's relationship with her most important client, it changed the way she dealt with other clients as well.

> *For me, the most difficult part of starting my own business was negotiating the fees. Beforehand, I would decide in my*

head what my services were worth, what the fees should be.
Then I would practice in front of a mirror until I didn't
think I was looking guilty.

I would just announce my fees and not budge. Some-
times I would get the clients, other times I would lose them.
This negotiation changed all that. I am much less inclined
to impose a set arrangement.

Carrie now designs her fee arrangements collaboratively, even with new clients. As they come to a better understanding of what they expect from each other, they can build an agreement that is tailored to the sort of relationship they envision.

In the strategic game of pushing and packaging, most people are reluctant to ask for help or reveal too much. If they show where they are vulnerable, they believe, they will be inviting someone to take advantage of them. That may be true in certain situations. You probably don't want to tip your hand to a car dealer or a prospective buyer for your condo. But as a general rule it holds less often than is assumed. For some people, asking for help on a problem and giving it are basic to how they do their work and support each other. Mutual inquiry builds on this instinctive helpfulness.[6] It's okay to admit you need help. It's okay to give it. It is also a given that people have different contributions to make to a negotiation. Even the language changes. "How can I help?" is a very different kind of inquiry question from "What are you looking for?"

We have described several other examples of the benefits of mutual inquiry. Marjorie, the VP for joint ventures (described in Chapter Four) used mutual inquiry with the director of South American operations to work out an agreement that neither had considered before. John, the marketing manager of mutual funds, used inquiry with his group to come up with an innovative way to deal with their market challenges (Chapter Five). Kate Griscomb and the engineers (Chapter Six) went together to the head of R&D to revamp the incentive structures that were creating internal conflict. In each case, engagement in mutual inquiry helped the participants see the situation differently. That different framing of the problem led them to agreements they could not have predicted. Each agreement resulted in *small wins* that improved the working of their organizations. In the process, relationships changed too, making any future conflicts more likely to have productive outcomes.[7]

A mutual sense of responsibility and involvement grows when people feel they can contribute to solving a problem and not just produce or react to a solution. Their relationship changes and that affects how they see the problem that they need to solve. It is in this way that problems and ultimately outcomes come to be transformed by mutual inquiry.

Midcourse Corrections

What happens in the shadow negotiation always intersects with the way bargainers discuss specific issues and those issues in turn alter the tenor of the shadow negotiation. However clearheaded bargainers try to be in assessing the problem and evaluating proposals, their own as well as those of others, they do not always succeed. They bring to the negotiation biases and feelings, memories of what has worked for them in the past and what has been less successful. These feelings can mask or distort the discussion of the issues. Sometimes the real issues never surface; they are disguised in other terms.

We all know how important it is to prepare for a negotiation. We think through every possible scenario that comes to mind. But we are not omniscient and the other side can have a surprise or two in store for us. We go into a negotiation expecting a rational discussion and find ourselves in the midst of emotional turmoil. We prepare for a tough encounter only to find the other person distinctly amenable and open to new ways of thinking. Successful negotiation requires a certain amount of flexibility. In other words, you have to be ready to change course when the situation dictates.

Sharon, a teacher turned educational consultant, recognizes the complex ways in which the shadow negotiation permeates the resolution of any issue and how easily these intersections can send any negotiation veering in unexpected directions.

> *An argument about where to take a family vacation may really be about who picked up their socks that morning. The socks remain in the background all the time we're discussing the vacation. I don't bring them up because I don't like to nag, but they are still there. Similar things happen at the office. There are the equivalents of socks in almost every negotiation. They remain in the background when you are dealing with an issue or trying to understand what is really bugging someone.*

From Packaging to Pushing

Sharon's metaphorical socks play out in the shadow negotiation. They are quite distinct but no less powerful than admitted interests, however astutely those might be probed. When gender, or race, or sexual orientation, or age rather than socks is the undiscussable factor, efforts at packaging or mutual inquiry can be rebuffed for apparent but undiscussable reasons. Under these circumstances, a negotiator can be forced to switch to a pushing strategy. These undiscussables once derailed Sharon's attempt to reach a mutual agreement when she pursued the job of principal for an upper school. But she was, however, able to use them to advantage when the negotiation reverted to pushing.

Sharon had been head of a girls' K–12 school for four years when it merged with a boys' school. She was the only sitting school head who was going to continue on after the merger. The trustees had selected an outside person to be headmaster. "This decision," in Sharon's opinion, "was exactly the one the trustees should have made." That appointment was not the issue in dispute between Sharon and the board. Sharon wanted to be principal of the upper school, while the trustees were pressing her to take over the middle school. She knew, as did the trustees, that "in our society prestige goes with older kids."

For the merger to succeed, Sharon believed, it had to be a true merger rather than an absorption of the girls' school. Quite apart from her personal stake in the issue, her appointment as principal of the upper school would make a symbolic statement. Focused on what was best for the school, Sharon calmly tried to turn the board's challenges so that they could concentrate on that central issue.

> *The board members raised all kinds of objections that had nothing to do with education. I'd assure them that I was quite capable of stopping a fight between two teenage boys and then try to move the discussion back to the educational and institutional issues. I understood something about what they were feeling. They were worried that appointing a woman would diminish the school's prestige. I tried to be flexible. I offered to accept a contract for two years. Then*

*they would be able to measure my performance. They
rejected that proposal and the other ideas I put to them.*

Even though Sharon did not agree with the reasons underlying the trustees' objections, she tried to address their fears through the options that she presented to the board. Despite her persistence and widespread support among alumnae and faculty, Sharon was gradually being backed into a corner.

*Only when I realized that the trustees were dead set
against me for no clear reasons that they would state did I
stop trying to engage them. After that I just kept restating
my position, clearly.*

Fatigue, stress, and frustration began to take a toll.

*They continued to call me at home at all hours of the night,
trying to persuade me not to go after the job. While all this
was going on, I was still running the school.*

 *One night I was so tired, I felt like just saying, "Fine,
I'll take the middle school." Then my husband cautioned
me. It was the smartest advice I've ever been given: Make
them say the words. Don't give it to them. Make them say
the words. That you cannot have that job. Ultimately, it
worked. I got the job.*

When push came to shove, the trustees could not verbalize their true reasons. That would have been an admission of their bias. They had framed the negotiation as a power struggle with a gendered leitmotif, but no one wanted to admit it publicly. Over the course of the negotiation, the trustees' continual rejection of Sharon's proposals forced her to push back, harder and harder. At the outset, she experimented with creative packages and made connected overtures to ease the discussion toward mutual inquiry. But as the position of the trustees hardened, she did not hesitate to hold firm and push her own agenda. That deliberate choice is what effective advocacy is all about.

From Pushing to Mutual Inquiry

Midcourse corrections can as easily lead in the other direction—from an emphasis on pushing to a discovery of mutuality. Bringing more voices into the negotiation precipitated a fundamental change in Lori's dealings with the hospital that was her firm's most important customer.

Lori's promotion to the hospital account was a mixed blessing. When she settled into her new job, she discovered her company had rarely emerged from contract negotiations with this particular hospital with a favorable fee schedule. The hospital management constantly whittled away at the profit margin, her firm always on the losing end. The relationship was intrinsically adversarial. When the contract came up for renewal, Lori realized that redirecting this dynamic would be difficult. The health-care environment was competitive, highly political, and prone to constant change. She had one advantage, however.

> *On a day-to-day basis, my relationships on the floors and with the various departments were good. Traditional boundaries separating customer and vendor were largely absent. The hospital's operation was decentralized, cross-functional. There weren't many strict lines of authority and so I could wander around and see what was happening.*

The team in charge of negotiating the new contract for the hospital was not nearly so cordial. Although satisfied with the quality and level of service Lori's firm provided, members of the team concentrated on extracting further price concessions. Lori resisted. She could not reduce charges further without seriously damaging her company's bottom line.

Lori set out to move the discussion away from the single issue of price. At first she focused on showing the team the added value in her firm's services. With several carefully executed strategic moves, she began to foster coalitions with her day-to-day contacts in the various departments while at the same time making sure that as many influential people as possible knew about the renewal agreement. But a peculiar thing happened as Lori began to walk the halls, talking to people on the floors and in their offices. Because the organization was so decentralized, no one outside top management had much of a sense of how everything fit together. On the floors, they only knew the problems they had. As she made her rounds, Lori got her departmental contacts to open up.

After I had a feel for each department's needs, I would follow up with a written report outlining their difficulties and possible ways of working together to solve them.

What started out as a search for a package deal, as an effort to shift the negotiation away from a fixation on price and pushing, turned into something very different when Lori consolidated her department write-ups. Her information gathering had already sparked debate within the departments. Complaints that "there must be a better way to do this systems stuff" became a common refrain. Lori's report brought those needs out in the open and provided a context for expanding discussions across departments.

Previously isolated because of the hospital's decentralized decision-making patterns and organization, people in each department saw a given problem as peculiar to them, something they had to solve on their own. They began to see that they shared common problems that needed a more comprehensive solution. Lori started floating ideas about how her firm's expertise might be helpful. The firm, a pioneer in systems and forms management in complex organizations, had a depth of experience that could be brought to bear on the hospital's communication problems.

Before Lori started walking the halls, price was the only way the hospital could define the problem. What she learned about the deeper issues broadened the focus. Opposing, adversarial positions yielded to mutual inquiry. The initial question on the table—the terms of a contract renewal—gave way to a discussion of how the hospital's forms and systems management could be revamped. The collective sense of the issues at stake allowed the systemic problems to surface. These required a solution that had little to do with price or even with clever packaging. Instead of being forced to accept or reject additional price concessions, Lori negotiated an expanded contract.

Pushing, Packaging, Mutual Inquiry, and the Shadow Negotiation

Pushing, packaging, and mutual inquiry are models for making agreements. Which you choose depends on the situation and your personal preference. It is also conditioned by what takes place in the shadow negotiation, where bargainers work out how they feel about each other. Their interactions here determine how open they are when they come to discuss the issues dividing them, how candidly they talk about what matters to them and what they really want. It is in the shadow negotiation, as bargainers relate to each other, that they judge just how willing they are to participate in the problem solving of packaging, much less in the dialogue of mutual inquiry.

Karen was the first woman to be appointed codirector of the Strategic Information Institute (SII), a think tank in Washington. The institute's programs, marketed through Browne Associates, offered courses on strategic modeling to individuals and corporations in the information technology sector. Karen was involved in a negotiation with the head of Brown Associates that could have played out under any of our three scenarios: pushing, packaging, or mutual inquiry. Each approach calls on advocacy and connection differently and produces very different outcomes. Karen actually tried all three approaches sequentially, shifting the balance between advocacy and connection as she went along.

Karen is something of a contradiction in terms—a bubbly and enthusiastic workaholic. Only in her mid-thirties, she had landed a dream job at the think tank. Unfortunately, two weeks into her tenure, she stumbled badly in the negotiation with the institute's major contractor. She took Sam Browne, a big, smiling man, at face value, and he proceeded to exploit her lack of familiarity with the institute's past practices to make a great deal for himself.

That first exposure left a bad taste in Karen's mouth. Convinced Sam's good-natured joviality was all show, she distrusted his numbers and disliked him personally. She was not about to have a repeat performance the next time around. Whatever it took, she would make up for her dismal results when she got another chance.

Meanwhile, the success of the institute's basic program had encouraged Karen and her codirector, Rick, to develop advanced seminars for anyone who had completed the introductory course. Sam, who paid SII a fixed fee for each SII program he handled, saw the expanded offerings as another potential source of revenue. So the next issue on the table was the fee arrangements for the new program. Although the advanced program made sense for both parties, the negotiations did not begin on an auspicious note.

> *We met at our usual place for breakfast. Sam handed Rick and me his proposal. After we had a chance to look it over, it was clear to both of us that Sam intended to pay us considerably less for this program than we got for the basic course. Rick asked Sam what was going on. He thought Sam was taking advantage of us. From Rick's vantage point, the institute was the goose that laid golden eggs for Sam and his company.*

At this moment, Karen could have pursued the negotiation in three ways. She could have followed Rick's lead and *pushed* for a greater share for the institute. Alternatively, she could have tried to discover what Sam wanted and come up with a *package deal* that suited everyone. She could also have engaged Sam in *mutual inquiry*, although with the hostility level running so high that was an improbable approach to take right then.

Karen's Negotiation: The Pushing Option

As soon as Rick and Karen read through Sam's proposal, the stage was set for a win-lose negotiation. Sam had staked out an adversarial position by putting a ridiculously low number on the table. Predictably Rick and Karen reacted.

> *Rick negotiates right from the gut. If he thinks he's being treated unfairly, off he goes. That's what happened. He started to pull his things together, getting ready to leave.*

Karen sat quietly while Rick attacked Sam. She was even more cynical. She considered Sam's proposal "just more of his double-speak: talking about partnership and making a low-ball offer."

On the defensive, Sam immediately countered. His costs were high. He was taking all the risks. He deserved a bigger slice of the revenues. Rick got up to leave. "Fine," he said. "If this proposal is the deal, then it's off. Forget the new product offering—we'll stick with what we have or get another contractor."

At this point Karen took another look at where they were headed in this contest of wills. To her mind, Rick's options left them worse off. SII could end up without a contractor for the new course offering. The prospects had to be equally unappealing to Sam. The best he could hope for was to maintain the present arrangements, with no possibility of increasing his revenues by adding another program. At worst, he would lose the SII account altogether. Karen set aside Sam's numbers and made a case for greater flexibility. In the early years, no one guessed SII's course would be so successful. The costs and the risks were high. Those days were over, she argued, but Sam was still taking a big cut. The new course would probably have the same life cycle. Sam countered that there were no guarantees that history would repeat itself.

They agreed to table any new offerings for the moment. To increase revenues, they decided to offer more sessions of the introductory course. Everyone felt okay, but not great about this outcome. Each got something—more revenue from the additional sessions. If no one was dissatisfied, no one was really satisfied either. In a sense, this is an example of what Mary Parker Follett called a lose-lose outcome. The real issue—how to put on and market new courses—was not settled.

Karen's Negotiation: The Packaging Option

Rick had picked up his papers and was getting ready to leave. Karen's efforts to convince Sam of the need for greater flexibility had been unsuccessful. Instead of "pushing" further in this direction, Karen changed course and tried to come up with some creative packaging.

> *I'm not sure what clicked for me, but I started to ask myself why were we doing this? We both wanted to make a deal on the new offering. Why wasn't it working? Something was going on that I just didn't understand. Why was Sam resisting so hard? Rick was really ticked off. He wasn't joking when he threatened to get a new contractor.*

Karen came right out and asked Sam why the revenue-sharing scheme for the new program was so skewed in his favor. His explanation was simple. He could only recruit participants from the pool that had already attended the basic course. He was worried that the yield would be low, and he wouldn't make his numbers.

What caught Karen's attention was the risk profile that Sam's remarks revealed. The new advanced program was more risky for Sam than the basic offering. With the entire pool of possible attendees for the advanced course limited to the ten thousand people who had already completed the introductory course, he had no flexibility in his marketing. Karen suggested they meet again after she had a chance to talk with Rick.

The next day she gave Sam a proposal. Because he was concerned about the new program's risk, she suggested that the institute's share start low but ratchet up as the number of seminar participants increased. When enrollments reached a certain level, SII would begin taking in more. This skewing compensated SII for the concession during the earlier stages when it would be paid less. When Sam objected to the rapid ratcheting, Karen adjusted the proposal—postponing the point at which SII's share increased, but raising its percentage when that threshold was crossed.

The solution produced gains for both sides. The new course would move forward. Although it would not return as much revenue in the early stages as Karen and Rick had hoped, it was likely to generate considerable cash flow in the future—for both Sam and SII. The scheme addressed Sam's risks and the institute's interest in diversifying its programs and bringing in more revenues, but Karen and Sam were still preoccupied with who would get what and when. Sam pushed Karen for a slower ratcheting, while Karen argued for a higher payout in the later stages.

Karen's Negotiation: Mutual Inquiry

Karen started the negotiation with Sam with a negative attitude about him as a person and as a negotiator. But as Sam began his litany of objections to the ratcheting in the package deal she proposed, she kept thinking:

*I'm still missing something here. We haven't talked
enough. I don't understand what's going on. This scheme
works for both of us, but Sam is really upset. He's not just
stonewalling about the money. Maybe I don't understand
his business.*

This train of thought prompted Karen to ask Sam to talk
about his business in more detail.

*Well, he did. He told us a lot more. In order to cover his
costs, including the institute's fixed fee, he needed to bring
in 105 attendees each time a course was run. At the start of
a mailing cycle, he could never predict the yield. If the
numbers looked low, he'd send out more direct mail. Based
on a formula of one per thousand, he knew he could fill the
sessions if he sent out enough mail.*

Interesting, Karen thought. Sam's problem wasn't just the
fee structure. He couldn't fill the new course with a direct mail
campaign. He could only approach previous participants. If not
enough signed up, he was out of pocket. Karen mentioned she
was only beginning to see how risky the advanced program was
for him.

*That comment really set him off. He started to talk about
the risks of the business. He felt he had always borne all the
risks. When we started, he said, nobody knew the programs
would be so successful. He underwrote them. Now that they
had succeeded, not only was the institute unappreciative, we
wanted more.*

Sam's unguarded remarks brought to the surface a critical
element driving the shadow negotiation. Each party considered

the other greedy and interpreted their actions through that screen. Sam's story pulled Rick into the conversation.

The whole mood changed. Sam stopped being so defensive. Rick and I stopped being so negative. We both now realized that Sam had a lot riding on our work together.

Karen inquired more deeply into Sam's business—not just the nuts and bolts, but why he made the decisions he did. Her appreciative inquiries broke the impasse. They surfaced the resentments that prevented them from dealing with each other or the problem. Through mutual inquiry all three discovered the real incentives they had to work out an agreement together. They also transformed the problem. No longer focused on the fee arrangements for the new course, they concentrated on the methods they could use to fill the classes. That meant moving outside the limited pool of people who had completed the basic course. But how?

Karen came up with the idea of a two-day course that created "instant alumni." Instead of promoting the new course as a stand-alone offering, they would couple it with the introductory course. That way Sam could approach the ten thousand existing alumni and, at the same time, prospect for new attendees for the basic course. After the first day, new recruits would become "instant alumni" with the option to remain for the advanced program.

Rick loved the idea. Sam was more hesitant. He needed to work it through. I understood that. But it was different this time. Sam was excited about the new course and wanted to make it a go.

The solution was a real winner for everyone. The two-day program played to sellout crowds. SII got returns that were comparable to those of its basic course, a prerequisite for this program. Mutual inquiry enabled Sam, Karen, and Rick to look at their differences differently. They actually confronted the conflict between them. Rather than the lose-lose outcome that came from the pushing approach (there is no new program) or the trade-offs of the packaging scenario (the new program gets off the ground, but the method of sharing revenues remains a bone of contention), mutual inquiry opened new possibilities. As Sam, Rick, and Karen learned about each other and from each other, they gained respect for each other's talents and revalued their initial perspectives together.

Mutual inquiry departs significantly from the exploration that typically takes place in packaging. That probing focuses almost exclusively on interests as they are currently defined. Had Karen persisted in pursuing only Sam's interests in the fee arrangements, she would in all likelihood have elicited an elaboration of his well-worn themes. Instead, she moved onto more fertile ground by expressing a concern for the risks that Sam was taking. Her appreciation of his difficulties was key to opening up the conversation. She learned something critical from Sam that she could build on. Most important, the existing relationship between Sam and Rick and Karen changed through mutual inquiry. Once they looked at each other more charitably, they saw the mutual stake they had in working together.

The solution Karen and Sam came up with cannot be separated from the process of getting there. They created an agreement not by pushing or packaging self-interest, but by experiencing their mutual interests. As Sam elaborated on his situation and Karen and Rick had an opportunity to talk about their resentment over the existing arrangements, they began to make tentative steps toward a trust missing in their previous relationship. Once they set aside their earlier suspicions, they could listen to and learn from each other. In their previous negotiations, they had given lip service to the notion of partnership. For the first time, they actually began to experience themselves as partners.

o   o   o

Advocacy and connection are ways bargainers relate to each other in the shadow negotiation. The effects of each and the balance struck between them ripple through the discussion of issues and the kinds of agreements that are reached. In pushing situations, you concentrate on getting the best deal for yourself, and it is here that advocacy plays its most obvious role. The better prepared you are, psychologically and tactically, the better you will do. But even here connection has a part. You have to be able to gauge the effects of your moves and turns. Anticipating obstacles and pushing in a connected way, you make it easier for the other party to say yes.

Packaging is a form of problem solving. It works best when both sides have a healthy respect for the value each brings to the negotiation. That's what gives everyone the incentive to tailor solutions so that they meet the various interests around the table. For your suggestions to be considered, the other party has to think them worth the time and effort. They must believe that it is in their best interest to deal with you. The tools of advocacy position you to claim what you deserve and need. But you still require a clear picture of the other person's priorities. That information is the key to the kinds of package deals you can put together. You tap into priorities and interests by getting connected.

In mutual inquiry, advocacy and connection are integrated differently. Neither is yoked so exclusively to self-interest. The moves and turns that get you to the table yield to another kind of process. You work together to learn more about each other's experience, and agreements emerge not from floating attractive options but from exploring mutual and separate needs. In other words, new ideas don't come from brainstorming, as in problem solving, but from listening, learning, and creating together.

Whether a negotiation becomes a learning experience depends equally on effective inquiry and effective advocacy. Strategic moves and turns provide the incentives to keep the negotiation on track and protect your interests. But connection opens the negotiation up by making room for everyone's stories. Resistance, instead of being regarded as a stumbling block, becomes an impetus for more inquiry. Without having to worry about the risks of disclosing too much, negotiators can come at issues in new ways and experiment with new ideas. Very often the issue under dispute acquires a new definition, one that is constructed together. What seemed like opposing interests turn into mutual concerns if one probes deeper or shares more.

Chapter 8

Negotiating Change

Every day we negotiate the fabric of our work and our relationships. Sometimes we deliberately direct the process; other times, it takes place without our much noticing. Pieced together, these discrete negotiations create the patterns of our life. Chance, circumstances, all have a hand in their design. But the more conscious we are of our actions, the less likely it is that the results will take shape by default.

The tools of advocacy—its strategic moves and turns—help you guard against the temptation to let decisions slide in order to avoid conflicts, while the skills of connection allow you to open up new possibilities. If advocacy stretches notions of what is negotiable, connection expands our sense of what can be achieved by working together.

Linked over time, negotiated outcomes take on a cumulative force. Whether you actively negotiate change in your life or permit others to decide determines your opportunities in the future. If every negotiation has a history and a context, its participants also have a history and a context. Their constraints and resources, values and goals both shape and are shaped by the results they have negotiated in the past. As you go about your daily negotiations, the agreements made cast ripples into the future. If you agree to take on that new assignment with no increase in pay, you add to the expectation that you will make the same decision tomorrow.

In earlier chapters we selected vignettes from specific negotiation stories or focused on a single negotiation. Stopping the action, so to speak, allowed us to capture bargainers at precise points in a negotiation or within their careers. First, we wanted to show how others have grappled with the demands of a strong advocacy. What, we asked, do they tell us about gaining a voice at the table? Then we moved to stories about the challenges of getting connected. How can relational skills be used to open a dialogue with the other party?

To make specific points, we isolated aspects of these stories. But generally negotiations are neither so tidy nor so compartmentalized, particularly when it comes to the shadow negotiation. You don't systematically work through all the strategic moves and turns of effective advocacy and then summon your relational skills to foster a collaborative relationship with your counterpart. Then, too, focusing on one aspect of a negotiation can make the outcome seem inevitable. One of the characteristics of any negotiation is that you can never be sure how it is going to turn out. You can only anticipate the ending. Only in retrospect does the confrontational strategy that Chris Lydon employed in Chapter Five to force WBUR's hand seem foolhardy. At the time he probably considered standing firm a smart move. He could count on support from a loyal following, and the station's general manager had a reputation as a tough bargainer. Carrie in Chapter Seven was also determined—dead set against giving a major client so much control over her life. Yet Carrie, unlike Chris, eventually managed to articulate her "no" in a way that kept the job and her client. The path to deadlock or agreement, however, was by no means straight in either case.

As we talked with people around the country about their experiences, they didn't just describe complex situations and undiluted triumphs. They also touched on their feelings about negotiation. They assessed what they have learned about advocating for themselves and connecting with others, what they believe they still need to learn. They often attributed their success to luck. "Oh, I was in the right place at the right time," they'd say, or "I was lucky." It is not luck. In their accounts, success emerges as the product of constant improvisation, negotiating opportunity, evading roadblocks, creating value. It comes from managing both the tools of forceful advocacy and the relational skills of connection. That experience is cumulative, and in this chapter we want to look at negotiation over time—through the eyes of Shannon Galvin.

Shannon, the highest-placed woman in a major hotel chain, has the map of Ireland written across her face. Her fair skin blushes easily. Blunt-cut blond hair swings forward when she bends toward someone to listen. Her smile tips up one side of her mouth and goes right to her eyes. Now in her early forties, Shannon has a directness that can be mistaken for naïveté. Shannon has spent her entire professional life with the hotel chain. This tenure has pluses and minuses. Shannon knows the organization from bottom to top. "There are lots of people around who met me when I was a kid. Some of the telephone operators were here when I first worked the reservation desk. They call me dear."

The executive suite on the third floor of the chain's flagship hotel is an oasis of calm. No one rushes. The telephone rings constantly, but responses are measured, efficient, and warm. There is little hint that in the not-too-distant past the chain was reeling under the strain of three reorganizations in five years. Outside consultants still roam through the corporate offices, evaluating head counts and efficiency.

A woman carrying a stack of letters and wearing a red blazer and a charcoal skirt with knife pleats comes out of a corner office. She stops to say hello to the deliveryman unloading a case of bottled water in the pantry just off the reception area. "Thank you, John." It is Shannon. And she runs her hotel on a first-name basis. "I get a little help, you know. When I first came, I insisted on name tags—for everyone."

Shannon has been around the organization for twenty years, wearing many hats. For two and a half years, she sat at headquarters shepherding a massive organizational change. Before the shakeup, decisions got stuck someplace in the chain of command. Accountability fell through the cracks at the lower levels, and at the top the hotel managers assiduously tended their turf, spending a good portion of their time on what Shannon describes as political gamesmanship. "To be a service organization, those attitudes had to be turned around. That's quite an assignment in a place that hates change." Over the years Shannon had acquired the reputation of a consensus builder, and she put her energies to work building agreement on the need for change.

Once the reorganization was well under way, Shannon was promoted to head up operations and take charge of the chain's flagship hotel. Aside from her early experiences on the reservation desk and as an assistant manager, Shannon had never been "in the trenches, actually assigned to an operating hotel." Some members of the hotel staff, aware of her aversion to confrontation, consistently made moves that pushed her toward accommodation. They tried, in effect, to position her as they saw her.

There were no veterans in management's upper ranks when Shannon came to the hotel. Her senior team was all new. "We had to be extremely sensitive to how things came out of our mouths. If we saw things that were wrong, the people who had been here thought that we blamed them." If the "old hands" at the reservation desk and manning the telephones remembered a shy young kid, the rest of the staff was more distant. They tried to hide information, not maliciously but to protect themselves. "The impulse behind their moves was transparent. They were obviously thinking that what I didn't know couldn't hurt them." No one considered Shannon a strict disciplinarian, but they knew she was a crusader for customer satisfaction. By hoarding their problems, they avoided bringing any attention to them. She would hear comments like, "Oh, you don't want to be bothered about that." But Shannon is nonconfrontational with people, not issues. "Why wouldn't I want to hear? If there is an issue, it could be a problem for all of us. If we can't make something work, then we should talk about why, not paper over it."

Shannon arrived at the hotel at the beginning of a blustery January storm. The next day, the chief engineer paid her a visit. One of his men objected to shoveling snow. "Excuse me?" she said. "When it snows, everybody shovels, everyone on the team pitches in. This is winter. It snows." The chief engineer shifted from one foot to the other and then proceeded to fill Shannon in on the facts. "He told me I couldn't ask anyone over fifty to shovel. That was my vivid and rude introduction to unions."

A week later the contract with the hotel engineers, members of the International Brotherhood of Firemen and Oilers, came up for renewal. Although there were twelve union hotels in the city, Shannon's two primary competitors were nonunion and likely to remain so. Any contract she negotiated needed to meet two criteria. The agreement had to be fiscally sound for the hotel and at the same time allow its customers to be served well. Shannon identified the two objectives early on. How they could be realized remained a puzzle initially. Behind them lurked a bigger question: Can customers expect and get top-notch service in a union hotel without bankrupting the treasury?

Typically in the past, bargaining with the union had been conducted by a closed group. The chief engineer made his needs known going in, but the union president and the general manager of the hotel struck the final deal. Shannon was not prepared to negotiate the contract one-on-one, nor did she think the practice served her larger interests. Determined to get a different kind of contract, she realized that she needed to change the process.

Shannon, new on the job and completely inexperienced in union negotiations, could have relied on the hotel's labor attorney. Instead, she expanded participation on management's side, opening it to members of her advisory team. At this point she did not know anything about negotiating with a union. "My gut instinct told me that I needed to make a symbolic statement and that I needed to make it early." By including the advisory team, she signaled that management of the hotel would be a collaborative effort.

> *I wanted to run the hotel as a team, and these negotiations*
> *had to be conducted that way. This change disturbed our*

labor lawyer. He is extremely capable, but quite traditional. Suddenly not only were we breaking the mold, but he was dealing with a team with two women in key roles.

I had no desire to negotiate this contract with our attorney telling me what to do. That advice would have come from what happened in the past. But, face it, I also didn't have the experience or the inclination to do it on my own.

If Shannon's own attorney was disturbed by the change, the union president was at a total loss. He had been comfortable with her predecessor, whose confrontational posturing fitted his notion of how negotiations moved forward.

The previous manager liked the fight. Well, I don't like the fight. Foul language, pounding the table, threatening to walk out—that is not my style.

Concerned, Shannon called the union president and asked him to come by so she could introduce herself.

We had tea and cookies. The union president had no idea what to expect. He had never negotiated with a woman before. He'd gone out for beers with my predecessor, but a tea party? I had no stated agenda, but between sips of Earl Grey, I let him know what I expected from a working relationship and that I expected to have one with him. This was not what he had been used to hearing from my predecessor.

Shannon was essentially telling the union president that they were in this together. Off-line, before the formal proceedings began, she created an opportunity for him to get to know her. Equally significant, Shannon gave herself a chance to clarify her expectations for the upcoming talks. She emphasized her willingness to be reasonable within certain boundaries. Both the willingness and the boundaries were important to establish before the negotiations began.

Shannon was taking on a larger task than even she realized. She had a broader objective than keeping the annual increase in the union's hourly wage to a minimum. She wanted to focus on performance and tie compensation to that performance.

> *Every organization has some slugs. Everyone involved in these negotiations had to be thinking about serving our customers. From my perspective, the contract needed to sharpen that focus. You cannot serve customers well if you don't have flexibility, if a plumber cannot change a light bulb.*

The hotel had just had a terrific year, and prospects looked equally promising for the current year. The union representatives arrived at the first session with their confidence swelled by that success. They immediately put their demands on the table—all forty-five of them. The management team countered by raising the issue of performance-based pay. Conversations about performance measurement were not new. What was new was the idea of linking compensation to performance.

> *I wanted the union members to share my objective for the hotel—to be number 1 in service in the city. Starting with a dime, countering with a nickel, and settling for seven cents was not going to get us even close to where we needed to be.*

Shannon knew from the beginning that she did not want to pursue a pushing strategy. The most she could hope to achieve by pushing was a seven-cent compromise. The attitudes about work and the working relationships would remain unchanged. To ensure that customer satisfaction was in the front of everyone's mind, she needed to shake things up a bit. It could not be business as usual.

Performance-based pay has two components: an hourly wage and a bonus that is contingent on doing a good job. The union representatives rejected the concept in the first session. Their reaction came as no surprise to Shannon. "That was how the negotiations had always been conducted. You push, I push back, and we see where everyone is in the end." In the past, union officials had bargained for hikes in hourly wages across the board, and the union membership measured their success by the rate they achieved. Shannon appreciated the extent to which she was asking them to venture into uncharted territory. Not only would they have to relinquish a visible and comfortable scorecard, they would have to give up some of their traditional rights.

Rather than respond as an adversary, Shannon treated that first no as a starting point. Her tea-and-cookies meeting with the union president convinced her that the interests of the union and the hotel converged. The challenge was to find a way of enabling everyone to see how.

Luisa DiLorenzo, the head of human resources, began working behind the scenes, talking to people in the cafeteria. The message she heard was loud and clear. The union members wanted to hear from Shannon—who, thus far, had deliberately remained in the background.

I was the new kid on the block. I wanted to get to know the players better, watch and not take over. Besides, it was important for me that this negotiation be perceived as a team effort. If I started inserting myself into the sessions right from the beginning, everyone would just wait for me to talk.

However low a profile Shannon had kept, the union leadership still considered her the final authority, and she was an unknown quantity. Until they heard directly from her, they remained unsure of their ground. To get them to own the problem with her, she had to be candid about her objectives. To get where she wanted to go, everyone involved in the negotiations needed to recognize the goals they had in common and not concentrate on past practices and the contract details pulling them apart. "The union knew the *what* of performance-based pay. It was now time to talk about the *why*, and they wanted to get it from the horse's mouth. In their mind that horse was me."

Shannon began the "horse's mouth" session by sharing her goals for the hotel and how they were linked to performance. "Right off, I put my three objectives up on a flip chart: Serving our customers, looking out for our employees, and ensuring our financial health." Shannon considered these goals interconnected. Without satisfied employees, they wouldn't get satisfied customers. She also mentioned the changes in company ownership. As a public company, the hotel chain was accountable to its stockholders. Performance was monitored daily in the stock price.

With that introduction, Shannon made what to her was an impassioned plea for performance-based pay. Until some agreement was reached on performance, she argued, they could not even begin to discuss the union's forty-five issues. Shannon told the assembled crowd that they had three options in the talks: performance-based pay, traditional hourly pay, or contracting out the work based on what made economic sense. She believed the only viable choice was the first option. If they went the traditional route, all they could talk about was dollars, and she would fight as hard as possible for the best deal for the hotel. If they could not come to an agreement that was reasonable economically, she would be forced to contract the services out.

Shannon directly linked the kind of agreement they could forge with the negotiation process itself. Going the traditional route would replay the adversarial win-lose bargaining of the past. In her view, more structured participation, a process driven by dialogue, would lead to joint ownership of the issues on the table.

When Luisa again tapped into the hotel grapevine, she discovered that the union members had interpreted Shannon's remarks very differently from what she had intended to say. They believed she had drawn a line in the sand. Union leadership and the rank and file heard Shannon's list of options as a thinly veiled threat. Luisa told Shannon that if they did not back down on performance, they faced the real possibility of a strike. Union members now believed that if they did not back down on performance, they might well have no alternative but to go out on strike. "I didn't want to position myself that way," Shannon says. "I hadn't intended to send that particular message." A subtle self-deception is at work here. Shannon did fully intend to deliver a tough message; she did not, however, want to be perceived as being intractable or hard. Rather than misunderstanding the message, the union members got their first real glimpse of Shannon's primary objective.

At first, Shannon was horrified at the construction the union members placed on her remarks. Then she watched their effect. Rather than resisting her firm stand, the union members appreciated the "straight talk." If it took an unusual degree of bluntness to exert pressure to cooperate, Shannon was now happy to oblige.

That "horse's mouth" session laid out the potential costs to everyone of *not* coming to terms. Shannon's candor, instead of adding to the divisiveness, became the catalyst for more intense and open discussion. No one wanted a strike. This consensus provided a starting point from which both sides could test for other common interests. Behind the scenes, Luisa stepped up her invisible work of connection. In casual meetings with individual union members or small groups, she stressed management's intention to be flexible. Although management was not willing to give in on the performance concept, it was open to any suggestions about the weighting between the hourly figure and the bonus. Luisa gave the union members what amounted to an open invitation to participate in figuring out what that weighting should be.

At the same time, Shannon decided they could not let themselves get bogged down in specific details. "The most important thing we needed was buy-in on the concept of performance-based pay itself." For joint ownership to evolve, Shannon and her team had to keep the conversation (as opposed to the formal talks) going. Once the union understood why performance-based pay was so important, the details could be bundled or unbundled in lots of ways. "Just getting a performance component into the contract," Shannon believed, "would represent real progress." She needed the union's help to do that.

This clarity on the goal prevented Shannon from getting mired in the details of implementation. Walking around, talking to people, the management team learned more about what the union wanted. The views of the membership were not monolithic. Differences within the union camp encouraged Shannon to broaden the discussions so that they would include more players from the union side.

At the next session Shannon held out a proposal for the union's consideration. She stressed that the suggestion was not meant to define a position. Rather, it should be taken as just an idea, a what-if proposal, something to which they could react. She put muscle behind that statement by establishing work groups to develop other alternatives. Eventually all the engineers participated in these voluntary sessions.

> *They came up with truly innovative suggestions. They didn't want anyone to start with a history, and they were dead on there. They realized right away that poor performers would fare better than high performers under our opening proposal because they had more room for improvement. When they asked if we would be willing to change that, we said, "Sure, come back with a workable formula."*

These work groups affected the tenor of the negotiations in three ways. First, they reinforced Shannon's commitment to reaching a joint agreement. Second, because she could act on the recommendations coming out of the work groups, they provided concrete opportunities to back up that commitment. And, most important, everyone involved could build on the ideas the sessions produced.

All the time the hotel's labor attorney was whispering to the management team: "Listen harder. Don't be so concerned about your responses. It's okay to keep your mouth shut and your ears open." Shannon maintains they were listening; they just didn't know what they were listening for. From then on, they made sure that someone on the team just listened. "We got into the habit of rephrasing to make sure that we were hearing what they actually meant. We would say, 'We hear you. It might work if we did this. Is that okay?'" These kinds of inclusive questions ensured that everyone stayed involved. They also encouraged people to participate more actively. Their responses, in turn, contributed greater color and detail, expanding the understanding on both sides. As the various groups worked on specific problems, multiple perspectives emerged, and the discussions shifted imperceptibly in the direction of the subjunctive—from emphatic declarative statements and counterproposals to the inclusive inquiry, "What if—?"

Listening harder revealed flaws in Shannon's original logic. The discussions had become a learning process. Over the course of the negotiations she came to realize that you must approach dramatic changes gradually. People need time to work through the implications of new ideas. Performance-based pay naturally goes against the union grain, against established patterns of thinking. It is a compensation system that individualizes people and, as a result, runs counter to the group identification that membership in a union encourages.

To be responsive to these concerns, at first Shannon included a team component in the performance measurements, but in the end the engineers themselves decided to eliminate it. "They recognized, as we talked, that their ability to influence their own performance was greater than their ability to influence a team's." As union members evaluated various schemes, each was forced to consider their impact on his daily work life. As a result, they began to rethink how they worked individually and as members of a team.

After agreement was reached on the performance component, the discussions took on a different rhythm. "The formula wasn't everything I had hoped for," Shannon says, "but it was a start." At this point, she began to share with the union representatives as much financial information as she could. This openness was a major change for her labor attorney and for the union.

I looked at their original forty-five items and basically said: "It is impossible for us to deliver all of these. We have a budget. This is the pot of money we have. How do you want to spend it? Tell us what demands are most important."

The timing of this sharing is significant. Had Shannon furnished the financial information earlier, the union leadership would probably not have believed they were getting the whole story, and they would have been suspicious about the numbers they were given. Shannon, on the other hand, would have risked having that information used against her to extract concessions. Trust on both sides of the table was a precondition for her candor.

The way in which Shannon shared the information is also significant. With common financial data at hand, the union and management could agree on what was actually in the pot. Shannon left the spending to the union members. It was money available for their benefits. They knew best how to spend it.

If there was danger in sharing information, there was an equally potent benefit. It was an act of trust, a signal that they had the makings of a real dialogue.

I was going for trust, telling them as much as I could. Previously getting more was the goal—more concessions, squeezing. We were learning as we went along. This really comes down to how you define success, what it means to win.

Before these negotiations, Shannon had no hands-on experience dealing with unions. Her inexperience with the traditional adversarial model of collective bargaining, where pushing is the rule, worked to her advantage. She chose to define success in terms of shared decision making. Through mutual inquiry, she moved them all to a joint problem and a jointly constructed solution. For that definition of success to take hold, however, Shannon had to stand firm at critical junctures. Had she not, her inexperience would have been turned against her. Once she established her authority at the table beyond the dimensions conferred by her title, she could make connected overtures that were interpreted as such, rather than as signs of weakness.

"I knew where I wanted to go in these talks," Shannon says, "but I didn't have a clue how to get there." Against a history of adversarial pushing, she fashioned a participatory and collaborative process. Both sides learned together as they went along. They discovered the linkages between their concerns and reframed the issues separating them.

Shannon is an inclusive kind of person. She goes out of her way to draw people in, bends toward them when she listens, instinctively enlarges a conversation circle so no one is left out. But there are limits to how far participation can be taken in any organization. Shannon has discovered that effective advocacy is not just a prelude for making connection, it is important on its own.

"People want a lot of you. I take consensus to a fault. I'm inclusionary, say, 90 percent of the time and that 10 percent when I'm not becomes an issue." The more Shannon puzzled over the criticism she heard about the missing 10 percent, the more she realized that people needed boundaries. Without them, they resented the lack of participation or tested her, looking for the limits. Advocacy establishes your place at the table, but it also defines the limits you set.

> *It has always been my preference to have everyone move forward happily. I will drag people if I need to, but I don't like doing it. I now have a better understanding of what is actually going on. For example, when the union thought I was drawing a line in the sand with my impassioned plea for performance pay, I did not realize how necessary it was to draw that line. I now recognize that it's not only okay to be tough, it's actually necessary. They would not have let go of their original positions and moved forward without that strong statement from me.*

Shannon does not equate consensus with compliance. Although she still has an aversion to outright conflict, she is not interested in rubbing the rough edges off differences of opinion. She does not want to reach a place where everyone agrees, but rather one where differences can be spoken and heard.

The hotel and its parent have been going through a lot of change, of which the performance-based pay for union members is only a part. The last reorganization, which Shannon spearheaded, had been a painful growing process for a lot of people. Shannon is the first to admit that it has not been easy. Negotiating a change in attitude or behavior takes a personal and professional toll. There has been some difficult learning on everyone's part as old habits and sometimes actual turf have had to be surrendered. Change is also ongoing.

*I want everyone in the hotel to be thinking about the cus-
tomer. To know that they are accountable for our customers'
satisfaction and do everything they can to make our guests'
stay here pleasant. But that means we all have to pull in
the same direction.*

At times Shannon's role interferes with the communication
she wants. No matter how hard she tries to create an impression of openness, she is still perceived as the boss. And for a
very good reason. She is.

*It is tough. Last week I had bonus checks in my desk
drawer. I'd written letters to each of the managers, but I
wanted to give them their checks personally. When I saw
the manager of room service in the lobby, I asked him to
stop by my office whenever he got a minute.*

*Well, he panicked, all day long. I happened to catch
him in the human resources office downstairs with Luisa.
She said, "I don't break confidences, but, Shannon, you
have got to hear this. Nick has been wound up like a top
because you want to see him. I had to tell him you have his
bonus check."*

*That should have been a great day for Nick. Instead he
stewed unnecessarily for five hours. I thought, this is mind-
boggling. Sure I'm his boss, but he also needs to understand
that I wouldn't approach a problem by saying, "Hey, when
you get a minute, stop by my office."*

*Some managers would have been in my office in a split
second, ready to talk. What struck me was his immediate
response. He must have done something wrong. He didn't
think, "Gee, maybe she wants my opinion on something."
It's the same perception that makes it hard for him, and for
others, to ask for help. In their minds, it is an admission of*

incompetence, an acknowledgment that they cannot handle something on their own.

That incident gave Shannon pause. It reinforced her conviction that open communication and a fear of sanctions do not mix. The reaction of the room service manager was both her problem and his. To help him and others feel more comfortable raising difficult issues, Shannon began to build frameworks for what she calls "programmed communication." These are not occasions for her to channel discussion to her way of thinking. They provide recurrent opportunities for feedback.

If you don't actively seek input from people, provide for it, look for other opinions, where do they come from? How do you get people to the point of knowing they can bring bad news and their heads won't roll?

There is a hidden danger in introducing programmed communication. People instinctively recognize these techniques can be used for diametrically opposed purposes. They can encourage diverse opinions, but they can also mute dissent. When compliance is the order of the day, people are reluctant to put their opinions out for inspection. They won't take the chance. Their concerns may depart from what is being enforced. Structured opportunities for communication can raise suspicions. They also take time away from "real work." "I rarely dig my heels in," Shannon says, "but I dug my heels in on this issue. These sessions were worth the time and the effort. You have to give people a chance to sit around a table and lay their needs out. They have to know they will have everyone's undivided attention."

Only recently has Shannon admitted to herself that relationships as much as issues must be negotiated.

> *Remember at breakfast I told you that I never negotiated, that I was going into my first big negotiation—the labor talks. Well, the other day, two senior staff members came to me with an ongoing issue that they needed to resolve. They wanted me to broker the resolution for them. I told them it was not about either one of them positioning themselves individually with me. They needed to negotiate their relationship. That is part of what they get paid for. To work together. I would never have said that a couple of years ago.*

Behind the success of Shannon's negotiations is a conscious struggle. She is a firm believer that "no news is not good news." She subjects her own goals and the process to a hard-edged scrutiny. She explicitly contracts with those around her for the sharing of information and reliable feedback. She reflects on what she hears and constantly revises the way she approaches the practice of negotiation. The union members' reaction to her strong advocacy and its positive effect on the subsequent talks made her think about why she shied away from any appearance of toughness. For Shannon, negotiation has become a learning experience.

∘   ∘   ∘

Shannon negotiates changes as an insider with a powerful job. She has also benefited from the backing of a powerful mentor. Both her title and her support create perceptions when she negotiates. On one hand, she has less need to establish her voice in the shadow negotiation. She takes her credentials to the table with her. On the other, she also carries a reputation for disliking confrontation.

Despite her power (or perhaps because of it), Shannon has been slow to realize the need for continuous advocacy. "I don't like to throw my weight around, tell people what to do. Subconsciously, I did not recognize the difference between being tough and being an effective advocate. Now I realize they are not the same." That recognition separates her earlier efforts at consensus building from the negotiations of mutual inquiry in which she now engages.

Shannon has resolved the catch-22 most people face when they negotiate—how to be forceful advocates so you get what you want, but not so tough that you alienate the other person. She has come to grips with the paradox by no longer considering advocacy and connection, strategic moves and responsive inquiry, as mutually exclusive approaches. She has come to see that both are equally necessary to the effective practice of negotiation. Forceful moves and turns, Shannon has discovered, can define the boundaries and set the conditions for a participatory, expansive process that goes beyond consensus.

Every decision point is a potential issue to be negotiated, whether she decides to take it up or not. Not every encounter leads to connection. Nor is she as inclusionary in one situation as she might be in another. There are many lessons in Shannon's story, but perhaps the most important is this exercise of choice. "No" begins a process of engagement—with herself, trying to figure out the reasons blocking progress, and with those on the other side of the table.

o   o   o

Shannon Galvin is one negotiator. She builds into the negotiation process the possibility for mutual inquiry. As the tenor of negotiation moves from pushing and defensive posturing or clever packaging, the focus shifts from specific agendas or interests to solutions people hadn't considered before. Together they invent new options and create wins, sometimes small and sometimes large. Although not all negotiations contain the seeds of transformative change, they all produce change at some level. The question is whose voices will participate in fashioning those changes.

The story of Shannon Galvin and the experiences recounted in this book reveal what an inevitable part of our lives negotiation is. It is the way people work their way through conflict and put their stamp on change. Negotiated outcomes all resolve conflict in one way or another. They can reinforce existing relations, including the calculus of power at the table, or they can modulate those relations. There is a choice involved here, but it is one that depends ultimately on the recognition that choice is possible. Outcomes can be purposefully shaped. The decision to play an active role in that shaping is perhaps the most important one you as a negotiator make in coming to the table. That primary decision opens up multiple avenues for effective advocacy and participative inquiry.

Three threads weave through all our stories. The awareness embedded in each expands not only the choices available to you in a negotiation but the possibilities as well.

- **Negotiation is a central part of life at work.**
  To see negotiation as a possibility and to take up the challenge can mean wins for you and for your organization.

- **Everyday negotiations take place on many levels.**
  Bargainers work out relations of power and define their roles in a shadow negotiation that parallels their debate on the issues. How issues are interpreted and recast depends

fundamentally on the relationships established in this shadow negotiation. The impressions that govern those relationships are not static. They can be confronted, resisted, and modified by active intervention—through strategic moves and turns that empower us as negotiators.

o **The outcome of any negotiation is a function of the process used to get there.**
Through mutual inquiry, bargainers can rethink their biases and expectations together. In what Mary Parker Follett called a constant process of relating and revaluing, they can come to see each other differently and gain new perspectives on the issues dividing them. Through mutual inquiry, people learn from their negotiations and they carry these lessons into the future.

These threads, woven together, subtly transform our notions of what it means to be an effective negotiator. When equal weight is granted to the shadow negotiation, it becomes clear how important relational matters are to the outcome of any negotiation.

Negotiations involve both self-interest and a concern for others. The balance between them constantly shifts. But, as Shannon Galvin and our other storytellers illustrate, there are many ways to manage the shadow negotiation, many ways of advocating for your own interests at the same time that you connect with others to give greater depth to the understanding of the issues at stake. Collectively these stories show that you can use negotiation to make personal progress *and* at the same time promote constructive change in the workplace.

Notes

INTRODUCTION: RECOGNIZING THE HIDDEN AGENDAS
IN EVERYDAY NEGOTIATION

1. Books that have influenced thinking about negotiation include Roger Fisher, William Ury, and Bruce Patton, *Getting to Yes;* William Ury, *Getting Past No;* Howard Raiffa, *The Art and Science of Negotiation;* David Lax and James Sebenius, *The Manager as Negotiator;* and Max Bazerman and Margaret Neale, *Negotiating Rationally.*

2. Recent work, especially in the international field, has begun to pay more attention to how a negotiation is constructed as an ongoing process. Two Harvard Business School case studies are particularly interesting: James Sebenius and Daniel F. Curran, "To Hell with the Future, Let's Get On with the Past: George Mitchell in Northern Ireland," and Michael Watkins, "Getting to Dayton: Negotiating an End to the War in Bosnia."

3. The orange story illuminates central elements of the mutual-gains approach to negotiation. We use it as a proxy, but at the same time recognize that it doesn't begin to cover all the permutations within mutual-gains analysis.

4. This composite of the "effective negotiator" comes from the stereotype work of Kray and others ("Battle of the Sexes") and Mnookin and others *(Beyond Winning).* Kray, Galinsky, and Thompson show how powerful stereotypes can be, and with each stereotype comes a whole constellation of expectations about behavior, ability, and so on.

5. On "enlightened self-interest," see, for example, Jeffrey Rubin, "Some Wise and Mistaken Notions About Conflict and Negotiation."

6. Anthropologists and linguists emphasize the extent to which meaning in any exchange comes not just from what is said but from how it gets said. See Gregory Bateson, *Steps to an Ecology of Mind.*

7. We are using the concept of *position* in a way that differs from its use in most writing on negotiation. In *Getting to Yes*, for example, a position is a demand a negotiator makes and is to be distinguished from the interests that stand behind that position or demand. We use *position* as a verb. This verbal form suggests how a negotiator comes to be placed in the process, whether she positions herself to advocate for what she wants—the subject position—or is at the whim of how others define her—the object position. This object/subject relation has been a primary focus in women's studies. See, for example, Chris Weedon, *Feminist Practice and Poststructuralist Theory*, and Sylvia Gherardi, *Gender, Symbolism, and Organizational Culture*. Sara Cobb takes up its impact on conflict resolution in "A Narrative Perspective on Mediation."

8. Linda Carli describes the two-edged sword that assertiveness can be for women in "Gender, Language, and Influence," and Mary Crawford offers a pointed critique of the assertiveness-training solution in *Talking Difference: On Gender and Language*.

9. Because influence typically follows gender lines, issues of gender and power can and do affect men and women differently when they negotiate. For men, gender may be invisible. For women, however, it can be a significant factor, particularly when stereotypical expectations are triggered. As one commentator put it, an emphasis on caring and nurturing, qualities often attributed to women, can amount to a "setup to be shafted" (Catharine MacKinnon, "Feminist Discourses"). In an unequal world, MacKinnon argues, difference will always mean less and women will generally get less when they negotiate.

CHAPTER ONE: STAYING OUT OF YOUR OWN WAY

1. In a summary of early research in *The Psychology of Bargaining and Negotiation*, for example, Jeffrey Rubin and B. R. Brown point to studies on gender differences. Some conclude that women are more cooperative than men are; others find the opposite. See also Deborah Kolb and Gloria Coolidge, "Her Place at the Table." Analysis of recent work turns up equally inconsistent findings. There is some evidence that, overall, women are slightly more cooperative than men unless they are caught in a tit-for-tat situation. When Alice Stuhlmacher and Amy Walters restricted their analysis to negotiation, however, the studies found that men negotiated significantly better outcomes than women did ("Gender Differences in Negotiation Outcomes: A Meta-Analysis"). Even when gender does not affect a bargainer's results, Carol Watson's research indicates that it does affect the bargainer's feelings. Women

tend to feel less confident and less satisfied regardless of the outcomes they achieve. See Carol Watson and L. R. Hoffman, "Managers as Negotiators: A Test of Power vs. Gender as Predictors of Feelings, Behaviors and Outcomes."

2. Lawrence Fouraker and Stanley Siegal first pointed to the determining impact that aspirations—the goals you set and the expectations you have about their success—can have on the outcome of a negotiation *(Bargaining and Group Decisionmaking)*.

3. Women are much less likely than men are to use self-promoting tactics like Pat employs in this story; they make fewer offers and counteroffers. These differences in approach and tactics account, in part, for the lower salaries women negotiate when they compete with men for the same job. See Lisa Barron, "Talk That Pays: Differences in Salary, Negotiator's Beliefs and Behaviors."

4. Myriad explanations have been put forth for the disparity in the salaries negotiated by men and women. Women have difficulty setting specific salary targets and putting a number on the table (Cynthia Stevens and others, "Gender Differences in the Acquisition of Salary Negotiation Skills"). Men get more because they ask for more, are more confident of success, and employ a more active strategy than do women (V. S. Kamen and C.E.J. Hartel, "Gender Differences in Anticipated Pay Negotiation Strategies and Outcomes"). Women do badly, in part, because they don't ask for much (Brenda Major and colleagues, "Social Comparisons and Pay Evaluations: Preferences for Same-Sex and Same-Job Wage Comparisons," Wayne H. Bylsma, lead author; "An Investigation of Sex Differences in Pay Expectations and Their Possible Causes"; and "Overworked and Underpaid"). Women determine what they deserve on the basis of what other women are earning rather than what the work itself commands. Or, others suggest, the work they do simply does not pay well (W. T. Bielby and J. N. Baron, "A Woman's Place Is with Other Women: Sex Segregation Within Organizations").

5. See Rhona Mahony, *Kidding Ourselves: Breadwinning, Babies, and Bargaining Power*; and Arlie Hochschild, *The Second Shift*.

6. For more on the concept of BATNA, see Roger Fisher, William Ury, and Bruce Patton, *Getting to Yes*.

CHAPTER TWO: MAKING STRATEGIC MOVES

1. In "Bargaining and Gender," Carol Rose contends, for example, that it does not matter whether women are or are not more inclined to cooperation and accommodation in their negotiations. The assumption

that they are makes the job of getting people to the table more difficult and the pressure to make concessions, once there, almost inevitable. This assumption holds broadly whenever the other party perceives a bargainer as being accommodating.

2. Abba Eban, *Diplomacy for the Next Century*.

3. *Unfreezing* is a concept developed, among others, by Kurt Lewin, *Resolving Social Conflicts: Field Theory in Social Science*.

4. Negotiations to secure the backing of a bargainer's own side are so critical to success in the main negotiation that they have been called the "second table." See Thomas Colosi, "Negotiation in the Public and Private Sectors"; Ray Friedman, *Front Stage, Backstage: The Dramatic Structure of Labor Negotiations*; and Richard Walton and Robert McKersie, *A Behavioral Theory of Labor Negotiations*.

5. See David Lax and James Sebenius, "Thinking Coalitionally."

6. "Clean encounters," conducted one-on-one privately, have another benefit. A negotiator may be willing to explore controversial issues or concessions in private but feel constrained in a more public forum.

7. On making change without explicit authority, see Allan R. Cohen and David L. Bradford, "Influence Without Authority: The Use of Alliances, Reciprocity, and Exchange to Accomplish Work." Peter Bachrach and Morton S. Baratz differentiate between direct and indirect uses of power in "The Two Faces of Power."

8. Influence in negotiation is relational. It is not fixed, as the notion of bargaining power implies; it is fluid, malleable. It can, within limits, be increased through strategic moves. For this reason, we prefer the concept of positioning—the active bettering of your odds at the table—to the static notion of bargaining power. On the intersection of power relations and gender relations, see Joan Scott, *Gender and the Politics of History*; Jane Flax, "Postmodernism and Gender Relations in Feminist Theory"; and *Thinking Fragments: Psychoanalysis, Feminism, and Postmodernism in the Contemporary West*.

9. On using strategic moves to get negotiations off the ground, see also Deborah Kolb and Judith Williams, "Breakthrough Bargaining."

CHAPTER THREE: RESISTING CHALLENGES

1. Erving Goffman shows in *The Presentation of Self in Everyday Life* the great lengths to which people go to present themselves in a positive light. Bargainers use moves and turns to ensure that a positive or flattering view of them prevails in the negotiation.

2. Judith Lorber suggests in *Paradoxes of Gender* that "doing gender" means, in part, that men do dominance while women do deference. The expectation that women will be accommodating causes problems in the shadow negotiation. Women sometimes hesitate to ask for much or to push their own advocacy, and other parties, expecting acquiescence, retaliate when they don't get it. For men, expectations play out somewhat differently. Although taking a strong stand conforms to expectations, male negotiators still run the risk of pushing too hard and being dismissed or triggering a contest. On the other hand, when men act in a more collaborative fashion—something that is not expected—they can gain advantage in the shadow negotiation.

3. See Linda Alcoff, "Cultural Feminism Versus Post-Structuralism: The Identity Crisis in Feminist Theory."

4. The exchange between Charlene Barshefsky and the Chinese trade representative is written up in James Sebenius, Rebecca Hulse, and Sarah G. Matthews, "Charlene Barshefsky (B)," a Harvard Business School case.

5. Maryanne's story is based on work done in collaboration with the Center for Women and Enterprise, a nonprofit organization in Boston.

6. "Focus on the problem, not the people" is a much-quoted dictum in Roger Fisher, William Ury, and Bruce Patton's *Getting to Yes*.

7. The authors of *Getting to Yes*, for example, urge readers to ignore personal challenges, rise above them, or deal with them outside the negotiation. When challenging moves in the shadow negotiation carry an abusive personal message, however, they *must* be answered directly.

8. Kathleen Reardon underscores this point in *They Don't Get It, Do They? Communication in the Workplace—Closing the Gap Between Women and Men*, emphasizing the confirming aspect of not confronting these challenges. The label sticks when no objection is raised.

9. Disruptive turns bring gender and sexism to the surface and expose the problems they can cause. Conflicts of this nature are generally avoided in organizations. See Joanne Martin, "Deconstructing Organizational Taboos: The Suppression of Gender Conflict in Organizations."

10. Because gender is transmitted and reenacted through communication, the tools of language—sarcasm, irony, exaggeration—come in handy in turning the insults of gender. See Kathy Ferguson, "Interpretation and Genealogy in Feminism"; Teresa DeLauretis, *Technologies of Gender: Essays on Theory, Film, and Fiction*; and Sylvia Gherardi, *Gender, Symbolism, and Organizational Culture*. The contention holds for insults that have roots in other stereotypes—racial, ethnic, age, whatever. As a

result, these resources are useful for turning demeaning moves that exploit other than gendered stereotypes.

11. Attractiveness is considered an attribute of success in male executives, but most often taken as a sign of sexuality among females. See Madeline Heilman and Melanie Stropek, "Attractiveness and Corporate Success: Different Causal Attributions for Males and Females."

CHAPTER FOUR: LAYING THE GROUNDWORK

1. For arguments that specifically link women and connection, see Carol Gilligan, *In a Different Voice;* Mary Belenky, Blythe Clinchy, Nancy Goldberger, and Jill Tarule, *Women's Ways of Knowing;* and Judith Jordan, Alexandra Kaplan, Jean Baker Miller, Irene Stiver, and Janet Surrey, *Women's Growth in Connection.*

2. Robert Mnookin, "Why Negotiations Fail: An Exploration of Barriers to the Resolution of Conflict"; and Max Bazerman and Margaret Neale, *Negotiating Rationally.*

3. On the narrative approach, see Victor Turner, *Drama, Fields, and Metaphor;* Jerome Bruner, *Active Minds, Possible Worlds;* Molly Hite, *The Other Side of the Story: Structures and Strategies of Contemporary Feminist Narratives;* Laura Tracy, "Catching the Drift: Authority, Gender and Narrative"; Jill Freedman and Gene Combs, *Narrative Therapy;* and Michael White and David Epston, *Narrative Means to Therapeutic Ends.*

4. We have adopted the exercise in circular questioning given in Figure 4.1 from Sara Cobb, who first introduced the technique to the negotiation field in "Narrative Perspective on Mediation."

5. Alison's story is adapted from "Amelia Rogers at Tassani Communications," a case used at the Harvard Business School.

CHAPTER FIVE: ENGAGING YOUR COUNTERPART

1. Unlike the other stories recounted in this book, the drama played out between Christopher Lydon and Jane Christo is taken entirely from the public record and not from interviews with the principals. As the two thrust and parried, their posturing unfolded in the press. Details of the yearlong negotiations were published in the *Wall Street Journal* and the *New York Times.* Private e-mail messages and memos quickly found their way into commentary by Mark Jurkowitz and Eileen McNamara of the *Boston Globe* and Dan Kennedy of the *Phoenix,* while the participants editorialized on the situation on their Web sites. The *Boston Globe*

articles cited in the chapter are by Mark Jurkowitz. We interviewed none of the principal players.

2. Obviously, without talking to the principals, we have no definitive way of knowing whether Christo and Lydon could have reached an agreement. From the outside, it certainly looked possible and as though tough tactics got in the way. But, as always, there may be more to the story.

3. See David Cooperrider and Suresh Srivastva, "Appreciative Inquiry in Organizational Life."

4. Victor Turner, *Drama, Fields, and Metaphor: Symbolic Action in Human Society,* and *The Ritual Process;* Clifford Geertz, *Local Knowledge.*

5. Dennis K. Mumby and Linda L. Putnam, "The Politics of Emotion: A Feminist Reading of Bounded Rationality."

6. Deborah Tannen, "Rethinking Power and Solidarity in Gender and Dominance."

7. Amy Sheldon calls this kind of exchange "double-voice discourse" to suggest that self-assertion is expressed without giving offense ("Saying It with a Smile: Girls' Conflict Talk as Double-Voice Discourse").

8. Steven R. Wilson, "Face and Facework in Negotiation"; and Erving Goffman, *The Presentation of Self in Everyday Life.*

9. This story happens to be about a woman. The dynamics, however, hold for anyone in a position of less power—whether male or female. Reviewing research on transcripts from "black boxes" after airline crashes, Deborah Tannen points out that a major contributor to the eventual tragedy is often the subordinate's reluctance to tell the captain bad news. Deference makes the subordinate cautious about giving unvarnished facts or opinions.

10. In "Breakthrough Bargaining," we argue that both connection and advocacy are needed to get stalled negotiations off the ground.

CHAPTER SIX: GETTING COLLABORATION TO WORK

1. Pauline Graham (ed.), *Mary Parker Follett—The Prophet of Management: A Celebration of Writings from the 1920s.* Quotes on pp. 189, 75, and 42.

2. See Jeffrey Z. Rubin, Dean G. Pruitt, and Song Hee Kim, *Social Conflict: Escalation, Stalemate and Settlement.*

3. Joyce Fletcher, *Disappearing Acts: Gender, Power, and Relational Practice at Work;* and Deborah M. Kolb, "Women's Work: Peacemaking Behind the Scenes."

4. Sara Cobb, "A Narrative Perspective on Mediation: Toward the Materialization of the 'Storytelling' Metaphor"; W. B. Pearce and V. E. Cronen, *Communication, Action, and Meaning: The Creation of Social Reality;* and Carlos Sluski, "Transformations: A Blueprint for Narrative Changes in Therapy."

5. Victor Turner, *The Ritual Process: Structure and Anti-Structure,* and *Drama, Fields, and Metaphor: Symbolic Action in Human Society.* Reference to "doffing" is in *Drama,* p. 243.

6. Conflicts over values require different processes than do simple disputes over interests. More direct interaction that brings people together to discuss and expose their differences is often recommended. See, for example, Kimberly A. Wade-Benzoni and others, "Barriers to Resolution in Ideologically Based Negotiations: The Role of Values and Institution." How those interactions should be structured, however, is elided in the recommendations. We suggest that storytelling is a good approach.

7. Ann Douglas, *Industrial Peacemaking.*

8. Jeffrey Rubin discusses this and other common traps in negotiation in "Some Wise and Mistaken Assumptions About Conflict and Negotiation." See also Rubin, Pruitt, and Kim, *Social Conflict: Escalation, Stalemate and Settlement.*

CHAPTER SEVEN: CRAFTING AGREEMENTS

1. More extensive commentary on win-lose or "distributive" negotiations can be found in the works by Howard Raiffa, Thomas Schelling, and David Lax and James Sebenius cited in the Bibliography. The most accessible accounts of win-win or "joint-gains" bargaining remain Roger Fisher, William Ury, and Bruce Patton's *Getting to Yes* and William Ury's *Getting Past No.*

2. Peter Senge talks about the learning that comes from "reciprocal inquiry-making" in *The Fifth Discipline,* but this inquiry is about understanding another person's reasoning, about getting the facts.

3. The work of Howard Raiffa and his students David Lax and James Sebenius has clarified how important differences, rather than commonalties, are in providing the ingredients for joint-gains negotiations. See also Dean Pruitt, "Strategic Choice in Negotiation."

4. Pauline Graham (ed.), *Mary Parker Follett—The Prophet of Management.* (The "window" dilemma is on p. 69.)

5. In *The Manager as Negotiator,* David Lax and James Sebenius characterize all negotiation as a parallel process of claiming value for your-

self and creating value together with your counterpart. There is an inevitable tension between the two impulses in pushing and packaging situations. It abates in mutual inquiry.

6. Judith Jordan and the other authors of *Women's Growth in Connection* consider the asking for and giving of help an essential factor contributing to the way women develop. Of course, mutual inquiry is not a gender-specific process. It isn't something only women can practice, but the experience of women provides valuable clues for creating mutual inquiry negotiations.

7. Debra Meyerson argues in *Tempered Radicals* that small wins are opportunities on which negotiators (and others) can capitalize to change organizational practices that undermine both effectiveness and equity. See also Debra Meyerson and Joyce Fletcher, "A Modest Manifesto for Shattering the Glass Ceiling."

Bibliography

Acker, Joan. "Gendering Organizational Theory," in *Gendering Organizational Theory*, eds. Albert J. Mills and Peta Tancred (Thousand Oaks, Calif.: Sage, 1992).

Alcoff, Linda. "Cultural Feminism Versus Post-Structuralism: The Identity Crisis in Feminist Theory," *Signs* 13, no. 3 (1988): 405–436.

Ayers, Ian. "Fair Driving: Gender and Race Discrimination in Retail Car Negotiations," *Harvard Law Review* 104, no. 4 (1991): 817–872.

Bacharach, Samuel, and Edward Lawler. *Bargaining* (San Francisco: Jossey-Bass, 1981).

Bachrach, Peter, and Morton Baratz. "The Two Faces of Power," *American Political Science Review* 56 (1962): 947–952.

Bailyn, Lotte. *Breaking the Mold: Women, Men and Time in the Corporate World* (New York: Free Press, 1993).

Barron, Lisa. "Talk That Pays: Differences in Salary, Negotiator's Beliefs, and Behaviors," unpublished dissertation, Anderson School, UCLA (1998).

Bateson, Gregory. *Steps to an Ecology of Mind* (New York: Ballantine, 1972).

Bateson, Mary Catherine. *Composing a Life* (New York: Plume, 1990).

Bazerman, Max, and Margaret Neale. *Negotiating Rationally* (New York: Free Press, 1992).

Belenky, Mary Field, Blythe McVicker Clinchy, Nancy Rule Goldberger, and Jill Mattuck Tarule. *Women's Ways of Knowing: The Development of Self, Voice, and Mind* (New York: Basic Books, 1986).

Bem, Sandra. *The Lenses of Gender: Transforming the Debate on Sexual Inequality* (New Haven, Conn.: Yale University Press, 1993).

Bielby, William T., and James N. Baron. "A Woman's Place Is with Other Women: Sex Segregation Within Organizations," in *Sex*

Segregation in the Workplace: Trends, Explanations, Remedies, ed. B. F. Reskin (Washington, D.C.: National Academy Press, 1984).

Bruner, Jerome. *Active Minds, Possible Worlds* (Cambridge: Harvard University Press, 1986).

Bylsma, Wayne H., and Brenda Major. "Social Comparisons and Pay Evaluations," *Psychology of Women Quarterly* 16 (1991): 193–200.

Carli, Linda. "Gender, Language, and Influence," *Journal of Personality and Social Psychology* 59 (1990): 941–951.

Chusmir, L. H., and J. Mills. "Gender Differences in Conflict Resolution Styles of Managers: At Work and at Home," *Sex Roles* 20 (1989): 149–163.

Cobb, Sara. "Empowerment and Mediation: A Narrative Perspective," *Negotiation Journal* 9 (1993): 245–259.

———. "A Narrative Perspective on Mediation: Toward the Materialization of the 'Storytelling' Metaphor," in *Directions in Mediation*, eds. Joseph P. Folger and Tricia S. Jones (Thousand Oaks, Calif.: Sage, 1994).

Cohen, Allen R., and David L. Bradford. "Influence Without Authority: The Use of Alliances, Reciprocity, and Exchange to Accomplish Work," in *Negotiation*, eds. Roy Lewicki, Joseph Litterer, John Minton, and David Saunders (Minneapolis, Minn.: Richard Irwin, 1994).

Colosi, Thomas. "Negotiation in the Public and Private Sectors," *American Behavioral Scientist* 27 (1983): 229–255.

Connell, R. W. *Gender and Power* (Stanford: Stanford University Press, 1987).

Cooperrider, David, and Suresh Srivastva. "Appreciative Inquiry in Organizational Life," *Research in Organizational Change and Development*, Vol. 1 (Greenwich, Conn.: JAI Press, 1987): 129–169.

Crawford, Mary. *Talking Difference: On Gender and Language* (London: Sage, 1990).

Crosby, Faye J. *Juggling: The Unexpected Advantages of Balancing Career and Home for Women and Their Families* (New York: Oxford University Press, 1991).

Deaux, Kay. "From Individual Differences to Social Categories: Analysis of a Decade's Research on Gender," *American Psychologist* 39 (1984): 105–116.

———. "Putting Gender into Context: An Interactive Model of Gender-Related Behavior," *Psychological Review* 94, no. 3 (1987): 369–89.

Deaux, Kay, and Brenda Major. "A Social Psychological Model of Gender," in *Theoretical Perspectives on Sexual Difference*, ed. Deborah Rhode (New Haven, Conn.: Yale University Press, 1990).

DeLauretis, Teresa. *Technologies of Gender: Essays on Theory, Film, and Fiction* (Bloomington: Indiana University Press, 1987).

Douglas, Ann. *Industrial Peacemaking* (New York: Columbia University Press, 1962).

DuPlessis, Rachel Blau. *Writing Beyond the Ending: Narrative Strategies of Twentieth-Century Women Writers* (Bloomington: Indiana University Press, 1985).

Eagly, Alice. *Sex Differences in Social Behavior: A Social Role Interpretation* (Hillsdale, N.J.: Erlbaum, 1987).

———. "The Science and Politics of Comparing Women and Men," *American Psychologist* 50 (1995): 145–158.

Eban, Abba. *Diplomacy for the Next Century* (New Haven, Conn.: Yale University Press, 1998).

Ely, Robin. "The Power of Demography: Women's Social Constructions of Gender Identity at Work," *Academy of Management Journal* 38 (1995): 589–634.

Epstein, Cynthia Fuchs. *Deceptive Distinctions: Sex, Gender, and the Social Order* (New Haven, Conn.: Yale University Press, 1988).

Graham, Pauline, ed. *Mary Parker Follett—The Prophet of Management: A Celebration of Writings from the 1920s* (Boston: Harvard Business School Press, 1995).

Ferguson, Kathy. "Interpretation and Genealogy in Feminism," *Signs* 16 (1991): 322–339.

———. *The Feminist Case Against Bureaucracy* (Philadelphia: Temple University Press, 1984).

Fisher, Roger, and Scott Brown. *Getting Together* (New York: Penguin, 1987).

Fisher, Roger, William Ury, and Bruce Patton. *Getting to Yes: Negotiating Agreement Without Giving In*, 2nd ed. (Boston: Houghton Mifflin, 1991).

Flax, Jane. "Postmodernism and Gender Relations in Feminist Theory," *Signs* 12 (1987): 621–643.

———. *Thinking Fragments: Psychoanalysis, Feminism, and Postmodernism in the Contemporary West* (Berkeley: University of California Press, 1990).

Fletcher, Joyce. "Castrating the Feminine Advantage: Feminist Standpoint Research and Management Science," *Journal of Management Inquiry* 3 (1994): 74–82.

———. *Disappearing Acts: Gender, Power, and Relational Practice at Work* (Cambridge: MIT Press, 1999).

Fouraker, Lawrence, and Stanley Siegal. *Bargaining and Group Decisionmaking* (New York: McGraw-Hill, 1960).

Freedman, Jill, and Gene Combs. *Narrative Therapy* (New York: Norton, 1996).

Friedman, Ray. "Interaction Norms as Carriers of Organizational Culture: A Study of Labor Negotiations at International Harvester," *Journal of Contemporary Ethnography* 18 (1989): 3–29.

———. *Front Stage, Backstage: The Dramatic Structure of Labor Negotiations* (Cambridge: MIT Press, 1994).

Geertz, Clifford. *Local Knowledge: Further Essays in Interpretive Anthropology* (New York: Basic Books, 1983).

Gerhart, B. "Gender Differences in Current and Starting Salaries: The Role of Performance, College Major, and Job Title," *Industrial and Labor Relations Review* 43 (1990): 418–433.

Gerhart, B., and S. Rynes. "Determinants and Consequences of Salary Negotiations by Male and Female MBA Graduates," *Journal of Applied Psychology* 76 (1991): 256–262.

Gerson, Judith M., and Kathy Peiss. "Boundaries, Negotiation, Consciousness: Reconceptualizing Gender Relations," *Social Problems* 32, no. 4 (1985): 317–331.

Gherardi, Sylvia. *Gender, Symbolism, and Organizational Culture* (Thousand Oaks, Calif.: Sage, 1996).

Gilligan, Carol. *In a Different Voice* (Cambridge: Harvard University Press, 1982).

Goffman, Erving. *Interaction Ritual: Essays in Face-to-Face Behavior* (New York: Doubleday/Anchor, 1967).

———. *The Presentation of Self in Everyday Life* (Woodstock, N.Y.: Overlook Press, 1973).

———. *Frame Analysis* (New York: HarperCollins, 1974).

———. "The Arrangement Between the Sexes," *Theory and Society* 4 (1977): 301–331.

Goleman, Daniel. *Emotional Intelligence* (New York: Bantam, 1997).

———. *Working with Emotional Intelligence* (New York: Bantam, 1998).

Gray, Barbara. "The Gender-Based Foundations of Negotiation Theory," *Research on Negotiations in Organizations*, 4 (Greenwich, Conn.: JAI Press, 1994).

Griscomb, Joan. "Women and Power: Definition, Dualism, and Difference," *Psychology of Women Quarterly* 16 (1992): 389–414.

Heilman, Madeline E., and Melanie H. Stopeck. "Attractiveness and Corporate Success: Different Causal Attributions for Males and Females," *Journal of Applied Psychology* 70, no. 2 (1985): 379–388.

Helgesen, Sally. *The Feminine Advantage: Women's Ways of Leadership* (New York: Doubleday, 1990).

Henley, Nancy. *Body Politics, Sex, and Nonverbal Communication* (Upper Saddle River, N.J.: Prentice Hall, 1984).

Hill, Linda, and Melinda Conrad. "Amelia Rogers at Tassani Communications," Harvard Business School Case Study 9-492-034 (1995).

Hite, Molly. *The Other Side of the Story: Structures and Strategies of Contemporary Feminist Narratives* (Ithaca, N.Y.: Cornell University Press, 1989).

Hochschild, Arlie. *The Second Shift: Working Parents and the Revolution at Home* (New York: Viking Press, 1989).

Hyde, Janet. "Meta-analysis and the Psychology of Differences," *Signs* 16, no. 1 (1990): 55–73.

Ibarra, H. "Homophily and Differential Returns: Sex Differences in Network Structure and Access in an Advertising Firm," *Administrative Science Quarterly* 37 (1992): 422–447.

Jamieson, Kathleen Hall. *Beyond the Double Bind: Women and Leadership* (New York: Oxford University Press, 1995).

Jordan, Judith V., Alexandra G. Kaplan, Jean B. Miller, Irene P. Stiver, and Janet L. Surrey. *Women's Growth in Connection: Writings from the Stone Center* (New York: Guilford Press, 1991).

Kamen, V. S., and C.E.J. Hartel. "Gender Differences in Anticipated Pay Negotiation Strategies and Outcomes," *Journal of Business and Psychology* 9 (1994): 183–197.

Keashley, L. "Gender and Conflict: What Does Psychological Research Tell Us?" in *Gender and Conflict*, eds. Anita Taylor and Judi Beinstein Miller (Cresskill, N.J.: Hampton Press, 1994): 167–190.

Kessler-Harris, Alice. *A Woman's Wage: Historical Meanings and Social Consequences* (Lexington: Kentucky University Press, 1990).

Kolb, Deborah M. "Women's Work: Peacemaking Behind the Scenes," in *Hidden Conflict in Organizations: Uncovering Behind-the-Scenes Disputes*, eds. Deborah M. Kolb and Jean Bartunek (Thousand Oaks, Calif.: Sage, 1992).

Kolb, Deborah M., and Gloria Coolidge. "Her Place at the Table: A Consideration of Gender Issues in Negotiation," in *Negotiation Theory and Practice*, eds. J. W. Breslin and Jeffrey Rubin (Cambridge: Program on Negotiation, Harvard Law School, 1991).

Kolb, Deborah M., Lisa Jensen, and Vonda Shannon. "She Said It All Before, or What Did We Miss About Ms. Follett in the Library?" *Organizations* (January 1996): 153–160.

Kolb, Deborah M., and Linda L. Putnam. "Through the Looking Glass: Negotiation Theory Refracted Through the Lens of Gender," in *Frontiers in Dispute Resolution in Industrial Relations and*

Human Resources, ed. S. Gleason (Ann Arbor: Michigan State University Press, 1997).

Kolb, Deborah M., and Judith Williams. "Professional Women in Conversation: Where Have We Been and Where Are We Going?" *Journal of Management Inquiry* 2 (1993): 14–26.

———. "Breakthrough Bargaining," *Harvard Business Review* (February 2001): 88–102.

Korn/Ferry International. *Decade of the Executive Woman: A Joint Study by Korn/Ferry International and UCLA Anderson Graduate School of Management* (Boston: Korn/Ferry International, 1993).

Kramer, Roderick, and David Messick, eds. *Negotiation as a Social Process* (Thousand Oaks, Calif.: Sage, 1995).

Kray, L. J., L. Thompson, and A. Galinsky. "Battle of the Sexes: Gender Stereotype Confirmation and Reactance in Negotiations," *Journal of Personality and Social Psychology* 80 (2001): 942–958.

Kriesberg, Louis, and Stuart Thorson. *Timing and the De-escalation of International Conflicts* (Syracuse, N.Y.: Syracuse University Press, 1991).

Kunda, Gideon. *Engineering Culture: Control and Commitment in a High-Tech Corporation* (Philadelphia: Temple University Press, 1992).

Lakoff, Robin. *Language and Woman's Place* (New York: Octagon Books, 1976).

Lax, David, and James Sebenius. *The Manager as Negotiator* (New York: Free Press, 1986).

———. "Thinking Coalitionally," in *Negotiation Analysis,* ed. P. Young (Ann Arbor: University of Michigan Press, 1992).

Lewicki, Roy, Joseph Litterer, John Minton, and David Saunders, eds. *Negotiation* (Minneapolis: Richard Irwin, 1994).

Lewin, Kurt. *Resolving Social Conflicts: Field Theory in Social Science* (Washington, D.C.: American Psychological Association, 1997).

Lopresti, Pamela J. "Gender Differences in Wage and Job Mobility," *American Economic Review* 82, no. 2 (May 1992): 821–831.

Lorber, Judith. *The Paradoxes of Gender* (New Haven, Conn.: Yale University Press, 1994).

Lott, Bernice. *Women's Lives: Themes and Variations in Gender Learning* (Pacific Grove, Calif.: Brooks Cole, 1987).

MacKinnon, Catharine A. "Feminist Discourse," *Buffalo Law Review* 34 (1985).

Mahony, Rhona. *Kidding Ourselves: Breadwinning, Babies, and Bargaining Power* (New York: Basic Books, 1995).

Major, Brenda, and B. Forcey. "Social Comparisons and Pay Evaluations: Preferences for Same-Sex and Same-Job Wage Comparisons," *Journal of Experimental Social Psychology* 21 (1985): 393–405.

Major, Brenda, and E. Konar. "An Investigation of Sex Differences in Pay Expectations and Their Possible Causes," *Academy of Management Journal* 27 (1984): 777–792.

Major, Brenda, D. McFarlin, and D. Gagnon. "Overworked and Underpaid," *Journal of Personality and Social Psychology* 47 (1984): 1399–1412.

Maniero, L. "Coping with Powerlessness: The Relationship of Gender and Job Dependency to Empowerment Strategy Usage," *Administrative Science Quarterly* 31, no. 4 (1986): 633–653.

Martin, Joanne. "Deconstructing Organizational Taboos: The Suppression of Gender Conflict in Organizations," *Organization Science* 1 (1990): 339–359.

Menkel-Meadow, Carrie. "Portia in a Different Voice: Speculating on a Woman's Lawyering Process," *Berkeley Women's Law Journal* 1, no. 1 (1985): 39–63.

———. "Portia Redux: Another Look at Gender, Feminism, and Legal Ethics," *Virginia Journal of Social Policy & the Law* 2, no. 1 (Fall 1994): 75–113.

Meyerson, Debra. "From Discovery to Resistance: A Feminist Read and Revision of the Stress Discourse," *Organization Science* 9 (1998): 103–118.

———. *Tempered Radicals: How People Use Difference to Inspire Change at Work* (Boston: Harvard Business School Press, 2001).

Meyerson, Debra, and Joyce K. Fletcher. "A Modest Manifesto for Shattering the Glass Ceiling," *Harvard Business Review* (January-February, 2000): 127–136.

Miller, Barbara. *Sex and Gender Hierarchies* (New York: Cambridge University Press, 1993).

Miller, Jean Baker. *Toward a New Psychology of Women* (Boston: Beacon Press, 1976).

Mills, Albert J., and Peta Tancred, eds. *Gendering Organizational Theory* (London: Sage, 1992).

Mnookin, Robert H. "Why Negotiations Fail: An Exploration of Barriers to the Resolution of Conflict," *Ohio State Journal of Dispute Resolutions* 8, no. 2 (1993): 235–249.

Mnookin, Robert H., Scott R. Peppet, and Andrew S. Tulumello. *Beyond Winning: Negotiating to Create Value in Deals and Disputes* (Cambridge: Harvard University Press, 2000).

Monk, Gerald, John Winslade, Kathie Crocket, and David Epston, eds. *Narrative Therapy in Practice: The Archaeology of Hope* (San Francisco: Jossey-Bass, 1997).

Mumby, Dennis K., and Linda L. Putnam. "The Politics of Emotion: A Feminist Reading of Bounded Rationality," *Academy of Management Review* 17 (1992): 465–486.

Neale, Margaret, and Max Bazerman. *Cognition and Rationality in Negotiation* (New York: Free Press, 1994).

Offerman, Lynn R., and Cheryl Beil. "Achievement Style of Women Leaders and Their Peers," *Psychology of Women Quarterly* 16 (1992): 37–56.

Parry, Alan, and Robert Doan. *Story Revisions: Narrative Therapy in the Postmodern World* (New York: Guilford Press, 1994).

Pearce, W. B., and V. E. Cronen. *Communication, Action, and Meaning: The Creation of Social Reality* (New York: Praeger, 1980).

Pierce, Jennifer. *Gender Trials: Emotional Lives in Contemporary Law Firms* (Berkeley: University of California Press, 1995).

Pruitt, Dean. *Negotiation Behavior* (New York: Academic Press, 1981).

———. "Strategic Choice in Negotiation," *American Behavioral Scientist* 27, no. 2 (1983): 167–194.

Raiffa, Howard. *The Art and Science of Negotiation* (Cambridge: Harvard University Press, 1982).

Rapaport, Rhona, Lotte Bailyn, Deborah Kolb, and Joyce Fletcher. *Relinking Life and Work: Toward a Better Future*. A Report to the Ford Foundation on a Research Project in Collaboration with Xerox Corporation, Tandem Computers Inc., and Corning Inc. (New York: Ford Foundation, 1996).

Reardon, Kathleen Kelley. *They Don't Get It, Do They? Communication in the Workplace—Closing the Gap Between Women and Men* (New York: Little, Brown, 1996).

Rhode, Deborah, ed. *Theoretical Perspectives on Sexual Difference* (New Haven, Conn.: Yale University Press, 1990).

Rose, Carol. "Bargaining and Gender: Feminism, Sexual Distinctions, and the Law," *Harvard Journal of Law and Public Policy* 18, no. 2 (1995): 547–563.

Rosener, Judith. "Ways Women Lead," *Harvard Business Review* (November-December, 1990): 119–125.

———. *America's Competitive Secret: Using Women as a Competitive Strategy* (New York: Oxford University Press, 1997).

Rubin, Jeffrey Z. "Some Wise and Mistaken Assumptions About Conflict and Negotiation," in *Negotiation Theory and Practice*, eds. J. William Breslin and Jeffrey Z. Rubin (Cambridge: Program on Negotiation, Harvard Law School, 1991).

Rubin, Jeffrey Z., and B. R. Brown. *The Psychology of Bargaining and Negotiation* (New York: Academic Press, 1975).

Rubin, Jeffrey Z., Dean G. Pruitt, and Song Hee Kim. *Social Conflict: Escalation, Stalemate and Settlement* (New York: McGraw-Hill, 1993).

Sebenius, James, and Daniel F. Curran. "To Hell with the Future, Let's

Get on with the Past: George Mitchell in Northern Ireland," Harvard Business School Case Study, N9–801–393 (2001).

Sebenius, James, Rebecca Hulse, and Sarah G. Matthews. "Charlene Barshefsky (B)," Harvard Business School Case Study N9–801–422 (2001).

Senge, Peter. *The Fifth Discipline: The Art and Science of a Learning Institution* (New York: Doubleday, 1990).

Sheldon, Amy. "Saying It with a Smile: Girls' Conflict Talk as Double-Voice Discourse," in *Current Issues in Linguistic Theory*, eds. M. Eid and G. Iverson (Amsterdam: John Benjamins, 1993).

Sluski, Carlos. "Transformations: A Blueprint for Narrative Changes in Therapy," *Family Process* (1992): 217–230.

Smeltzer, Larry, and Kittie W. Watson. "Gender Differences in Verbal Communication During Negotiations," *Communication Research Reports* 3 (1986): 74–79.

Stamato, L. "Voice, Place, and Process: Research on Gender, Negotiation, and Conflict Resolution," *Mediation Quarterly* 9, no. 4 (1992): 375–386.

Stevens, Cynthia, K. Bavetta, and M. Gist. "Gender Differences in the Acquisition of Salary Negotiation Skills: The Role of Goals, Self-Efficacy, and Perceived Control," *Journal of Applied Psychology* 78, no. 5 (1993): 722–735.

Stuhlmacher, Alice F., and Amy E. Walters. "Gender Differences in Negotiation Outcomes: A Meta-Analysis," *Personnel Psychology* 52, no. 3 (1999): 653–667.

Tannen, Deborah. *You Just Don't Understand: Women and Men in Conversation* (New York: Ballantine, 1990).

———. "Rethinking Power and Solidarity in Gender and Dominance," in *Gender and Conversation Interaction*, ed. Deborah Tannen (New York: University Press, 1993).

———. *Talking from 9 to 5: Women and Men in the Workplace: Language, Sex and Power* (New York: Avon, 1994).

Tracy, Laura. *"Catching the Drift": Authority, Gender, and Narrative* (New Brunswick, N.J.: Rutgers University Press, 1988).

Turner, Victor. *The Ritual Process: Structure and Anti-Structure* (Ithaca, N.Y.: Cornell University Press, 1969).

———. *Drama, Fields, and Metaphor: Symbolic Action in Human Society* (Ithaca, N.Y.: Cornell University Press, 1974).

Turner, Victor, and Jerome Bruner, eds. *The Anthropology of Experience* (Chicago: University of Chicago Press, 1986).

U.S. Department of Labor. *Report on the Glass Ceiling Initiative* (Washington, D.C.: U.S. Government Printing Office, 1991).

———. *Working Women: A Chartbook* (Washington, D.C.: U.S. Government Printing Office, 1991).

———. *Employment and Earnings* (Washington, D.C.: U.S. Government Printing Office, 1993).

Ury, William. *Getting Past No* (New York: Bantam, 1990).

Valian, Virginia. *Why So Slow? The Advancement of Women* (Cambridge, Mass.: MIT Press, 1998).

Wade-Benzoni, Kimberly A., Andrew J. Hoffman, Leigh Thompson, Don A. Moore, James J. Gillespie, and Max Bazerman, "Barriers to Resolution in Ideologically Based Negotiations: The Role of Values and Institution," *Academy of Management Review* 27, no. 1 (January 2002): 41–58.

Walton, Richard, and Robert McKersie. *A Behavioral Theory of Labor Negotiations* (New York: McGraw-Hill, 1965).

Watkins, Michael. "Getting to Dayton: Negotiating an End to the War in Bosnia," Harvard Business School Case Study, 1–800–134 (1999).

Watson, Carol. "Gender Differences in Negotiating Behavior and Outcomes: Fact or Artifact?" in *Conflict and Gender,* eds. Anita Taylor and Judi Beinstein Miller (Cresskill, N.J.: Hampton Press, Inc., 1994).

———. "Gender Versus Power," in *Women, Men and Gender,* ed. Mary Roth Walsh (New Haven, Conn.: Yale University Press, 1997).

Watson, Carol, and L. R. Hoffman, "Managers as Negotiators: A Test of Power vs. Gender as Predictors of Feelings, Behaviors and Outcomes," *Leadership Quarterly* 7, no. 1 (1996): 63–86.

Weedon, Chris. *Feminist Practice and Poststructuralist Theory* (Oxford: Blackwell, 1987).

White, Michael, and David Epston. *Narrative Means to Therapeutic Ends* (New York: Norton, 1990).

Wilson, Steven R. "Face and Facework in Negotiation," in *Communication and Negotiation,* eds. Linda Putnam and Michael E. Roloff (Thousand Oaks, Calif.: Sage, 1992).

Zimmerman, Don, and Candace West. "Sex Roles, Interruptions and Silence in Conversations," in *Language and Sex,* eds. Barrie Thorne and Nancy Henley (Rowley, Mass.: Newbury House, 1979).

Index

About the Authors

Deborah M. Kolb is professor of management at Simmons Graduate School of Management and at the Center for Gender in Organizations there. From 1991 through 1994, she was executive director of the Program on Negotiation at Harvard Law School. She is currently a senior fellow at the Program, where she co-directs The Negotiations in the Workplace Project. Dr. Kolb is a principal in The Shadow Negotiation LLC, an e-learning company that provides negotiation training specially designed for women (see http://www.theshadownegotiation.com).

Professor Kolb is author of *The Mediators* (MIT Press, 1983), an in-depth study of labor mediation, and co-editor of *Hidden Conflict in Organizations: Uncovering Behind-the-Scenes* *Disputes* (Sage, 1992), a collection of field studies about how conflicts are handled in a variety of business and nonprofit organizations. She has published a study of the practice of successful mediators, *Making Talk Work: Profiles of Mediators* (Jossey-Bass, 1994). She is also the editor of *Negotiation Eclectics: Essays in Memory of Jeffrey Z. Rubin* (Program on Negotiation, 1999). She has authored more than fifty articles on the subjects of negotiation, conflict in organizations, and mediation, and is on the editorial boards of the *Negotiation Journal* and the *Journal of Conflict Resolution*.

She received her Ph.D. from MIT's Sloan School of Management, where her dissertation won the Zannetos Prize for outstanding doctoral scholarship. She has a BA from Vassar College and an MBA from the University of Colorado.

Judith Williams spent her early career in publishing and investment banking, serving as manuscripts editor for *Daedalus*, the journal of the American Academy of Arts and Sciences, and then as head of acquisitions for a private Boston investment firm.

In 1992 she secured seed money funding from a private foundation to establish a nonprofit corporation to develop documentaries and other media content on issues of specific concern to women. Two years ago, Williams and Kolb teamed up with Carol Frohlinger, lawyer and consultant, to form theshadownegotiation.com, the first Web site to offer negotiation training by women for women.

Dr. Williams earned a BA at Bryn Mawr College and a Ph.D. from Harvard University, as well as an MBA from the Simmons Graduate School of Management with highest honors. She has taught at both Boston College and Harvard.

Deborah Kolb and Judith Williams first collaborated on "Where Have We Been and Where Are We Going: A Conversation with Professional Women," in which executive women in Boston explored the effects (and noneffects) of the women's movement on corporate life. Subsequent collaboration produced

The Shadow Negotiation: How Women Can Master the Hidden Agendas That Determine Bargaining Success (Simon & Schuster, 2000), which was named one of the Ten Best Books of the year by the *Harvard Business Review* and won the Best Book Award from the International Association of Conflict Management.